T0257819

Petri Nets and Manufacturing Systems

Petri Nets and Manufacturing Systems

Edited by **Ruth Hinrichs**

LANRYE
INTERNATIONAL

New Jersey

Published by Clanrye International,
55 Van Reypen Street,
Jersey City, NJ 07306, USA
www.clanryeinternational.com

Petri Nets and Manufacturing Systems
Edited by Ruth Hinrichs

International Standard Book Number: 978-1-63240-406-0 (Hardback)

Printed in the United States of America.

Contents

Preface   VII

Manufacturing   1

Chapter 1   **Automated Petri-Net Modelling
            for Batch Production Scheduling**   3
            Dejan Gradišar and Gašper Mušič

Chapter 2   **A Computationally Improved Optimal Solution
            for Deadlocked Problems of Flexible Manufacturing
            Systems Using Theory of Regions**   27
            Yen-Liang Pan

Chapter 3   **Specifying and Verifying Holonic Multi-Agent Systems
            Using Stochastic Petri Net and Object-Z: Application
            to Industrial Maintenance Organizations**   51
            Belhassen Mazigh and Abdeljalil Abbas-Turki

Chapter 4   **Measurement of Work-in-Process and Manufacturing Lead
            Time by Petri Nets Modeling and Throughput Diagram**   75
            Tiago Facchin and Miguel Afonso Sellitto

Chapter 5   **Implementation of Distributed Control Architecture
            for Multiple Robot Systems Using Petri Nets**   87
            Gen'ichi Yasuda

Chapter 6   **Workflow Modelling Based on Synchrony**   107
            Chongyi Yuan

Chapter 7   **Control Interpreted Petri Nets –
            Model Checking and Synthesis**   143
            Iwona Grobelna

Chapter 8   **Construction and Application of Learning Petri Net**   **159**
Liangbing Feng, Masanao Obayashi,
Takashi Kuremoto and Kunikazu Kobayashi

Permissions

List of Contributors

Preface

This book concentrates on the applications of Petri Nets in manufacturing. Petri Nets are graphical and mathematical tools, and the synchronism of executed actions is the natural phenomenon because of which Petri Nets are considered as mathematical tools for modeling synchronous systems. The primary idea of this theory was modified by several researchers according to their needs, owing to the odd "flexibility" of this theory. The theory is still cultivating and some directions of investigations are also encompassed in this book.

Significant researches are present in this book. Intensive efforts have been employed by authors to make this book an outstanding discourse. This book contains the enlightening chapters which have been written on the basis of significant researches done by the experts.

Finally, I would also like to thank all the members involved in this book for being a team and meeting all the deadlines for the submission of their respective works. I would also like to thank my friends and family for being supportive in my efforts.

Editor

Manufacturing

Automated Petri-Net Modelling for Batch Production Scheduling

Dejan Gradišar and Gašper Mušič

Additional information is available at the end of the chapter

1. Introduction

Production scheduling is a fundamental function in production control. It has an immediate and considerable impact on the efficiency of related manufacturing processes and significantly influences the overall production performance.

The primary characteristic of batch production is that the output of the process appears in quantities of materials or lots called batches. All components are completed at a workstation before they move to the next one. These kinds of production environments appear in chemical, pharmaceutical, food and similar industries.

The control of batch processes poses difficult issues as these processes are neither continuous nor discrete, but have the characteristics of both. ISA society introduced a multi-part S88 standard where the first part [1] defines the models and terminology for batch plants and control systems. S88 provides a framework for the development of technologies that not only support control activities of batch processes but also management activities, such as scheduling. This is illustrated in [14] where a generic framework is defined for interpreting a multi-purpose/product batch plant in terms of S88 constructs for scheduling purposes.

In order to cope with the behaviour of a batch production process an appropriate mathematical model is needed. When the behaviour is described by such a model, formal methods can be used, which usually improve the understanding of systems, allow their analysis and help in implementation. MILP based formulations of batch process features are typically used as shown in [12]. Nevertheless, Petri nets have also been applied in different aspects of modelling, qualitative and quantitative analysis, control, planning and scheduling of batch processes [4]. Independently of the chosen framework, the modelled behaviour is often extremely complex. Within the changing production environment the effectiveness of batch production modelling is, therefore, a prerequisite for the effective design and operation of batch systems.

To determine a model, data from different existing information systems could be used. From production management systems, such as Manufacturing Resource Planning (MRP II) and Enterprise Resource Planning (ERP), data about the needs, product structure and process structure could be gained [21]. On the other hand, data from the production process could be used to determine the actual resource availability. MRP II and ERP systems are commonly used in discrete manufacturing for upper level production control, such as production planning. Standard production management tools, such as MRP, are also used in batch production environment [20]. As defined with standard S88.01 the required raw materials and their quantities are determined from a dedicated data structure named *Formula*. This way the formula can be linked to standard Bill of Materials (BOM) used within MRP II concept [7].

While in a discrete manufacturing processes BOM are used to determine process materials and their quantities needed for production of finished products, in batch production processes these data are given with Formula. The same is with information that defines a sequence of operations required to produce an item. In discrete manufacturing processes these are defined with Routing, and Manufacturing recipes are used in batch production.

These two groups of data items, together with the given resource units, form the basic elements of the production process. These data can be effectively used to build up a model of the batch production system with timed Petri nets. An algorithm will be introduced, which builds a Petri-net model from the existing data. The model is built directly in a top-down manner, starting from the Formula (BOM) and the Manufacturing recipes (routings) [21].

First a class of Petri nets used is presented in a formal manner with detailed discussion on time representation. Next a method to describe a Formula with Petri net structure is given. Root item, representing the product, is composed of sub-items (sub-processes). Later a method of describing the basic production activities with timed Petri net is presented. The obtained model is applied in optimisation of batch scheduling problem.

2. Timed PN

In the Petri net literature, three basic ways of representing time in Petri nets are used [2]: firing durations (FD), holding durations (HD) and enabling durations (ED). When using FD principle the transition firing has duration [23]. In contrast, when using HD principle, a firing has no duration but a created token is considered unavailable for the time assigned to transition that created the token, which has the same effect. With ED principle, the firing of the transitions has no duration while the time delays are represented by forcing transitions that are enabled to stay so for a specified period of time before they can fire. This is a more general concept since it allows for modelling of task interruption. Some authors use an even more general concept, which assigns delays to individual arcs, either inputs or outputs of a transition [10].

When modelling several performance optimisation problems, e.g. scheduling problems, such a general framework is not needed. It is natural to use HD when modelling most scheduling processes as operations are considered non-preemptive. The timed version of CPNs defined by [9] uses a HD equivalent principle, where the unavailability of the tokens is defined implicitly through the corresponding time stamps. While CPNs allow the assignment of delays both to transition and to output arcs, we further simplify this by allowing time delay inscriptions to transitions only. This is sufficient for the type of examples investigated here, and can be generalised if necessary.

To include a time attribute of the marking tokens, which determines their availability and unavailability, the notation of timed CPN will be adopted. Tokens are accompanied with a timestamp, which is written next to the token number and separated from the number by @. E.g., two tokens with time stamp 10 are denoted 2@10. A collection of tokens with different time stamps is defined as a multiset, and written as a sum (union) of sets of timestamped tokens. E.g., two tokens with time stamp 10 and three tokens with timestamp 12 are written as $2@10 + 3@12$. The timestamp of a token defines the time from which the token is available.

Time stamps are elements of a time set TS, which is defined as a set of numeric values. In many software implementations the time values are integer, i.e., $TS = \mathbb{N}$, but will be here admitted to take any positive real value including 0, i.e., $TS = \mathbb{R}_0^+$. Timed markings are represented as collections of time stamps and are multisets over $TS : TS_{MS}$. By using HD principle the formal representation of a P/T timed Petri net is defined as follows. $TPN = (\mathcal{N}, M_0)$ is a timed Petri net system, where: $\mathcal{N} = (P, T, Pre, Post, f)$ is a Timed Petri net structure, $P = \{p_1, p_2, ..., p_k\}, k > 0$ is a finite set of places, $T = \{t_1, t_2, ..., t_l\}, l > 0$ is a finite set of transitions. $Pre : (P \times T) \to \mathbb{N}$ is the input arc function. If there exists an arc with weight k connecting p to t, then $Pre(p,t) = k$, otherwise $Pre(p,t) = 0$. $Post : (P \times T) \to \mathbb{N}$ is the output arc function. If there exists an arc with weight k connecting t to p, then $Post(p,t) = k$, otherwise $Post(p,t) = 0$. $f : T \to TS$ is the function that assigns a non-negative deterministic time delay to every $t \in T$. $M : P \to TS_{MS}$ is the timed marking, M_0 is the initial marking of a timed Petri net.

To determine the availability and unavailability of tokens, two functions on the set of markings are defined. The set of markings is denoted by $\mathbb{M}$. Given a marking and model time, $m : P \times \mathbb{M} \times TS \to \mathbb{N}$ defines the number of available tokens, and $n : P \times \mathbb{M} \times TS \to \mathbb{N}$ the number of unavailable tokens for each place of a TPN at a given time τ_k. Note that model time also belongs to time set TS, $\tau_k \in TS$.

Using the above definitions, addition and subtraction of timed markings, and the TPN firing rule can be defined. Given a marked $TPN = (\mathcal{N}, M)$, a transition t is time enabled at time τ_k, denoted $M[t\rangle_{\tau_k}$ iff $m(p, M, \tau_k) \geq Pre(p,t), \forall p \in \bullet t$. An enabled transition can fire, and as a result removes tokens from input places and creates tokens in output places. The newly created tokens are accompanied by timestamps depending on the model time and the delay of transition that created the tokens. If marking M_2 is reached from M_1 by firing t at time τ_k, this is denoted by $M_1[t\rangle_{\tau_k} M_2$. The set of markings of TPN $\mathcal{N}$ reachable from M is denoted by $R(\mathcal{N}, M)$.

3. Modelling procedure

Petri nets are a family of tools that provide a framework, which can be used for various problems that appear during the life-cycle of a production system [18]. In this section we present the modelling of production system using timed Petri nets for the purpose of performance control. When timed Petri nets are used, it is possible to derive performance measures such as makespan, throughput, production rates, and other temporal quantities. The Petri net model is built based on the data stored in production management information systems, i.e., ERP system.

3.1. The class of production systems

With the method presented here several scheduling problems that appear in various production systems can be solved. In a discrete manufacturing different jobs are needed to produce a final product that is composed of several components. Similarly in batch production different activities have to be performed in order to produce a final product. However, here the resultant product is produced with some irreversible change, e.g. products are mixed from quantities of ingredients.

Different management systems (*ERP*) can be applied for different types of production systems to plan the production process activities. We are assuming here a management system that can provide plan for both, discrete and batch process. The system generates work orders that interfere with the demands for the desired products. Different jobs/procedures are needed to produce a desired product. Set of operations needed to produce one item represent a job. In general, more operations have to be performed using different resources in order to complete a specific job. To complete a specific product, more sub-products may be needed. To list these components a BOM is used in discrete manufacturing and formulas in batch manufacturing. These components determine sub-jobs that are needed to manufacture a parent item. In this way the general scheduling problem is defined that can be applied both in discrete or batch production environment and can be given as:

- n jobs are to be processed: $J = \{J_j\}, j = 1, ..., n,$
- r resources are available: $M = \{M_i\}, i = 1, ..., r,$
- each job J_i is composed of n_j operations: $O_j = \{o_{jk}\}, k = 1, ..., n_j,$
- each operation can be processed on (more) different sets of resources $S_{jkl} \in R; l$ determines the number of different sets,
- the processing time of each operation o_{jkl}, using resource set S_{jkl}, is defined with T_{jkl},
- precedence constraints are used to define that some operations within one job has to be performed before a set of operations in another job.

Using this definition, the following assumptions have to be considered:

- Resources are always available and never break down.
- Each resource can process a limited number of operations. This limitation is defined by the capacity of resources.
- Operations are non pre-emptive.
- When an operation is performed, it is desirable to free the resources so that they can become available as soon as possible. Intermediate buffers between processes are common solutions. It is common for batch processes that successive operations need to be performed on the same resource as predecessor. In this case the resource is free when the last operation is finished.
- Processing times are deterministic and known in advance.
- Work orders define the quantity of desired products and the starting times. Orders that are synchronised in time are considered jointly.

3.2. Modelling of production activities

Here we present a method of describing the production-system activities with timed Petri nets using the holding-duration representation of time. The places represent resources and jobs/operations, and the transitions represent decisions or rules for resources assignment/release and for starting/ending jobs.

To make a product, a set of operations has to be performed. We can think of an operation as a set of events and activities. Using a timed PN, events are represented by transitions and activity is associated with the presence of a token in a place.

An elementary operation can be described with one place and two transitions, see Figure 1. When all the input conditions are met (raw material and resources are available) the event that starts the operation occurs, t_1. This transition also determines the processing time of an operation. During that time the created token is unavailable in place p_2 and the operation is being executed. After that time the condition for ending the operation is being satisfied and t_2 can be fired. Place p_1 is not a part of the operation, it determines the input condition, e.g. the availability of the input material.

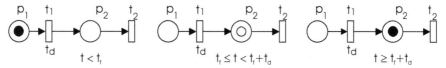

Figure 1. Operation described with timed Petri net.

When parallel activities need to be described the Petri-net structure presented in Figure 2 is used. Transition t_0 sets the input conditions for the parallel execution of two operations. In places p_{01} and p_{02} operations can wait for the available resource(s). The time delays of the transitions t_{11in} and t_{12in} define the duration of each operation. An available token in place p_{11} (p_{12}) indicates that operation is finished. Transition t_1 is used to synchronise both operations.

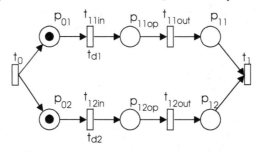

Figure 2. Two parallel operations.

An operation might need resources, usually with a limited capacity, to be executed; this is illustrated in Figure 3. Place p_{R1} is used to model a resource R_1. Its capacity is defined with the initial marking of that place. The resource is available to process the operation if there are enough available tokens in it. When the resource is used at the start of the operation the unavailable token appears in place p_{1op}. After the time defined by transition t_{1in} the token becomes available, t_{1out} is fired, and the resource becomes free to operate on the next job. For this reason zero time needs to be assigned to the transition t_{1out}. An additional place p_1 models the control flow. When the token is present in this place, the next operation can begin.

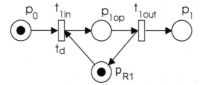

Figure 3. Operation that uses a resource with finite capacity.

A particular operation can often be done on more different (sets of) resources with different availability, and the time duration can be different on each set of resources. An example where an operation can be executed on two different sets of resources is shown in Figure 4. If the operation chooses resource R_3, its time duration is determined with the transition $f(t_{2in}) = t_{d2}$. Otherwise the set of resources, composed of R_1 and R_2, is being selected and its operation time is defined with $f(t_{1in}) = t_{d1}$.

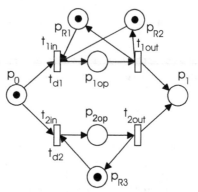

Figure 4. Operation that can be performed on two different sets of resources.

There are common situations where more operations use the same resource, e.g., an automated guided vehicle (AGV) in a manufacturing system or a mixing reactor in a batch system. This can be modelled as shown in Figure 5.

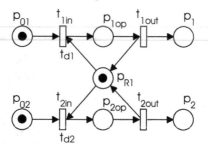

Figure 5. Shared resource.

Precedence constraints are used to define technological limitations and the sequence of operations. An example of two successive operations is shown in Figure 6, depicted as $Op1$ and $Op2$. In this figure an example of technological limitations is also shown. Here, the situation where operation $Op1$ precedes operation $Op3$ is considered. For this purpose an additional place p_{pr1} is inserted between the transition t_{1out} (ending $Op1$) and the transition t_{3in} (starting $Op3$). The weight n of the arc, which connects p_{pr1} to t_{3in}, prescribes how many items need to be produced by the first operation before the second operation can begin.

3.3. Modelling using the data from production-management systems

The most widely used production-management information system in practice are MRP II and ERP. Data stored in those systems can be used to build up a detailed model of the production system with Petri nets. In discrete manufacturing these data are bills of material and routing, while in batch manufacturing master formula and recipe are used to determine the production

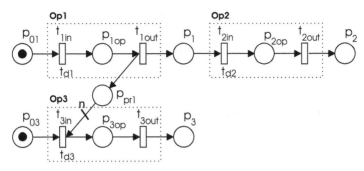

Figure 6. Precedence constraint.

process. Work orders are used to determine which and how many of finished products have to be produced.

3.3.1. Bill of materials (Formula)

The Bill of materials (BOM) is a listing or description of the raw materials and items that make up a product, along with the required quantity of each. In batch manufacturing other terms are used instead, i.e. Formula.

The BOM used in this work is defined as:

$BOM = (R, E, q, pre)$, where:

- $R = \{r_1\}$ is a root item.

- $E = \{e_1, ..., e_i\}$ is a finite set of sub-items,

- $q : E \rightarrow \mathbb{N}$ is the function that defines the quantities for each sub-item e_i. **q** represents an $i \times 1$ column vector whose ith entry is $q(e_i)$.

- $pre : (E \times E) \rightarrow \{0,1\}$ is a precedence-constraints function. It defines the precedence-constraints matrix **pre**, where $\mathbf{pre}(i, j) = 1$ indicates that the i-th item precedes the j-th item. It can also be interpreted as a directed graph.

R is a root item and represents the product that is composed of sub-items described with $e_i \in E$. The number of required sub-items is determined with the vector **q**. When any sub-item has to be produced before another, the precedence function pre is used to define it. All the sub-items have to be finished before the operation for the subsequent sub-items can begin. A required property of **pre** is that only zero values can be on its diagonal, i.e. a sub-item cannot precede itself. An item is never allowed to become (indirectly) a component of itself. In other words, if the BOM structure is seen as a directed graph, this graph should be cycle-free [21].

If any of the sub-items e_i are composed of any other sub-items, the same BOM definition is used to describe its dependencies. The items at the highest level of this structure represent a finished product, and those at the lower level represent raw materials. The items that represent raw materials do not have a BOM.

Table 1 shows an example of a BOM describing the production of product I, which is composed of three components, i.e., three items of J, one item of K and and two items of

Item	Sub-item	Quantity	Precedence constraints		
I	J	3	0	1	0
	K	1	0	0	0
	L	2	0	0	0

Table 1. Example of the BOM structure.

L. From the precedence-constraint matrix it is clear that all of the items J has to be completed before the production of item K can begin.

The mathematical representation of the BOM of item I would be represented as:

$$BOM = (R, E, \mathbf{q}, \mathbf{pre}), \text{ where } R = \{I\},$$

$$E = \{J\,K\,L\}, \quad \mathbf{q} = \begin{bmatrix} 3\,1\,2 \end{bmatrix} \quad \text{and} \quad \mathbf{pre} = \begin{bmatrix} 0\,1\,0 \\ 0\,0\,0 \\ 0\,0\,0 \end{bmatrix}.$$

To start with building a model, let us assume that, for each item from the BOM, only one operation is needed. As stated before, each operation can be represented with one place and two transitions (Figure 1). To be able to prescribe how many of each item is required the transition t_{Rin} and the place p_{Rin} are added in front, and p_{Rout} and t_{Rout} are added behind this operation. The weight of the arcs that connect t_{Rin} with p_{Rin} and p_{Rout} with t_{Rout} are determined by the quantity q_0 of the required items. In this way an item I is represented with a Petri net as defined in Figure 7.

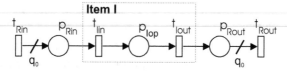

Figure 7. PN structure representing one item in the BOM.

As finished product is defined with a structure of BOMs, the construction of the overall Petri net is an iterative procedure that starts with the root of the BOM and continues until all the items have been considered. If the item requires any more sub-assemblies (i.e., items from a lower level) the operation, the framed area of the PN structure presented in Figure 7, is substituted with lower-level items. If there are more than one sub-items, they are given as parallel activities.

The substitution of an item with sub-items is defined as follows:

- Remove the place p_{Iop} and its input/output arcs.
- Define the PN structure for sub-components, as it is defined with a BOM. Consider the precedence constraints.
- Replace the removed place p_{Iop} by the sub-net defined in the previous step. The input and output transitions are merged with the existing ones.

The result of building the PN model of this example (Table 1) is given in Figure 8, where item I is composed of three subitems: J, K and L.

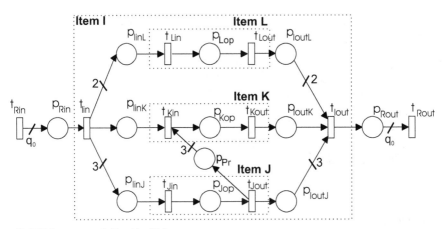

Figure 8. BOM structure defined by PN.

3.3.2. Routings (Recipe)

For each item that can appear in production process, and does not represent a raw material, a routing is defined. It defines a job with sequence of operations, each requiring processing by a particular resource for a certain processing time, which are needed for transforming raw material into the (sub)product. This information are provided by routing tables in discrete manufacturing, and by recipes in batch manufacturing industries. The table contains a header, where the item that is being composed is defined and the lines where all the required operations are described. For each operation one line is used.

As an example, the routing table for item K is given as presented in Table 2. Three operations are needed to produce this item; the first of these operations can be done on two different resources. Similar notation is used for other possible cases, e.g. an operation that needs three resources R_1 and two R_2, or one resource R_1 and three R_3 would be presented by $(3 \times R_1, 2 \times R_2)/(R_1, 3 \times R_3)$.

Operations	Duration	Resources
Op10	10s/9s	R1/R3
Op20	20s	R2
Op30	12s	R1

Table 2. Routing of product K.

The implementation of the routing data in one item of a BOM is defined as follows:

- Remove the place p_{Xop} and its input/output arcs.
- Define a PN structure for the sub-components, as it is defined with routing data. Also precedence constraints are considered here.
- Place p_{Xop} is replaced with the sub-net defined in previous step, where input and output transitions are merged with the existing ones.

Function that defines PN structure for every sub-component yields the corresponding sequence of production operations from the routing table and for each operation a timed Petri net is built as defined in section 3.3.1. All the placed operations are connected as prescribed by the required technological sequence, and each operation is assigned to the required places representing appropriate resources.

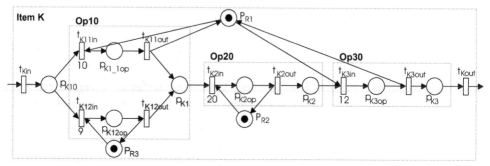

Figure 9. Routing of product *K* modelled with timed Petri net.

The PN structure in Figure 9 is achieved if the sequence of operations described with a routing table (Table 2) is modelled. The resulting PN structure is inserted into the main PN model, on the place where item *K* (p_{Kop}) was.

The routings/recipes are submodels that are inserted (by substitution, as defined previously) into the main model defined with the BOM structure. However, some activities of any sub-item may also be described with a BOM, i.e., in the case they are composed of semi-products. The construction of the overall Petri-net model can be achieved by combining all of the intermediate steps.

3.3.3. Work order

The work order ($WO = [R, q_0, st]$) determines which and how many of the finished products have to be produced. Each product (R) can be represented with a Petri-net model, shown in Figure 7, where one place is added in front and one at the end of the structure to determine the start and end of the work. As usually more products are produced at one time (one product is represented with one batch), the weight of the arc that connects t_{Rin} and p_{Rin} are used to determine the number of required batches (q_0). To be able to consider different starting times for different quantities of one product the general structure shown in Figure 10 is used. q_0 determines the number of products to be finished. Orders for products which should start with the production at the same time are merged and every group of products with the same starting time is modelled with places $p_1, p_2, ...p_n$ and with tokens located in them. The timestamps, which are assigned to these tokens determine the starting time of every group of products. Wights $q_1, q_2, ...q_n$ determine the number of products, where $q_1 + q_2 + ... + q_n$ is equal to q_0. The token in the place p_{end} implies that WO is finished.

3.4. Specifics of batch production processes

In previous sections (3.3.1 – 3.3.3) we present methods to represent formula, recipe and work orders with Petri nets. As given so far these elements can be equally used for discrete and batch process environments. However, as mentioned in 3.1 there are some specifics in batch production processes.

Actually batch production is more complicated and formula and recipe are more connected as are BOM and routings [7]. There are common situations where precedence constraints

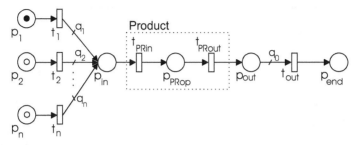

Figure 10. Petri net structure of a work order.

are not used only to define interdependencies between different (finished) items, but also for interdependencies between job operations of various items that are defined with recipes. In this situations the definition of BOM (Formula) has to be extended.

Definition of a sub-items set E is extended in a way that it contain also the information about operations that produce that item: $E = \{(e_1, o_{1k}), ...(e_i, o_{in_j})\}$.

Further also a precedence-constraint function *pre* is extended in order to include information about how many operations are needed for every item. As defined in 3.1, set of operations needed to produce j-th item is given as $O_j = \{o_{jk}\}$, where $k = 1, ..., n_j$. Size of the matrix is therefore defined with $[m \times m]$, where $m = \sum n_j$, $j = 1...n$. Here n is number of items that make up a product. In this way we can define an extended precedence-constraints function *pre* as $pre : ((E \times O) \times (E \times O)) \rightarrow \{0, 1\}$. Element from constraint matrix $pre(p_{ij}, p_{kl}) = 1$ indicates that the j-th operation from i-th item precedes l-th operation from k-th item. Here index p_{ij} in a matrix **pre** presents j-th operation of i-th item and p_{kl} l-th operation of k-th item.

3.5. Procedure for building the PN model

With WO demands for product to be finished are passed. For each WO a Petri net model has to be defined. The modelling procedure can be summarised in the Algorithm 1.

Algorithm 1 Read BOM

[R, q, st] = *readWO*()
For i = 1 **to** *length*(R)
    E = *readBOM*(R(i))
    PN = *placePN*(R(i), E, q(i), [ ], st(i), x0, y0)
    PN = *routing*(PN, R(i))
end

First, the data about the WO are read. The products that are needed to be produced are given in R; in vector **q** the quantities of the desired products are passed; and vector **st** is used to determine the starting time of each product. For each product the Petri-net structure, shown in Figure 10, is determined and placed on the model. The step when the *routing*() is called is described in more detail with algorithm 2.

First, the routing and the BOM data are read from the database (functions *readRouting*() and *readBOM*()). For each operation that comprises the routing, the algorithm checks whether it is made up of sub-item(s) or this is an operation. In the first case, the function *placePN*() is used to determine the PN structure of the given structure BOM. Precedence constraints are added

---

Algorithm 2 Read Routing

---

function PN = *routing*(PN, R)
datRoute = *readRouting*(R)
[E, q, pre] = *readBOM*(R)
for i = 1 **to** *length*(datRoute.Op)
   if datRoute.Resources ==BOM
     PN1 = *placePN*(R, E, q, pre, [ ])
     PN = *insertPN*(PN, PN1)
     for j = 1 **to** *length*(E)
       PN1 = *routing*(PN1, E(j))
     end
   else
     PN = *constructPN*(PN, datRoute(i))
     PN = *insertPN*(PN, PN1)
   end
  end

---

if they exist. With the function *insertPN()* the resulting subnet is inserted into the main PN structure. If the operation represents the production operation, the function *constructPN()* is called. With it, basic elements (Figures 1–6) are recognised, joined together and placed in the model, again using the function *insertPN()*. All the data about resources and time durations are acquired from the routing table. The described algorithm has been implemented in Matlab.

The resulting model is stored in a XML-based format employing Petri Net Markup Language (PNML) [6].

3.6. Verification

When the model is built up, it should be verified to see whether it reflects the system operation as defined with data about the production process. Some interesting properties of the model can be checked with the P-invariant analysis. Several P-invariants can be identified in the model. Their number is defined with the sum of all the resources, the number of product routes and the number of all precedences that are present in the model. It can be stated that the weighted sum of tokens that belongs to every P-invariant, which is a consequence of a resource, is equal to the capacity of that resource. The weighted sum of all other invariants is defined with the common number of batches of demanded product.

If possible, the model is later simplified in a way, that eliminated nodes do not influence the model behaviour.

4. Scheduling

Scheduling is one of the most important management functions and is a fundamental problem in the control of any resource-sharing organisation. Scheduling problems are very complex and many have been proven to be NP hard [8].

Literature on deterministic scheduling classifies the manufacturing scheduling problems according to machine environment structure, processing characteristics and constraints, and objectives. Standard machine environment structures lead to standard scheduling problems, e.g., open shop, flow shop and job shop problems, which are commonly studied. All three problem classes address a problem of sequencing n jobs (tasks) through a set of r machines (resources) where every job has to be processed once on every machine and every such job operation requires a specified processing time. The problems differ in restrictions on the job routings.

The scheduling problems related to batch plants possess a more complicated structure compared to standard scheduling problems. Batch plants are flexible and alternative resources can be used for conveying recipe operations. There may be different operation processing time assignments based on which equipment is used for processing and there may be specific requests on precedences or allowable intermediate storage time. This significantly complicates the problem of operations scheduling in batch processes. A comprehensive review of the state-of-the art of short-term batch scheduling is presented in [12]. Different types of batch scheduling problems are specified and the types of optimization models are reviewed. The presented models result in a formulation of MILP optimization problem and its solution yields an optimal schedule.

Petri nets can be used to effectively model all standard deterministic scheduling problem classes. Furthermore, the modelling power of Petri nets allows for derivation of models also for problems, which do not have standard problem structure but are closer to real process specifics. This is typical e.g. in batch systems where complex interconnections among process equipment are possible and vary considerably with used batch recipes. Even when the models are not as general as the above mentioned MILP problem representations, Petri nets can be used to model main model components of a two stage batch scheduling approach as defined in [12]. In contrast to monolithic approach the two stage approach assumes that the number of batches of each size is known in advance. The scheduling stage therefore concentrates on the allocation of processing resources to the batches while the plant work load is determined in a previous stage.

4.1. Petri net based derivation of optimal or sub-optimal schedules

To derive a feasible schedule, the obtained Petri net model can be simulated by an appropriate simulation algorithm. During the simulation, the occurring conflicts are resolved 'on the fly', e.g. by randomly choosing a transition in conflict that should fire. Instead, heuristic dispatching rules [5], such as Shortest Processing Time (SPT), can be introduced when solving the conflicting situations. The schedule of process operations can be determined by observing the marking evolution of the net. Depending on the given scheduling problem a convenient rule should be chosen. Usually, different rules are needed to improve different predefined production objectives (makespan, throughput, production rates, and other temporal quantities).

A more extensive exploration of the reachability tree is possible by PN-based heuristic search method proposed by [11]. It is based on generating parts of the Petri net reachability tree, where the branches are weighted by the time of the corresponding operations. The chosen transition firing sequence corresponds to a schedule, and by evaluating a number of sequences a (sub)optimal schedule can be determined. The method is further investigated in [22], where a modified heuristic function is proposed and tested on a number of benchmark tests. The problems of the approach are in the complexity of the reachability tree, which can generally not be completely explored. The search has to be limited to predefined maximum tree size in order to complete in a reasonable time. In addition to that, the heuristic function used within the search has to be chosen such that the search is directed more into the depth of the tree, which makes the obtained solution very sensitive to decisions taken at initial levels of the tree and in many cases the quality of the obtained solutions is rather low.

Recent reports in scheduling literature show an increased interest in the use of meta-heuristics, such as genetic algorithms (GA), simulated annealing (SA), and tabu search (TS). Meta-heuristics have also been combined with Petri net modelling framework to solve complex scheduling problems [19]. With such an approach, the modelling power of Petri nets can be employed, and relatively good solutions of scheduling problems can be found with a reasonable computational effort, although the convergence to the optimum can not be guaranteed. Compared to reachability tree based search methods, meta-heuristics require less memory.

The problem is that these methods require a sort of neghbouring solution generation strategy. This is easily accomplished for well structured problems, e.g. standard scheduling problems, but may be problematic for general models. In contrast, reachability tree methods as well as priority rule based methods can be used with any type of Petri net model. This motivates the investigation of combined methods, such as the combination of dispatching rules and local search [13].

Dispatching rules, however, do not always enable to reach the optimum even if combined with optimization methods. Using the rule based conflict resolution strategy the solution space is explored in a time driven manner where a transition is fired whenever at least one transition is enabled. In contrast, the reachability tree based methods enable to explore the solution space in an event driven manner. It is possible that a chosen firing sequence imposes one or more intervals of idle time between transitions, i.e. some transitions are enabled but do not fire due to waiting for enablement of another transition in accordance to the chosen sequence. The difference is important in cases when the optimal solution can be missed unless some idle time is included in the schedule as shown in [15]. In other words, the optimal solution generally belongs to the class of semi-active schedules [16]. The schedules generated by an event-driven reachability tree search are semi-active schedules.

4.2. Algorithmically generated Petri net models and schedules

In contrast to academic investigation of static scheduling problems the real manufacturing environment is far more dynamic. Planned work orders are often changing, priority orders are inserted, planned resources may become unavailable. A fast derivation of models that adequately represent the current situation in the process is therefore of extreme importance for a usable scheduling system. The above described automatic generation of Petri net models can be effectively used for these purposes.

The proposed algorithm also allows for specific process sequence structures typical for batch processes. E.g., the scheduling literature typically addresses a type of problems where a resource required by an operation is released as soon as the operation is finished. This is typical in the discrete industry, where intermediate products are stored in buffer zones in between machines. In batch processes the situation is different in the sense that a resource, e.g. a reactor is used both for processing and intermediate storage. The resource can be occupied by a number of successive operations, which can be easily modelled by Petri nets. Furthermore, the use of timestamped tokens provides a convenient representation of the time status of the processed work orders.

4.3. Evaluation of schedules

As the majority of commonly used scheduling objective functions are based on completion times of the jobs or work orders and due dates, the timed Petri net modelling framework yields a possibility to use the same kind of model with an objective function tailored to the needs of the particular production scenario.

In the field of deterministic scheduling the objective to be minimised is always a function of the completion times of the jobs or work orders [16]. This fits well in the timed Petri net scheduling framework where the time evolution of the net marking depends on timestamps associated with the tokens. If the schedule is modelled properly, the work order completion times can be read from the timestamps of tokens in the final marking obtained by timed Petri net simulation.

Let o_{ji} denote the i-th operation of work order j. Let C_{ji} denote the completion time of the operation o_{ji}. The completion time of the work order, i.e. the completion of the last operation of the work order is denoted by C_j.

During the timed Petri net marking evolution, start of o_{ji} corresponds to triggering of a related transition t_{ji}. Associated delay $f(t_{ji})$ corresponds to duration of o_{ji}. Following the firing rule, the transition output places are marked with tokens whose time attribute is set to $@(\rho_{ji} + f(t_{ji}))$ if ρ_{ji} denotes the moment of transition firing, i.e., the release time of o_{ji}. The generated timestamp equals the completion time of o_{ji}: $C_{ji} = \rho_{ji} + f(t_{ji})$.

Assuming the timed Petri net model of scheduling problem as described above, let $p_{WO\_j\_end} \subset P$ denote the j-th work order end place, i.e. the place that holds a token representing finished status of the work order. Let M_f denote the final marking reached after all the operations had been finished. If a token in $p_{WO\_j\_end}$ corresponds to finishing the last operation of work order WO_j then $M_f(p_{WO\_j\_end}) = 1@C_j$. Therefore the completion times can be read from $M_f(p_{WO\_j\_end})$: $C_j = M_f(p_{WO\_j\_end}) \subset TS_{MS}$.

4.3.1. Makespan

Makespan C_{max} is equivalent to the completion time of the last finished work order: $C_{max} = max(C_1, \ldots, C_n)$. Considering the above notation

$$C_{max} = max(M_f(p_{WO\_j\_end})), j = 1 \ldots n \tag{1}$$

4.3.2. Total weighted completion time

The sum of weighted completion times gives an indication of the inventory costs related to a schedule [16]. Given a final marking M_f the cost can be calculated as

$$\sum w_j C_j = \sum_{j=1}^{n} w_j M_f(p_{WO\_j\_end}) \tag{2}$$

4.3.3. Tardiness

If a set of due dates d_j is adjoined to the work orders, the tardiness of a work order is defined as the difference $C_j - d_j$ if positive, and 0 otherwise:

$$T_j = max(M_f(p_{WO\_j\_end}) - d_j, 0) \qquad\qquad (3)$$

In contrast to objective measures, which are related to final marking, the initial marking can be used to specify release dates of work orders. If a token in $p_{WO\_j\_st}$ corresponds to the initial request of work order WO_j, and r_j is a corresponding release date then $M_0(p_{WO\_j\_st})$ should contain a token $1@r_j$.

5. A case study: Multiproduct batch plant

The applicability of our approach will be demonstrated on the model of a multiproduct batch plant designed and built at the Process Control Laboratory of the University of Dortmund. The demonstration plant is relatively simple compared to industrial-scale plants, but poses complex control tasks. A detailed description of the plant can be found in [17].

In the following a brief description of the plant will be given. From the data given in production management systems a timed Petri-net model is built. With the help of a simulator/scheduler using different scheduling rules, different schedules can be achieved. At the end the results for the given problem are presented and compared with the results achieved with other techniques.

5.1. Description of the plant

The process under consideration is a batch process that produces two liquid substances, one blue, one green, from three liquid raw materials. The first is coloured yellow, the second red and the third is colourless. The colourless sodium hydroxide (NaOH) will be referred to below as white. The chemical reaction behind the change of colours is the neutralisation of diluted hydrochloric acid (HCl) with diluted NaOH. The diluted HCl acid is mixed with two different pH indicators to make the acid look yellow if it is mixed with the first one and red when mixed with the second one. During the neutralisation reaction the pH indicators change their colour when the pH value reaches approximately 7. The first indicator changes from yellow to blue, and the second from red to green.

The plant consists of three different layers, see Figure 11. The first layer consists of the buffering tanks B11, B12 and B13, which are used for holding the raw materials "Yellow", "Red" and "White". The middle layer consists of three stirred tank reactors, R21, R22 and R23. Each reactor can be filled from any raw-material buffer tank. The production involves filling the reactor with one batch of "Yellow" or "Red" and then neutralising it with one batch of "White". The lower layer consists of two buffer tanks, B31 and B32, in which the products are collected from the middle layer. Each of them is used exclusively for "Blue" or "Green" and can contain three batches of product. The processing times of the plant are presented in Table 3. The system can be influenced through different inputs, pumps P1-P5 and valves V111-V311.

5.2. The scheduling problem

The plant provides a variety of scheduling problems. In our case we are dealing with a problem, where we have a demand to produce a certain amount of finished products. Also the starting times of every work order are given. Our task is to determine when raw materials must be available and when the overall production process will be finished. Our goal is to finish the production in the shortest time.

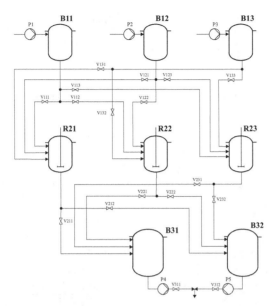

Figure 11. Multiproduct batch plant.

Process	Time(s)
Pumping 1 batch "Yellow" into B11	12
Pumping 1 batch "Red" into B12	12
Pumping 1 batch "White" into B13	12
Draining 1 batch "Yellow" into R21	15
Draining 1 batch "Red" into R21	11
Draining 1 batch "White" into R21	10
Draining 1 batch "Yellow" into R22	12
Draining 1 batch "Red" into R22	13
Draining 1 batch "White" into R22	9
Draining 1 batch "Yellow" into R23	12
Draining 1 batch "Red" into R23	14
Draining 1 batch "White" into R23	13
Draining 1 batch "Blue" from R21 into B31	12
Draining 1 batch "Green" from R21 into B32	13
Draining 1 batch "Blue" from R22 into B31	12
Draining 1 batch "Green" from R22 into B32	12
Draining 1 batch "Blue" from R23 into B31	12
Draining 1 batch "Green" from R23 into B32	12
Pumping 3 batches "Red" out of B31	30
Pumping 3 batches "Green" out of B32	30

Table 3. Processing times.

Work orders, given in table 4, illustrate the problem, where six batches of "Blue" (PB) and six batches of "Green" (PG) products have to be produced. It follows that we need six batches of "Yellow" and "Red" raw materials and twelve batches of "White" raw material.

Product	Code	Amount	Starting time
Blue	PB	6	0
Green	PG	6	0

Table 4. Work orders.

5.3. Structure of the production facility given in production management system

Data about the production process and its structure can be obtained from the production management information systems. These data can be presented in a form of a recipe and the formula as described in chapter 3.4.

There are two recipes available, which are specifying a sequence of operations needed to produce product "PB" and product "PG". They are given with tables 5 and 6.

	Operation	Duration	Resources
PB	Op10	–	BOM_B
	Op20 draining R2x in B31	12/12/12	[R_1](R21/R22/R23), B31
	Op30 pumping from B31	30	$(3 \times 1) \times$ B31
Y	Op10 pumping Y in B11	12	[BY_1](B11)
	Op20 draining B11 in R2x	15/12/12	[R_3](R21/R22/R23), [BY_2](B11)
WB	Op10 pumping W in B13	12	[BW_1](B13)
	Op20 draining B13 in R2x	10/9/13	[R_2](R21/R22/R23), [BW_2](B13)

Table 5. Recipe of a product "PB".

	Operation	Duration	Resources
PG	Op10	–	BOM_ G
	Op20 draining R2x in B32	13/12/12	[R_ 1](R21/R22/R23), B32
	Op30 pumping from B32	30	$(3 \times 1) \times$ B32
R	Op10 pumping Y in B12	12	[BR_ 1](B12)
	Op20 draining B12 in R2x	11/13/14	[R_ 3](R21/R22/R23), [BR_ 2](B12)
WG	Op10 pumping W in B13	12	[BW_ 1](B13)
	Op20 draining B13 v R2x	10/9/13	[R_ 2](R21/R22/R23), [BW_ 2](B13)

Table 6. Recipe of a product "PG".

To produce Blue product ("PB"), firstly operation *Op10* has to be carried out. This operation determines only that a sub-product, defined with formula "B", is needed. When this sub-product is ready, two more operations are needed. *Op20* gives information about draining the product into the buffer tank *B31* and *Op30* about pumping the final product out of that buffer tank. The fact, that buffer tank could not be emptied before three batches of sub-product "B" are poured in it, is described with this notation: $(3 \times 1) \times B31$.

In batch manufacturing situations when one task has to be executed with a (group of) resource(s), that were used to execute a previous task already are common. These resources are in our case labelled with an additional mark, i.e. code with serial number in square brackets is added in front of this resource(s). For example, this occurs in our case when one of the reactor is being used. Code [R_1] is assigned to the reactor (from a group of reactors R2x) which is needed for operation *Op20* when producing product "B" and indicates that this resource can now be released. Note, that this resource was assigned with an operation where code [R_3] was used already (*Op10* of a sub-product "Y").

Formula given in Table 7 lists the raw materials needed to produce items "B" and "G". Item "B" represents a sub-product that is needed for operation *Op10* of a recipe "PB". The production of one item "B" requires one "Yellow" ("Y") and one "White" ("WB") batches (items). Each of these two items are produced with two operations. Note that some batch-specific precedence constraints exists. Operation *Op20* of item "Y" precede operation *Op20* of item "WB". The structure of item "G" is given in a similar way.

Item	Sub-item	Quantity	Preced. constr.			
B	Y, Op10	1	0	0	0	0
	Y, Op20		0	0	0	1
	WB, Op10	1	0	0	0	0
	WB, Op20		0	0	0	0
G	R, Op10	1	0	0	0	0
	R, Op20		0	0	0	1
	WG, Op10	1	0	0	0	0
	WG, Op20		0	0	0	0

Table 7. Formula for the items "B" and "G".

5.4. Modelling

In this subchapter production process described previously is modelled with timed Petri nets. To build a model the algorithm from Chapter 3.5 is used. This model can later be used to schedule all the tasks, that are necessary to produce as much final products as required by work orders.

From work orders, given in table 4 it is recognised which and how much of each products are required. Let start with the procedure on building the Blue product ("PB"). When applying the first step of our algorithm, the PN structure shown in figure 12 is achieved.

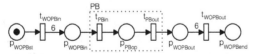

Figure 12. PN model of PB product.

In the second step, additional information are added into this model (framed part of figure 12). Data about all the details are gathered from recipe list of product "PB" (table 5). Information about emptying the buffer tank *B31* (*Op30*) and draining the reactor *R2x* (*Op20*) are added. As operation (*Op20*) needs resources, that are used by previous operations, not all details are added yet at this place. A model, shown in Figure 13 is achieved.

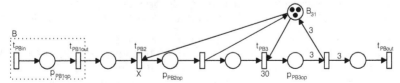

Figure 13. PN model of PB product.

Operation *Op10* (place P_{PB10p}) is defined with formula for item "B" (see table 7). It represents a mixing operation of two raw materials "Y" and "WB". Both sub-items are described with two operations, where precedence constraints are included as given with formula. Figure 14 shows how this formula information is modelled with Petri nets.

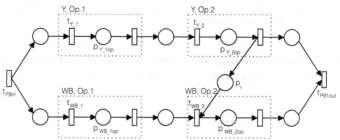

Figure 14. PN model of PB product with inserted BOM information.

In figure 15 some parts of a model given in figure 14 are simplified and information about the usage of rectors R_{2x} is added.

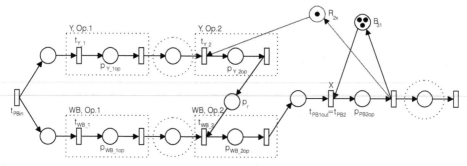

Figure 15. PN model of PB product.

As there are three possible reactors (R_{21}, R_{22} or R_{23}) that can be used to perform these operations this model is extended with the structure given in figure 16.

With this procedure a detailed timed Petri-net model of the production of the blue product ("PB") is obtained. The same procedure was performed to model also the production of green product ("PG"), and a Petri net model given in figure 17 is achieved.

5.5. Results

The resulting model was at the end verified using P-invariant analysis. We can find out eleven P-invariant, where eight of them refer to resources and three of them to the production routes.

In this way a Petri net model of a multiproduct batch plant was achieved on which different scheduling algorithms can be performed in order to obtain the most effective production. Petri-net simulation was used to evaluate different schedules of tasks that are needed to produce the desired amount of final products. Makespan was the performance measure of interest. The schedule allows an easy visualisation of the process and ensures that sufficient raw materials ("Yellow", "Red" and "White" batches) are available at the right time. It respects

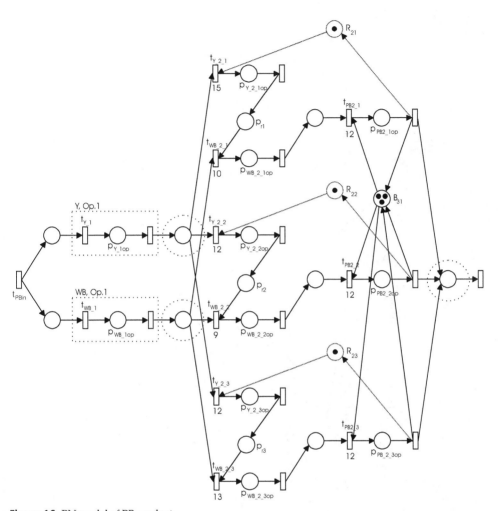

Figure 16. PN model of PB product.

all the production constraints and the duration of the whole process can be identified. A schedule of the batch process using SPT priority rule is given with Gantt chart (figure 18).

The results were compared with the results obtained using various algorithms and are presented in table 8.

Algorithm	Makespan
SPT rule	315s
LPT rule	331s
Branch and Bound ([17])	323s
MS Project ([3])	329s

Table 8. Results.

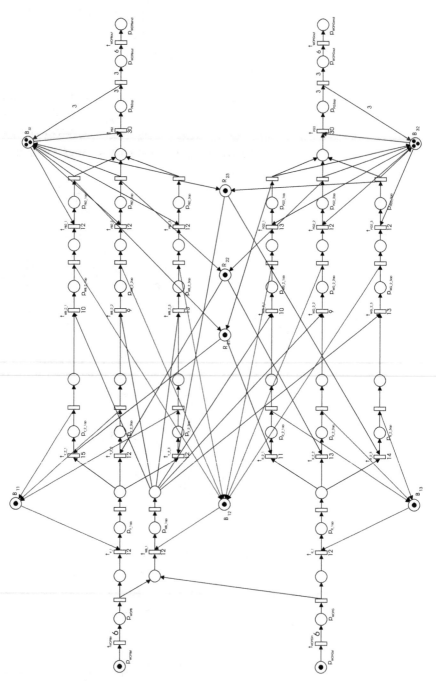

Figure 17. PN model of the production plant.

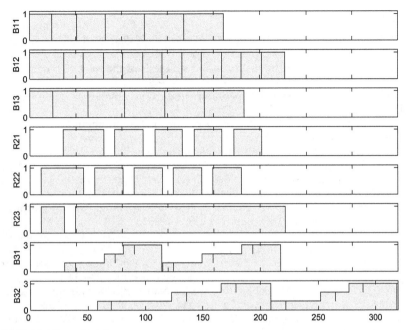

Figure 18. Production schedule.

6. Conclusion

A procedure for using existing data from production management systems to build the Petri-net model was developed. Timed Petri nets with the holding-duration principle of time implementation were used to model basic production activities. For the purposes of scheduling, different heuristic rules can be used within Petri net simulation. The applicability of the proposed approach was illustrated on a practical scheduling problem, where the data about the production facility is given with the formula and recipe. The model achieved with the proposed method was used to determine a schedule for production operations. The proposed method is an effective way to get an adequate model of the production process, which can be used to develop different analyses of the treated system, e.g. schedules.

Acknowledgements

The work was done in the frame of the Competence Centre for Advanced Control Technologies. Operation is partly financed by the Republic of Slovenia, Ministry of Education, Science, Culture and Sport and European Union (EU) - European Regional Development Fund.

Author details

Dejan Gradišar
Jožef Stefan Institute, Slovenia

Gašper Mušič
Faculty of Electrical Engineering, University of Ljubljana, Slovenia

7. References

[1] ANSI/ISA [1995]. *ANSI/ISA-88.01-1995 Batch Control Part 1: Models and Terminology (Formerly ANSI/ISA-S88.01-1995)*, ANSI/ISA.

[2] Bowden, F. D. J. [2000]. A brief survey and synthesis of the roles of time in Petri nets, *Mathematical and Computer Modelling* 31(10-12): 55–68.

[3] Gradišar, D. & Mušič, G. [2004]. Scheduling production activities using project planning tool, *Electrotechnical Review* 71(3): 83–88.

[4] Gu, T. & Bahri, P. A. [2002]. A survey of Petri net applications in batch processes, *Computers in Industry* 47(1): 99–111.

[5] Haupt, R. [1989]. A survey of priority rule-based scheduling, *OR Spectrum* 11(1): 3–16.

[6] Hillah, L., Kindler, E., Kordon, F., Petrucci, L. & Treves, N. [2009]. A primer on the Petri net markup language and ISO/IEC 15909-2, *Petri Net Newsletter* 76: 9–28.

[7] ISA [2008]. *ISA-TR88.95.01 Using ISA-88 and ISA-95 Together*, ISA.

[8] Jain, A. & Meeran, S. [1999]. Deterministic job-shop scheduling: Past, present and future, *European Journal of Operational Research* 113(2): 390–434.

[9] Jensen, K. [1997]. *Coloured Petri nets. Basic concepts, analysis methods and practical use*, Springer-Verlag, Berlin.

[10] Lakos, C. & Petrucci, L. [2007]. Modular state space exploration for timed Petri nets, *International Journal on Software Tools for Technology Transfer* 9: 393–411.

[11] Lee, D. & DiCesare, F. [1994]. Scheduling flexible manufacturing systems using Petri nets and heuristic search, *IEEE Trans. on Robotics and Automation* 10(2): 123–132.

[12] Méndez, C., Cerdá, J., Grossmann, I. E., Harjunkoski, I. & Fahl, M. [2006]. State-of-the-art review of optimization methods for short-term scheduling of batch processes, *Computers & Chemical Engineering* 30(6-7): 913–946.

[13] Mušič, G. [2009]. Petri net base scheduling approach combining dispatching rules and local search, *21st European Modeling & Simulation Symposium*, Vol. 2, Puerto de La Cruz, Tenerife, Spain, pp. 27–32.

[14] Nortcliffe, A. L., Thompson, M., Shaw, K. J., Love, J. & Fleming, P. J. [2001]. A framework for modelling in S88 constructs for scheduling purposes, *ISA Transactions* 40(3): 295–305.

[15] Piera, M. A. & Mušič, G. [2011]. Coloured Petri net scheduling models: Timed state space exploration shortages, *Math.Comput.Simul.* 82: 428–441.

[16] Pinedo, M. L. [2008]. *Scheduling: Theory, Algorithms, and Systems*, 3rd edn, Springer Publishing Company.

[17] Potočnik, B., Bemporad, A., Torrisi, F., Mušič, G. & Zupančič, B. [2004]. Hybrid modelling and optimal control of a multi product bach plant, *Control Engineering Practice* 12(9): 1127–1137.

[18] Silva, M. & Teruel, E. [1997]. Petri nets for the design and operation of manufacturing systems, *European Journal of Control* 3(3): 182–199.

[19] Tuncel, G. & Bayhan, G. [2007]. Applications of petri nets in production scheduling: a review, *The International Journal of Advanced Manufacturing Technology* 34(7-8): 762–773.

[20] Wijngaard, J. & Zijlstra, P. [1992]. MRP application the batch process industry, *Production Planning & Control* 3(3): 264–270.

[21] Wortmann, H. [1995]. Comparison of information systems for engineer-to-order and make-to-stock situations, *Computers in Industry* 26(3): 261–271.

[22] Yu, H., Reyes, A., Cang, S. & Lloyd, S. [2003]. Combined Petri net modelling and AI based heuristic hybrid search for flexible manufacturing systems-part II: Heuristic hybrid search, *Computers and Industrial Engineering* 44(4): 545–566.

[23] Zuberek, W. M. [1991]. Timed petri nets: definitions, properties and applications, *Microelectronics and Reliability* 31(4): 627–644.

Chapter 2

A Computationally Improved Optimal Solution for Deadlocked Problems of Flexible Manufacturing Systems Using Theory of Regions

Yen-Liang Pan

Additional information is available at the end of the chapter

1. Introduction

While competing for a finite number of resources in a flexible manufacturing system (FMS), e.g., robots and machines, each part has a particular operational flow that determines the order in which such resources are needed. However, such competition for shared resources by concurrent job processes can lead to a system deadlock. It occurs when parts are blocked waiting for shared resources held by others that will never be granted. Its related blocking phenomena often incur unnecessary overhead cost, e.g., a long downtime and low utilization rate of some critical and expensive resources, possibly leading to a catastrophic outcome in some highly automated FMS. Therefore, an efficient deadlock control policy must be developed to ensure that deadlocks do not occur. Having received considerable attention in literature, deadlock is normally prevented by using an offline computational mechanism to control the resource requests in order to avert deadlocks. Fanti and Zhou[1] introduce three fundamental methods (i.e. prevention, detection and avoidance) to solve the deadlock problems. Deadlock prevention aims to impose system constraints to prevent a deadlock. Importantly, deadlock prevention algorithms do not require run-time costs since the problems are solved in system design and planning stages. This study belongs to the deadlock prevention field.

Petri nets (PN)[2] have been recognized as one of the most powerful formal methods for modeling FMS. The reason is that they are well suited to represent such FMS characteristics as precedence relations, concurrence, conflict and synchronization. Their analysis methods used for deadlock prevention in FMS include structural analysis and reachability graphs. Deadlock prevention and avoidance schemes have been developed for controlling FMS[3-8] by using the former. In particular, deadlock prevention problems are solved using the concept of siphons[3-6]. Li & Zhou propose an elementary siphon control policy (ESCP) to reduce the redundant siphons to obtain structurally simpler controllers[9-10]. However, they cannot obtain optimal ones. Reachability graph methods are used to obtain the live system behavior[11-14]. Without confining to a certain class of FMS, they can provide an optimal deadlock controller by adopting the theory of regions[15]. The theory is originally developed for a transition system (TS). A state-based representation with arcs labeled with symbols from an alphabet of events in a TS can be mapped into a PN model. For an elementary TS (ETS) there exists a PN with minimum transition count (one transition for each label) with a reachability graph isomorphic to the original TS.

Uzam[12] follows the theory of regions[15] to define a deadlock-zone (DZ) and deadlock-free zone (DFZ) for preventing deadlocks. Hence, the concept of DZ and DFZ is used to solve ESSPs. An optimal controller can be obtained but suffers from many redundant control places. Ghaffari et al.[13] propose a unique interpretation of the theory of regions and define M_F (forbidden marking), M_D (dangerous marking), M_L (legal marking), and Ω (the set of marking/transition-separation instances or MTSI). An optimal PN controller synthesis method for FMS is proposed based on both MTSI and the theory of regions. Unfortunately, redundant MTSIs cannot be entirely avoided for large FMS cases.

To reduce redundant control places, Li et al.[16] adopt a combined algorithm based on siphon control and the theory of regions[15]. Its advantage is that the number of separation instances is significantly reduced after some sets of elementary siphons of a system are controlled. However, it fails to determine all sets of MTSIs and its application seems limited to some special nets only.

Uzam and Zhou propose an iterative control policy of liveness enforcement for PNs based on the theory of regions[17]. Less computation is required to obtain a controller. However, as indicated by Li et al[18], it requires the repeated calculation of reachability graphs. Piroddi et al. propose a combined selective siphons and critical markings in a reachability graph algorithm to obtain optimal controllers via iterations[19]. They successfully identify the critical uncontrolled siphons and control them to make a deadlock-prone PN live. However, their algorithm also requires the repeated calculation of reachability graphs. Eventually, the controllers are not ordinary (i.e. they contain weighted arcs).

This work in this chapter aims to develop a computationally more efficient optimal deadlock control policy by using the theory of regions. It focuses on dead markings in a reachability graph. The concept of a crucial MTSI (CMTSI) is proposed to synthesize optimal controllers. The proposed method can reduce the computational burden of the MTSI method[13] and redundant control places[12-13]. The experimental results indicate that it is the most efficient policy among all known ones[12-13, 16] that can design optimal controllers.

Section 2 presents the basic definitions and properties of PNs and the theory of regions. Section 3 describes the proposed policy. Section 4 presents the experimental results. Section 5 gives the comparisons. Conclusions are made in Section 6.

2. Preliminaries

2.1. Petri nets[2]

A Petri net (PN) is a 5-tuple $N = (P, T, F, W, M_0)$ where P is a finite set of places; T is a finite set of transitions, with $P \cup T \neq \varnothing$ and $P \cap T = \varnothing$; $F \subseteq (P \times T) \cup (T \times P)$ is the set of all directed arcs, $W: (P \times T) \cup (T \times P) \rightarrow \mathbf{N}$ is the weight function where $\mathbf{N} = \{0, 1, 2, ...\}$, and $M_0: P \rightarrow \mathbf{N}$ is the initial marking. A PN is said to be ordinary, denoted as (P, T, F), if $\forall f \in F$, $W(f) = 1$. $[N]^+(p, t) = W(p, t)$ is the input function that means the multiplicity of a directed arc from p to t if $(p, t) \in F$. $[N]^-(p, t) = W(t, p)$ is the output function that means the multiplicity of a directed arc from t to p if $(t, p) \in F$. The set of input (resp., output) transitions of a place p is denoted by $\bullet p$ (resp., $p \bullet$). Similarly, the set of input (resp., output) places of a transition t is denoted by $\bullet t$ (resp., $t \bullet$). A PN structure (P, T, F, W) is denoted by N. A PN with a given initial marking is denoted by (N, M_0).

A PN is said to be pure if no place is both input and output places of the same transition. The so-called incidence matrix $[N]$ of a pure Petri nets is defined as $[N] = [N]^- - [N]^+$. A transition t is said to be enabled at marking M, if $\forall p \in \bullet t$, $M(p) \geq W(p, t)$, or p is marked with at least $W(p, t)$ tokens, as denoted by $M[t>$. A transition may fire if it is enabled. In an ordinary net, it is enabled iff $\forall p \in \bullet t$, $M(p) \geq 1$. Firing t at M gives a new marking M' such that $\forall p \in P$, $M'(p) = M(p) - W(p, t) + W(t, p)$. It is denoted as $M[t>M'$. M indicates the number of tokens in each place, which means the current state of the modeled system. When M_n can be reached from M_0 by firing a sequence of transitions σ, this process is denoted by $M [\sigma > M_n$ and satisfies the *state equation* $M_n = M + [N] \vec{\sigma}$. Here, $\vec{\sigma}$ is a vector of non-negative integers, called a *firing vector*, and $\vec{\sigma}(t)$ indicates the algebraic sum of all occurrences of t in σ. The set of all reachable markings for a PN given M_0 is denoted by $R(N, M_0)$. Additionally, a definition of linearized reachability set (using the state equation) is defined as $\mathbf{R}(N, M_0) = \{M: M = M_0 + [N](\bullet \vec{\sigma})\}$. This definition is suitable for the incorporation of the state equation into a set of linear constraints. The markings in $\mathbf{R}(N, M_0) - R(N, M_0)$ are called *spurious ones* (with respect to the state equation)[20]. They may also be the solutions of the state equation but not reachable markings. In this work, ones just focus on the reachable markings.

A transition t is said to be *live* if for any $M \in R(N, M_0)$, there exists a sequence of transitions whose firing leads to M' that enables t. A PN is said to be *live* if all the transitions are live. A PN contains a *deadlock* if there is a marking $M \in R(N, M_0)$ at which no transition is enabled. Such a marking is called a dead marking. Deadlock situations are as a result of inappropriate resource allocation policies or exhaustive use of some or all resources. Liveness of a PN means that for each marking $M \in R(N, M_0)$ reachable from M_0, it is finally possible to fire t, $\forall t \in T$ through some firing sequence. (N, M_0) is said to be *reversible*, if $\forall M \in R(N, M_0)$, $M_0 \in R(N, M)$. Thus, in a reversible net it is always possible to go back to initial marking (state) M_0. A marking M' is said to be a *home state*, if for each marking $M \in R(N, M_0)$, M' is reachable from M. Reversibility is a special case of the home state property, i.e. if the home state $M' = M_0$, then the net is reversible.

2.2. Theory of regions and synthesis problem[13]

The theory of regions is proposed for the synthesis of pure nets given a finite TS[15], which can be adopted to synthesize the liveness-enforcing net supervisor (LENS) for a plant model[12-13]. For convenience, our method follows the interpretation of the theory of regions in[13].

First of all, let T be a set of transitions and G be a finite directed graph whose arcs are labeled by transitions in T. Assume that there exists a node v in G such that there exists a path from it to any node. The objective of the theory of regions is to find a pure PN (N, M_0), having T as its set of transitions and characterized by its incidence matrix $[N](p, t)$ and its initial marking M_0, such that its reachability graph is G and the marking of node v is M_0. In the following, M denotes both a reachable marking and its corresponding node in G.

Consider any marking M in net (N, M_0). Because (N, M_0) is pure, M can be fully characterized by its corresponding incidence vector $[N](p, \cdot)\vec{\Gamma}_M$ where $\vec{\Gamma}_M$ is the firing vector of path Γ_M. For any transition t that is enabled at M, i.e., t is the label of an outgoing arc of the node M in G

$$M'(p) = M(p) + [N](p, \cdot)\vec{\Gamma}_{M \to M'}, \forall (M, M') \in G \wedge M [\, t > M' \tag{1}$$

Consider now any oriented cycle γ of a reachability graph. Applying the state equation to a node in γ and summing them up give the following cycle equation:

$$\sum_{t \in T}[N](p, t)\vec{\gamma}(t) = 0, \forall \gamma \in C \tag{2}$$

where γ is an oriented cycle of G, $\vec{\gamma}(t)$ is a firing vector corresponding to γ, and C is the set of oriented cycles of G.

According to the definition of G, there exists an oriented path Γ_M from M_0 to M. Applying (1) along the path leads to $M(p) = M_0(p) + [N](p, \cdot)\vec{\Gamma}_M$. There are several paths from M_0 to M. Under the cycle equations, the product $[N](p, \cdot)\vec{\Gamma}_M$ is the same for all these paths. As a result, Γ_M can be arbitrarily chosen. The reachability of any marking M in G implies that

$$M(p) = M_0(p) + [N](p, \cdot)\vec{\Gamma}_M \geq 0, \forall M \in G \tag{3}$$

The above equation is called the reachability condition. Notably, (3) is necessary but not sufficient. Hence, spurious markings are beyond this paper.

It is clear that the cycle equations and reachability conditions hold for any place p. For each pair (M, t) such that M is a reachable marking of G and t is a transition not enabled at M, t should be prevented from happening by some place p. Since the net is pure, t is prevented from happening at M by a place p iff

$$M_0(p) + [N](p, \cdot)\vec{\Gamma}_M + [N](p, t) \leq -1 \tag{4}$$

The above equation (4) is called the event separation condition of (M, t). The set of all possible pairs (M, t) where M is a reachable marking and t is not enabled at M is called the *set of event separation instances* or *marking/transitions-separation instances* (MTSI)[13]. Symbol Ω is used to represent the set of MTSI in this paper. To solve the control problem, Ω is identified. The corresponding control places can then be found to prevent the transitions of the controlled system from firing in order to keep all legal markings only.

3. Controller synthesis method

In this section, an efficient controller synthesis method is developed based on the theory of regions. Please note that all transitions of the PN models are regarded as controllable ones.

3.1. Supervisory control problem

It is assumed that a deadlock-prone PN model contains at least a dead marking in its reachability graph at which no transition is enabled. Its reachability graph contains dead and live zones. Consequently, this study attempts to propose a method to prevent the controlled systems from entering a dead zone/marking.

A dead marking cannot enable any transition and thus cannot go to any other markings. We can formally define the dead marking M_D as follows.

Definition 1: The set of *dead markings* $M_D = \{M \in R(N, M_0) \mid$ at M, no transition is enabled$\}$.

Definition 2: A zone consisting of all dead markings is called a *dead zone*, denoted by Z_D.

Once a marking enters a dead zone, the system is dead. If there is no dead zone in a reachability graph, the system is called a live one.

The goal of the work is to control a deadlock-prone system such that it is live. All markings of a reachability graph can be divided into three groups: legal markings (M_L), quasi-dead markings (M_Q), and dead markings (M_D).

Definition 3: The set of *quasi-dead markings* $M_Q = \{M \in R(N, M_0) \mid M$ must eventually evolve to a dead one regardless of transition firing sequences$\}$.

Definition 4: A zone consisting of all quasi-dead markings is called a *quasi-dead zone*, denoted by Z_Q.

Definition 5: A zone consisting of all quasi-dead and dead markings, i.e., $Z_I = Z_D \cup Z_Q$, is called an *illegal zone*.

Markings except quasi-dead and dead markings are legal ones. Once a legal marking is enforced into the illegal zone, the net will eventually become deadlock.

Definition 6: A zone consisting of all legal markings is called a *legal zone*, i.e., $Z_L = R(N, M_0) - Z_I$.

Ramadge and Wonham show that a system has the maximally permissive behavior if the system behavior equals Z_L[21]. In other words, one must remove all the markings in illegal zone (i.e. quasi-dead and dead markings) from $R(N, M_0)$ if one wants to obtain the maximally permissive behavior. Ghaffari *et al.* propose the MTSI method to achieve their deadlock prevention based on the theory of regions[13]. However, the set of all MTSIs from the reachability graph must be identified. As a result, we can conclude that their method is computationally inefficient. A more efficient method is thus needed as described next.

3.2. Crucial MTSI (CMTSI)

Two types of CMTSIs are defined as follows.

Definition 7: Type I CMTSI: $\Omega' = \{(M, t) | M \in M_L, t \in T,$ and $\exists M' \in M_D, M'' \in M_L,$ and $t' \in T$ such that $M [t > M'$ and $M [t' > M'']\}$. Denote the set of all the dead markings related to Ω' as M'_D, i.e., $M'_D = \{M' \in M_D \mid \exists (M, t) \in \Omega'$ such that $M [t > M'\}$. They are called type I deadlocks.

Definition 7 explains a legal marking that can evolve into a dead or legal zone as shown in Figure 1 through a single transition's firing. For those dead markings that are not type I deadlocks, we need to introduce Type II CMTSI and deadlocks.

Definition 8: A zone consisting of all type I deadlocks (M'_D) is called type I dead zone, denoted by Z'.

Definition 9: σ_k is defined as a transition firing sequence starting in a quasi-dead marking (M_Q) and ending in a deadlock marking in M_D where $i = |\sigma_k|$ is the number of transitions in σ_k, called its length. Denote a firing sequence with the shortest length (i.e., smallest i) from any quasi-dead marking to M' as $\sigma^*(M')$ given $M' \in M_D - M'_D$.

Definition 10: Type II CMTSI : $\Omega'' = \{(M, t) | M \in M_L, t \in T,$ and $\exists M' \in M_Q, M'' \in M_L, M''' \in M_D, t' \in T,$ and a firing sequence $\sigma = \sigma^*(M''')$ from M' to M''' such that $M [t > M', M [t' > M'',$ and $M' [\sigma > M'''\}$. The set of dead markings associated with Type II CMTSI is denoted as M''_D, called type II deadlocks. $M''_D = \{M''' \in M_D \mid \exists (M, t) \in \Omega'', M' \in M_Q$ and a firing sequence σ from M' to M''' such that $M[t > M'$ and $\sigma = \sigma^*(M''')\}$.

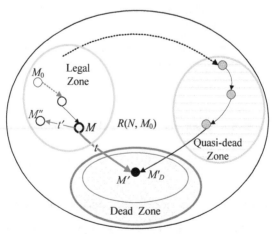

Figure 1. A structure of Type I CMTSI.

A Computationally Improved Optimal Solution
for Deadlocked Problems of Flexible Manufacturing Systems Using Theory of Regions

33

Definition 11: A zone consisting of all type II deadlocks (M''_D) is called type II dead zone, Z''.

A Type II CMTSI contains a legal marking that cannot reach a dead marking with one single transition's firing as shown in Figure 2. Given a dead marking in M''_D, the shortest transition firing sequence needs to be found. The main reason is based on the fact that, for a dead marking, the length of the firing sequence from the initial marking to CMTSI is the longest path than those from the initial marking to MTSIs. Hence, the solutions of MTSIs will be totally covered by the solution of CMTSI. For example, as shown in Figure 3, σ^* is the shorter path since $|\sigma^*| < |\sigma'|$ (i.e. $|\sigma^*| = 1$ and $|\sigma'| = 3$).

Remark 1: A dead marking is always with its corresponding CMTSI. As a result, the corresponding CMTSI is of either Type I or II. Type I may be viewed as a special case of Type II CMTSI by defining $\sigma^* = 0$ (no need to enter Z_Q but directly to Z_D). Type I CMTSI will be processed first in our proposed method. In the following, Theorems 1-3 will help readers to understand how to choose CMTSIs, which are with the same firing sequence of legal markings, from Types I and II.

Theorem 1: If a dead marking $M \in M'_D$ is associated with two different CMTSIs, only one CMTSI needs to be controlled.

Proof: Assume that a dead marking M is with both CMTSIs $\{M_i, t_m\}$ and $\{M_j, t_n\}$ as shown in Figure 4. According to the state equation, $M_i + [N](\bullet t_m) = M_j + [N](\bullet t_n) = M$. Arranging the above equation, $M_0 + [N](\bullet \vec{\sigma}_{M_0 \to M_i}) + [N](\bullet t_m) = M_0 + [N](\bullet \vec{\sigma}_{M_0 \to M_j}) + [N](\bullet t_n)$. According to (4), realizing either CMTSI, e.g., $\{M_i, t_m\}$, leads to $M_0 + [N](\bullet \vec{\sigma}_{M_0 \to M_i}) + [N](\bullet t_m) \leq -1$, which in turn implies $M_0 + [N](\bullet \vec{\sigma}_{M_0 \to M_j}) + [N](\bullet t_n) \leq -1$ and vice versa. Hence, only one CMTSI needs to be controlled.

Remark 2: Based on Theorem 1, if a dead marking $M \in M'_D$ is associated with more than two CMTSIs, only one of them needs to be controlled.

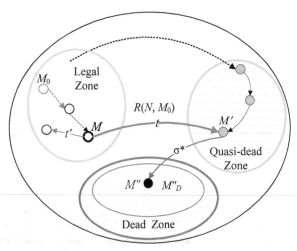

Figure 2. A structure of Type II CMTSI.

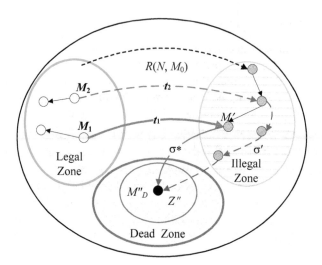

Figure 3. The shorter path σ* in Type II CMTSI given a dead marking.

Theorem 2: If a dead marking $M \in M''_D$, is associated with two CMTSIs whose markings can reach a same quasi-dead marking M' via their respective single transition's firing, only one CMTSI needs to be controlled.

Proof: Assume that a dead marking M is associated with Type II CMTSIs $\{M_p, t_r\}$ and $\{M_q, t_s\}$. M_p and M_q reaches a quasi-dead markings M' via t_r and t_s's firing, respectively as shown in Figure 5.

According to the state equation, $M_p + [N](\bullet t_r) + [N](\bullet \vec{\sigma}^*) = M_q + [N](\bullet t_s) + [N](\bullet \vec{\sigma}^*)$ M. Arranging the above equation, one can realize that $M_p + [N](\bullet t_r) = M_q + [N](\bullet t_s)$. According to (4), realizing either CMTSI, e.g., $\{M_p, t_r\}$, leads to $M_0 + [N] (\bullet \vec{\sigma}_{M_0 \to M_p}) + [N](\bullet t_r) \leq -1$, which in turn implies $M_0 + [N] (\bullet \vec{\sigma}_{M_0 \to M_q}) + [N](\bullet t_s) \leq -1$ and vice versa. Hence, only one CMTSI needs to be controlled.

Theorem 3: A dead marking $M \in M''_D$, is associated with two CMTSIs whose markings can reach two different quasi-dead markings M'_p and M'_q via two different single transitions' firing. Both need to be controlled if $[N](\bullet \vec{\sigma}_r^*) \neq [N](\bullet \vec{\sigma}_s^*)$.

Proof: Assume that a dead marking M is associated with both Type II CMTSIs $\{M_p, t_r\}$ and $\{M_q, t_s\}$. M_p and M_q reach two different quasi-dead markings M'_p and M'_q via t_r and t_s's firing, respectively as shown in Figure 6.

According to the state equation, $M_p + [N](\bullet t_r) + [N](\bullet \vec{\sigma}_r^*) = M_q + [N](\bullet t_s) + [N](\bullet \vec{\sigma}_s^*) = M''_D$. Arranging the above equation, $M'_p + [N](\bullet \vec{\sigma}_r^*) = M'_q + [N](\bullet \vec{\sigma}_s^*)$. Since $[N](\bullet \vec{\sigma}_r^*) \neq [N](\bullet \vec{\sigma}_s^*)$, M'_p is not equal to M'_q. And also according to the definition of the event separation condition equation, the first set of CMTSI $\{M_p, t_r\}$ leads to the first event separation condition equation is $M_0 + [N](\bullet \vec{\sigma}_{M_0 \to M_p}) + [N](\bullet t_r) \leq -1$; and the second set of CMTSI $\{M_q, t_s\}$ leads to the another event separation condition equation is $M_0 + [N](\bullet \vec{\sigma}_{M_0 \to M_q}) + [N](\bullet t_s) \leq -1$. Hence, one can infer that M'_p and M'_q are two different quasi-dead markings if $[N](\bullet\ \vec{\sigma}_r^{\ *}) \neq [N](\bullet$ $\vec{\sigma}_s^{\ *})$. It hints the two event separation condition equations are different. As a result, both CMTSIs need to be controlled.

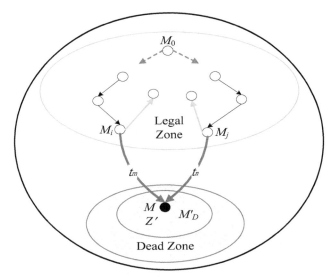

Figure 4. A type I deadlocks associated with two CMTSIs.

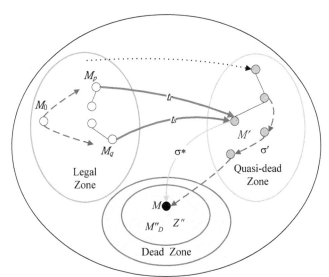

Figure 5. Two CMTSIs connected to the same quasi-dead marking.

Definition 12: A legal marking $M \in M_L$ can be led to a quasi-dead marking M_q via a single transition firing. M_q must eventually evolve to a dead one M_d (i.e. $M_d \in M_D$) after a sequence $\sigma_n = t_1 t_2 \ldots t_n$ fires. Denote the set of all the markings on the path from M_q to M_d as $M_{q\text{-}d}$.

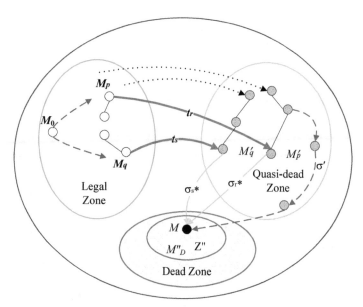

Figure 6. Two CMTSIs connected to two quasi-dead markings.

Remark 3: Based on Theorem 3, both CMTSIs still need to be controlled even if $M_P = M_q$ for the case shown in Figure 7.

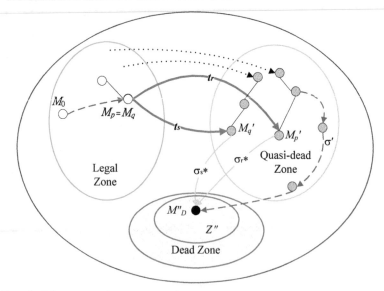

Figure 7. Two CMTSIs connected to two quasi-dead markings M'_p and M'_q with $\sigma_r{}^* = \sigma_s{}^* = \sigma^*(M''_D)$.

Control places are then found after CMTSIs. They are used to keep all markings of the controlled system within the legal zone.

A Computationally Improved Optimal Solution
for Deadlocked Problems of Flexible Manufacturing Systems Using Theory of Regions

37

Theorem 4: $(\Omega' \cup \Omega'') \subseteq \Omega$

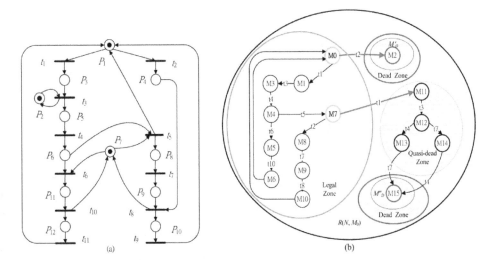

Figure 8. (a) A Petri net model.[22] (b) Its reachability graph.

Here, Figure 8(a) taken from existing literatures[22] is used to demonstrate how to identify two types of CMTSIs from its reachability graph (i.e. Figure 8(b)). Assume that all transitions of PN models are immediately in this case. Therefore, one can easy identify there are two dead markings M'_D (i.e. M_2) and M''_D (i.e. M_{15}) and four quasi-dead markings (i.e. M_{11}, M_{12}, M_{13} and M_{14}). Additionally, the markings M_0, M_1, M_3-M_{10} are the legal markings. Based on the mentioned above, there are two sets of CTMSIs in the reachability graph system due to the two dead markings in the system. As a result, one can infer that $\{M_0, t_2\}$ belongs to type I CMTSI and $\{M_7, t_1\}$ belongs to type II. In this Petri net system model, there are only one type I CMTSI and only one type II.

3.3. Procedure of deadlock prevention policy

Next, quasi-dead, dead, and legal markings are identified. Based on[12-13], the maximally permissive behavior means all of legal markings (M_L) and the number of reachability condition equations equals $|M_L|$. Additionally, all CMTSIs can be obtained such that the legal markings do not proceed into the illegal zone. The proposed deadlock prevention algorithm is constructed as Figure 9.

Theorem 5: The proposed deadlock prevention policy is more efficient than the method proposed by Ghaffari et al.[13]

Proof: The theory of regions is used to prevent the system deadlocks by both our deadlock prevention policy and the conventional one. All MTSIs can be controlled by the two control policies. Since $(\Omega' \cup \Omega'') \subseteq \Omega$, the use of CMTSI can more efficiently handle the synthesis problem than that of MTSI[13].

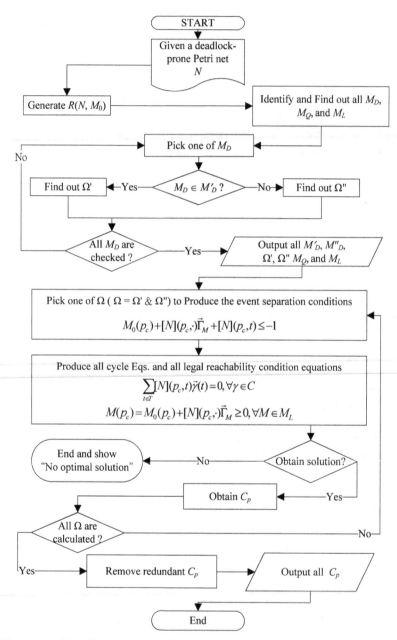

Figure 9. The Proposed Deadlock Prevention Flowchart.

4. Experimental results

Two FMS examples are used to evaluate our deadlock prevention policy[12-23].

A Computationally Improved Optimal Solution
for Deadlocked Problems of Flexible Manufacturing Systems Using Theory of Regions

39

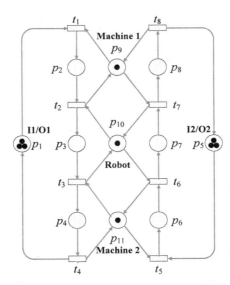

Figure 10. An FMS PN Model[12].

Example I: An FMS is shown in Figure 10[12]. This PN is a system of simple sequential processes with resources (S³PR), denoted by (N_1, M_0). To do our deadlock prevention policy, $R(N_1, M_0)$ of the PN system can be constructed as shown in Figure 11.

Two dead markings (i.e. M_7 and M_{12}) can then be identified. Next, $\Omega'_1 = \{(M_3, t_5)\}$ and $\Omega'_2 = \{(M_{15}, t_1)\}$ are obtained. The event separation condition equations can be obtained through them as follows.

$$M_7(p_c) = M_0(p_c) + 2[N](p_c, t_1) + [N](p_c, t_2) + [N](p_c, t_5) \leq -1 \tag{5}$$

$$M_{12}(p_c) = M_0(p_c) + [N](p_c, t_1) + 2[N](p_c, t_5) + [N](p_c, t_6) \leq -1 \tag{6}$$

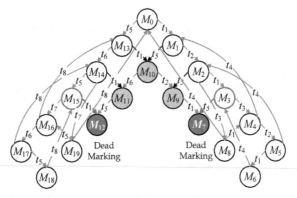

Figure 11. $R(N, M_0)$ of Example I.

Two cycle equations are as follows.

$$[N](p_c, t_1) + [N](p_c, t_2) + [N](p_c, t_3) + [N](p_c, t_4) = 0 \tag{7}$$

$$[N](p_c, t_5) + [N](p_c, t_6) + [N](p_c, t_7) + [N](p_c, t_8) = 0 \tag{8}$$

After listing all reachability conditions, all legal markings can be determined. In detail, M_0-M_6, M_8, and M_{13}-M_{19} are legal. Hence, the following reachability conditions are obtained.

$$M_0(p_c) \geq 0 \tag{9}$$

$$M_1(p_c) = M_0(p_c) + [N](p_c, t_1) \geq 0 \tag{10}$$

$$M_2(p_c) = M_0(p_c) + [N](p_c, t_1) + [N](p_c, t_2) \geq 0 \tag{11}$$

$$M_3(p_c) = M_0(p_c) + 2[N](p_c, t_1) + [N](p_c, t_2) \geq 0 \tag{12}$$

$$M_4(p_c) = M_0(p_c) + 2[N](p_c, t_1) + [N](p_c, t_2) + [N](p_c, t_3) \geq 0 \tag{13}$$

$$M_5(p_c) = M_0(p_c) + 2[N](p_c, t_1) + 2[N](p_c, t_2) + [N](p_c, t_3) \geq 0 \tag{14}$$

$$M_6(p_c) = M_0(p_c) + 3[N](p_c, t_1) + 2[N](p_c, t_2) + [N](p_c, t_3) \geq 0 \tag{15}$$

$$M_8(p_c) = M_0(p_c) + [N](p_c, t_1) + [N](p_c, t_2) + [N](p_c, t_3) \geq 0 \tag{16}$$

$$M_{13}(p_c) = M_0(p_c) + [N](p_c, t_5) \geq 0 \tag{17}$$

$$M_{14}(p_c) = M_0(p_c) + [N](p_c, t_5) + [N](p_c, t_6) \geq 0 \tag{18}$$

$$M_{15}(p_c) = M_0(p_c) + 2[N](p_c, t_5) + [N](p_c, t_6) \geq 0 \tag{19}$$

$$M_{16}(p_c) = M_0(p_c) + 2[N](p_c, t_5) + [N](p_c, t_6) + [N](p_c, t_7) \geq 0 \tag{20}$$

$$M_{17}(p_c) = M_0(p_c) + 2[N](p_c, t_5) + 2[N](p_c, t_6) + [N](p_c, t_7) \geq 0 \tag{21}$$

$$M_{18}(p_c) = M_0(p_c) + 3[N](p_c, t_5) + 2[N](p_c, t_6) + [N](p_c, t_7) \geq 0 \tag{22}$$

$$M_{19}(p_c) = M_0(p_c) + [N](p_c, t_5) + [N](p_c, t_6) + [N](p_c, t_7) \geq 0 \tag{23}$$

Furthermore, two optimal control places C_{P1} and C_{P2} can be obtained when (5) and (7)-(23) are solved. Their detailed information is: $M_0(C_{P1}) = 1$, $t_1 = t_5 = -1$, $t_2 = t_6 = 1$, $t_3 = t_4 = t_7 = t_8 = 0$; and $M_0(C_{P2}) = 1$, $t_2 = t_5 = -1$, $t_3 = t_6 = 1$, $t_1 = t_4 = t_7 = t_8 = 0$. By the same way, using (6) and (7)-(23), one can find two optimal control places, C_{P3} and C_{P4}. $M_0(C_{P3}) = 1$, $t_1 = t_6 = -1$, $t_2 = t_7 = 1$, $t_3 = t_4 = t_5 = t_8 = 0$; and $M_0(C_{P4}) = 1$, $t_1 = t_5 = -1$, $t_2 = t_6 = 1$, $t_3 = t_4 = t_7 = t_8 = 0$. Notably, C_{P1} and C_{P4} are the same. Therefore, a redundant control place (C_{P4}) can be removed. As a result, the system net can be controlled with the three control places C_{P1}, C_{P2} and C_{P3}. The optimally controlled system net (N_{1H}, M_0) is obtained as shown in Table 1.

It is worthy to emphasize that the three control places are obtained by using two CMTSIs and 36 equations under our control policy. However, six MTSIs/ESSPs and 108 equations have to be solved in two existing literatures[12, 24].

A Computationally Improved Optimal Solution
for Deadlocked Problems of Flexible Manufacturing Systems Using Theory of Regions

41

Additional Control Places	$M_0(C_{pi})$	$\bullet(Cp)$	$(Cp)\bullet$
Cp_1	1	t_2, t_6	t_1, t_5
Cp_2	1	t_3, t_6	t_2, t_5
Cp_3	1	t_2, t_7	t_1, t_6

Table 1. Control Places of the Net (N_{1H}, M_0)

Example II: This example is taken from[23] and is used in [12, 16, 24]. Here, the PN model of the system, denoted as (N_2, M_0), is shown in Figure 12.

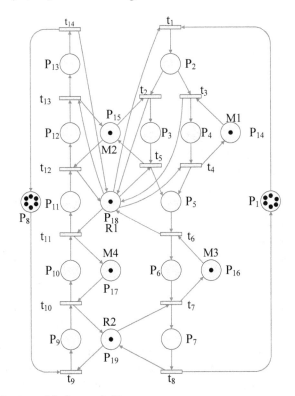

Figure 12. The Petri nets model of example II.

To prevent deadlock, 282 reachable markings (M_1 to M_{282}) are identified according to the software INA[25]. 16 dead markings M_9, M_{19}, M_{70}, M_{71}, M_{76}, M_{77}, M_{78}, M_{83}, M_{84}, M_{94}, M_{99}, M_{100}, M_{105}, M_{106}, M_{112}, and M_{113} are then located. Next, 61 quasi-dead markings M_6, M_7, M_8, M_{14}, M_{15}, M_{16}, M_{17}, M_{18}, M_{25}, M_{48}, M_{66}, M_{67}, M_{68}, M_{69}, M_{72}, M_{73}, M_{74}, M_{75}, M_{79}, M_{80}, M_{81}, M_{82}, M_{87}, M_{101}, M_{102}, M_{103}, M_{104}, M_{108}, M_{109}, M_{110}, M_{111}, M_{124}, M_{130}, M_{135}, M_{136}, M_{141}, M_{142}, M_{143}, M_{150}, M_{162}, M_{198}, M_{203}, M_{204}, M_{210}, M_{250}, M_{251}, M_{257}, M_{258}, M_{259}, M_{260}, M_{261}, M_{262}, M_{263}, M_{265}, M_{269}, M_{270}, M_{272}, M_{273}, M_{274}, M_{277}, and M_{278} are found based on Definition 3 in this paper. Hence, the number of legal markings (i.e. $288 - (16 + 61) = 205$) can be determined. Type I and II CMTSIs can be obtained as shown in Table 2. Notice that $\{(M_{56}, t_9)\}$ in M_{77} is a redundant one.

M'_D	Ω'_C	M''_D	Ω''_C
M_9	$\{(M_{65}, t_1)\}$	M_{19}	$\{(M_{56}, t_1)\}$ / $\{(M_{56}, t_9)\}$
M_{70}	$\{(M_{43}, t_9)\}$	M_{76}	$\{(M_{65}, t_{11})\}$
M_{71}	$\{(M_{51}, t_9)\}$	M_{77}	$\{(M_{56}, t_9)\}$ / $\{(M_{56}, t_{11})\}$
M_{78}	$\{(M_{171}, t_9)\}$	M_{83}	$\{(M_{128}, t_{11})\}$
M_{94}	$\{(M_{93}, t_1)\}$	M_{84}	$\{(M_{60}, t_9)\}$ / $\{(M_{60}, t_{11})\}$
M_{99}	$\{(M_{98}, t_1)\}$	M_{105}	$\{(M_{93}, t_{11})\}$
M_{100}	$\{(M_{98}, t_4)\}$	M_{106}	$\{(M_{98}, t_{11})\}$
		M_{112}	$\{(M_{122}, t_{11})\}$
		M_{113}	$\{(M_{96}, t_{11})\}$

Table 2. The Dead Markings and Their Relative CMTSIs.

M'_D	Event Separation Condition Equations
M_9	$M_0 + 3t_1 + t_2 + t_3 + 2t_9 + t_{10} \leq -1$
M_{70}	$M_0 + 3t_1 + t_2 + 2t_3 + 2t_4 + t_6 + 2t_9 + t_{10} \leq -1$
	$M_0 + 3t_1 + 2t_2 + t_3 + t_4 + t_5 + t_6 + 2t_9 + t_{10} \leq -1$
M_{71}	$M_0 + 3t_1 + t_2 + 2t_3 + t_4 + t_5 + t_6 + 2t_9 + t_{10} \leq -1$
	$M_0 + 3t_1 + 2t_2 + t_3 + 2t_5 + t_6 + 2t_9 + t_{10} \leq -1$
	$M_0 + 2t_1 + t_2 + t_3 + t_4 + t_5 + t_6 + 2t_9 + t_{10} \leq -1$
M_{78}	$M_0 + 2t_1 + 2t_2 + 2t_5 + t_6 + 2t_9 + t_{10} \leq -1$
	$M_0 + 2t_1 + 2t_3 + 2t_4 + t_6 + 2t_9 + t_{10} \leq -1$
M_{94}	$M_0 + 2t_1 + t_3 + 3t_9 + 2t_{10} + t_{11} + t_{12} \leq -1$
M_{99}	$M_0 + 3t_1 + 2t_3 + t_4 + t_6 + 3t_9 + 2t_{10} + t_{11} + t_{12} \leq -1$
	$M_0 + 3t_1 + t_2 + t_3 + t_5 + t_6 + 3t_9 + 2t_{10} + t_{11} + t_{12} \leq -1$

Table 3. The Dead Markings and Relative Event Separation Condition Equations of Type I CMTSI.

Tables 3-4 show the event separation condition equations based on 18 CMTSIs. Here, the procedure of our method is introduced as follows. Due to the space limitation, we use only one example (i.e. dead marking M_9) to illustrate how to prevent legal markings from leading to dead one M_9 by using a CMTSI. To do so, $\Omega'_{C1} = \{(M_{65}, t_1)\}$ can be located due to M_9. The event separation condition equation can then be identified as follows.

$$M_9(C_{P1}) = M_0(C_{P1}) + 3t_1 + t_2 + t_3 + 2t_9 + t_{10} \leq -1 \qquad (24)$$

Next, three different cycle equations are:

$$t_1 + t_2 + t_5 + t_6 + t_7 + t_8 = 0 \qquad (25)$$

$$t_1 + t_3 + t_4 + t_6 + t_7 + t_8 = 0 \qquad (26)$$

$$t_9 + t_{10} + t_{11} + t_{12} + t_{13} + t_{14} = 0 \qquad (27)$$

A Computationally Improved Optimal Solution
for Deadlocked Problems of Flexible Manufacturing Systems Using Theory of Regions

43

Finally, 205 reachability condition equations can be listed. They represent the sequence of all legal markings from the initial one. Moreover, control place C_{P1} can be computed, i.e., M_0 $(C_{P1}) = 2$, $\bullet C_{P1} = \{t_6, t_{13}\}$, and $C_{P1}\bullet = \{t_1, t_{11}\}$. Similarly, other control places are obtained as shown in Tables 5-6.

M''_b	Event Separation Condition Equations
M_{19}	$M_0 + 4t_1 + t_2 + 2t_3 + t_4 + t_6 + t_9 + t_{10} \leq -1$
	$M_0 + 4t_1 + 2t_2 + t_3 + t_5 + t_6 + t_9 + t_{10} \leq -1$
	$M_0 + 3t_1 + t_2 + 2t_3 + t_4 + t_6 + 2t_9 + t_{10} \leq -1$
	$M_0 + 3t_1 + 2t_2 + 2t_3 + t_5 + t_6 + 2t_9 + t_{10} \leq -1$
M_{76}	$M_0 + 2t_1 + t_2 + t_3 + 2t_9 + t_{10} + t_{11} \leq -1$
M_{77}	$M_0 + 3t_1 + t_2 + 2t_3 + t_4 + t_6 + t_9 + t_{10} + t_{11} \leq -1$
	$M_0 + 3t_1 + 2t_2 + t_3 + t_5 + t_6 + t_9 + t_{10} + t_{11} \leq -1$
M_{83}	$M_0 + t_1 + t_2 + 2t_9 + t_{10} + t_{11} \leq -1$
M_{84}	$M_0 + 2t_1 + t_2 + t_3 + t_4 + t_6 + t_9 + t_{10} + t_{11} \leq -1$
	$M_0 + 2t_1 + 2t_2 + t_5 + t_6 + t_9 + t_{10} + t_{11} \leq -1$
	$M_0 + 3t_1 + t_2 + 2t_3 + t_4 + t_6 + 2t_9 + t_{10} \leq -1$
	$M_0 + 3t_1 + 2t_2 + t_3 + t_5 + t_6 + 2t_9 + t_{10} \leq -1$
M_{105}	$M_0 + t_1 + t_3 + 3t_9 + 2t_{10} + 2t_{11} + t_{12} \leq -1$
M_{106}	$M_0 + 2t_1 + 2t_3 + t_4 + t_6 + 3t_9 + 2t_{10} + 2t_{11} + t_{12} \leq -1$
	$M_0 + 2t_1 + t_2 + t_3 + t_5 + t_6 + 3t_9 + 2t_{10} + 2t_{11} + t_{12} \leq -1$
M_{112}	$M_0 + 3t_9 + 2t_{10} + 2t_{11} + t_{12} \leq -1$
M_{113}	$M_0 + t_1 + t_3 + t_4 + t_6 + 3t_9 + 2t_{10} + 2t_{11} + t_{12} \leq -1$
	$M_0 + t_1 + t_2 + t_5 + t_6 + 3t_9 + 2t_{10} + 2t_{11} + t_{12} \leq -1$

Table 4. The Dead Markings and Relative Event Separation Condition Equations of Type II CMTSI.

M'_b	Ω'_C	$M_0(C_{pi})$	$\bullet(C_{pi})$	$(C_{pi})\bullet$
M_9	$\{(M_{65}, t_1)\}$	2	t_6, t_{13}	t_1, t_{11}
M_{70}	$\{(M_{43}, t_9)\}$	3	t_6, t_{11}	t_2, t_4, t_9
		3	t_5, t_7, t_{11}	t_2, t_6, t_9
		3	t_7, t_{11}	t_4, t_5, t_9
M_{71}	$\{(M_{51}, t_9)\}$	3	t_7, t_{11}	t_4, t_5, t_9
M_{78}	$\{(M_{171}, t_9)\}$	3	t_7, t_{11}	t_4, t_5, t_9
M_{94}	$\{(M_{93}, t_1)\}$	2	t_6, t_{13}	t_1, t_{11}
M_{99}	$\{(M_{98}, t_1)\}$	4	t_7, t_{11}	t_1, t_9
M_{100}	$\{(M_{98}, t_4)\}$	3	t_7, t_{11}	t_4, t_5, t_9

Table 5. Control Places from TYPE I CMTSI.

Finally, the controlled net is obtained by adding the six control places as shown in Table 7. It is live and maximally permissive with 205 reachable markings. However, 59 ESSPs and nine control places are required in [12]. It hints that 59 sets of inequalities are needed in [12], while only 18 sets of inequalities suffice using our algorithm. Hence, our policy is more efficient than that in [12].

Li *et al.* solve this problem by using elementary siphons controlled policy (ESCP) and the theory of region [16]. A two-stage deadlock prevention method is used. First, ESCP is used to replace a siphon control method[5]. Therefore, the number of dead markings is reduced. Second, the theory of regions is used to obtain the optimal solution. Three elementary siphons (i.e. $S_1 = \{p_2, p_5, p_{13}, p_{15}, p_{18}\}$, $S_2 = \{p_5, p_{13}, p_{14}, p_{15}, p_{18}\}$ and $S_3 = \{p_2, p_7, p_{11}, p_{13}, p_{16}-p_{19}\}$) can be identified. As a result, three control places $V_{S1}-V_{S3}$ as shown in Table 8 are needed to handle three elementary siphons. Then a partially controlled PN system, denoted as (N_{2L1}, M_0), can be obtained after the first stage.

M''_D	Ω''_C	$M_0(C_{pi})$	$\bullet(C_{pi})$	$(C_{pi})\bullet$
M_{19}	$\{(M_{56}, t_1)\}$	2	t_6, t_{13}	t_1, t_{11}
		4	t_7, t_{11}	t_1, t_9
	$\{(M_{56}, t_9)\}$	3	t_5, t_7, t_{11}	t_2, t_6, t_9
		4	t_7, t_{11}	t_1, t_9
M_{76}	$\{(M_{65}, t_{11})\}$	1	t_5, t_{13}	t_2, t_{11}
M_{77}	$\{(M_{56}, t_{11})\}$	1	t_5, t_{13}	t_2, t_{11}
M_{83}	$\{(M_{128}, t_{11})\}$	1	t_5, t_{13}	t_2, t_{11}
M_{84}	$\{(M_{60}, t_9)\}$	3	t_5, t_7, t_{11}	t_2, t_6, t_9
	$\{(M_{60}, t_{11})\}$	1	t_5, t_{13}	t_2, t_{11}
M_{105}	$\{(M_{93}, t_{11})\}$	1	t_5, t_{13}	t_2, t_{11}
M_{106}	$\{(M_{98}, t_{11})\}$	1	t_5, t_{13}	t_2, t_{11}
M_{112}	$\{(M_{122}, t_{11})\}$	1	t_5, t_{13}	t_2, t_{11}
M_{113}	$\{(M_{96}, t_{11})\}$	1	t_5, t_{13}	t_2, t_{11}

Table 6. Control Places from TYPE II CMTSI.

Additional Control Places	$M_0(C_{pi})$	$\bullet(C_{pi})$	$(C_{pi})\bullet$
C_{p1}	1	t_5, t_{13}	t_2, t_{11}
C_{p2}	2	t_6, t_{13}	t_1, t_{11}
C_{p3}	3	t_6, t_{11}	t_2, t_4, t_9
C_{p4}	3	t_5, t_7, t_{11}	t_2, t_6, t_9
C_{p5}	3	t_7, t_{11}	t_4, t_5, t_9
C_{p6}	4	t_7, t_{11}	t_1, t_9

Table 7. Control Places for the Net (N_{2H}, M_0).

However, (N_{2L1}, M_0) has a dead marking. Figure 13 shows a partial reachability graph and the deadlock marking M_{57} is included. M_{57} is one of the 210 reachable markings (i.e. the reachable markings M_1-M_{210} as denoted in [16]. In [16], 210 reachable markings are divided into two categories: legal and illegal zones. The illegal zone consists of quasi-dead markings (i.e. M_{54}, M_{55}, M_{56} and M_{60}) and a dead marking (i.e. M_{57}). Obviously, some legal markings (i.e. M_{43}, M_{44}, M_{47}, M_{48}, M_{49}, M_{53}, M_{59} and M_{74}) can enter the illegal zone (i.e. $Z_I = Z_Q \cup Z_D$). One can realize that they use the theory of regions to prevent these legal markings from entering Z_I. Therefore, they must resolve 8 MTSIs (i.e. $\{(M_{43}, t_9)\}$, $\{(M_{44}, t_9)\}$, $\{(M_{47}, t_9)\}$, $\{(M_{48}, t_9)\}$, $\{(M_{49}, t_9)\}$, $\{(M_{53}, t_4)\}$, $\{(M_{59}, t_1)\}$, $\{(M_{74}, t_2)\}$) and many equations in this example. Then the additional three control places can be obtained as shown in Table 9. Eight MTSIs are needed. Hence, their control policy[16] does not seem efficiently enough when the MTSI at the second stage is used to obtain control places.

To compare the efficiency of the deadlock prevention methods, the proposed one is examined in the system net (N_{2L1}, M_0). One can realize that M_{57} is the only deadlock marking in $R(N_{2L1}, M_0)$. Based on our method, only the dead marking M_{57} needed to be controlled. Here, only one $\Omega' = \{(M_{44}, t_9)\}$ is needed. Obviously, the involved necessary equations are much less than those of the conventional one. We can obtain the same controlled net as that in [16]. Hence, the proposed concept of CMTSIs can be used in their approach [16] to improve its computational efficiency significantly as well.

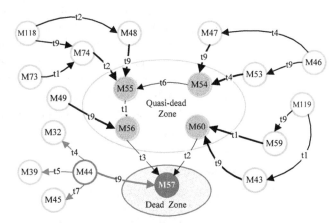

Figure 13. A Partial Reachability Graph of the Net (N_{2L1}, M_0)[16].

Additional Control Places	$M_0(C_{pi})$	$\bullet(C_{pi})$	$(C_{pi})\bullet$
V_{S1}	1	t_5, t_{13}	t_2, t_{11}
V_{S2}	2	t_4, t_5, t_{13}	t_1, t_{11}
V_{S3}	3	t_7, t_{11}	t_4, t_5, t_9

Table 8. Additional Control Places for the Net (N_{2L1}, M_0)

Additional Control Places	$M_0(C_{pi})$	$\bullet(C_{pi})$	$(C_{pi})\bullet$
C_{p1}	3	t_6, t_{11}	t_2, t_4, t_9
C_{p2}	3	t_5, t_7, t_{11}	t_2, t_6, t_9
C_{p3}	4	t_2, t_4, t_7, t_{11}	t_1, t_6, t_9

Table 9. Control Places for (N_{2L1}, M_0) by Two-Stage Method.

5. Comparison with existing methods

One can attempt to make a comparison with the previous methods[12, 16, 24] in terms of efficiency. The first one proposed by Uzam[12], called *Algorithm U*, is totally based on the theory of regions. It solves six ESSPs in Example I. Then three control places are added on the net such that the controlled net is live and reversible. As for Example II, it solves 59 MTSIs. Nine control places are obtained. However, the proposed deadlock prevention policy called *Algorithm P* solves only two and 18 CMTSIs in Examples I and II, respectively.

The other one is proposed by Li *et al.*[16, 24] called *Algorithm L* in which only the theory of regions is used in Example I. Notice that both the controlled results of *Algorithms L* and *U* are the same in Example I. In Example II, using *Algorithm L*, eight MTSIs are solved and six control places are computed. However, under the two-stage control policy, only one set of MTSI is needed by using our new policy to obtain the controlled result that is as the same as *Algorithm L* in Example II. Note that both the definitions of ESSP and MTSI are the same. Hence, ESSP and CMTSI can be regarded as MTSI for the comparison purpose. The detailed comparison results are given in Table 10. However, only 18 MTSIs among 59 MTSIs are needed by using *Algorithm P*.

EXAMPLE	# of Places	# of Resource Places	MTSI U, L, P	Control Places U, L, P	Reachable Markings
I	11	3	6, 6, 2	3, 3, 3	15
II	19	6	59, /, 18	9, /, 6	205
II (two stages)			/, 8, 1	/, 6, 6	

Table 10. Comparison of the Controlled Systems.

For Example II, eight MTSIs are required to obtain the six control places under *Algorithm L*. Hence, one can infer that its performance is better than that of *Algorithm U*. Only one set of CMTSI is needed to obtain the same control result by *Algorithm P*. As a result, one can conclude that our proposed policy is more efficient than the other two methods.

To examine and compare the efficiency of the proposed method with those in[16, 24] in a system with large reachability graphs, one can use eight different markings of p_1, p_8, p_{15}, p_{18}, and p_{19}: $[6, 5, 1, 1, 1]^T$, $[7, 6, 2, 1, 1]^T$, $[7, 6, 1, 2, 1]^T$, $[7, 6, 1, 1, 2]^T$, $[9, 8, 2, 2, 2]^T$, $[12, 11, 3, 3, 3]^T$, $[15, 14, 4, 4, 4]^T$, and $[18, 17, 5, 5, 5]^T$. Tables 11 and 12 show various parameters in the plant and partially controlled net models, where M (p_{15}), M (p_{18}), and M (p_{19}) vary; $|R|$, $|M_L|$, $|R_D|^U$, $|R_D|^L$, indicate the number of reachable markings (states), legal markings, and dead markings under *Algorithms U* and *L*, respectively. Additionally, MTSIs of *Algorithms U*, *L*, and *P* are symbolized by $|\psi|^U$, $|\psi|^L$ and $|\psi|^P$, respectively. The last column is $r_a = |\psi|^P / |\psi|^U$ in Table 11, and $r_b = \psi|^P / |\psi|^L$ in Table 12. Notably, *Algorithm G*[13] can be regarded as

Algorithm U in Table 11 since the number of MTSIs and ESSPs are the same. In table 11, here, N_{sep} represents the number of MTSIs, and the N_{sep}/U, N_{sep}/L and N_{sep}/P represent the number of MTSIs of *Algorithms U, L,* and *P,* respectively. Obviously, the number of $|\psi|^{U}$ in the plant model grows quickly from cases 1 to 8. For instance, when M (p_{15}) = M (p_{18}) = M (p_{19}) = 5, $|\psi|^{U}$ = 4311, meaning that one must solve 4311 MTSIs when *Algorithm U* is used. However, since $|\psi|^{P}$ = 228, only 228 equations (MTSIs) need to be solved under *Algorithm P.* As a result, *Algorithm P* is more efficient than *Algorithm U* in a large system.

CASES	$|R|$	$|M_L|$	$|R_D|^{U}$	$|\psi|^{U}$	$|\psi|^{P}$	r_a
1	282	205	16	59	18	30.5%
2	600	484	27	95	28	29.5%
3	972	870	26	103	26	25.2%
4	570	421	16	107	19	17.8%
5	4011	3711	42	288	42	14.6%
6	27152	26316	84	886	84	9.5%
7	124110	122235	145	2115	145	6.9%
8	440850	437190	228	4311	228	5.3%

Table 11. Parametersin the Plant and Partially Controlled Models with Varying Markings: *U* vs. *P.*

CASE	$|R|$	$|M_L|$	$|R_D|^{L}$	$|\psi|^{L}$	$|\psi|^{P}$	r_b
1	282	205	1	8	1	12.5%
2	600	484	1	8	1	12.5%
3	972	870	6	10	6	60.0%
4	570	421	1	8	1	12.5%
5	4011	3711	9	15	9	60.0%
6	27152	26316	28	48	28	58.3%
7	124110	122235	60	105	60	57.1%
8	440850	437190	108	192	108	56.3%

Table 12. Parametersin the Plant and Partially Controlled Models with Varying Markings: *L* vs. *P.*

In Table 12, the number of MTSIs calculated by *Algorithm L* can be controlled, but *Algorithm P* is more efficient in these cases. For instance, when M (p_{15}) = M (p_{18}) = M (p_{19}) = 5, $|\psi|^{L}$ = 192, meaning that one still has to solve 192 MTSIs when *Algorithm L* is used. However, $|\psi|^{P}$ =108. Only 108 MTSIs need to be solved by using *Algorithm P.* Importantly, the computational cost can be reduced by using our proposed method when it is compared with those in[12, 16]. In conclusion, *Algorithm P* is more efficient in large reachability graph cases than those in[12-13].

6. Conclusion

The proposed policy can be implemented for FMSs based on the theory of regions and Petri nets, where the dead markings are identified in its reachability graph.   The underlying notion of the prior work is that many inequalities (i.e. MTSIs) must be solved to prevent legal markings from entering the illegal zone in the original PN model. One must generate all MTSIs in a reachability graph and require high computation. This work proposes and uses CMTSI to overcome the computational difficulty. The detail information is also obtained in existing literatures.[26-29] The proposed method can reduce the number of inequalities and thus the computational cost very significantly since CMTSIs are much less than MTSIs in large models. Consequently, it is optimal with much better computational efficiency than those existing optimal policies[12-13, 16]. More benchmark studies will be desired to establish such computational advantages of the proposed one over the prior ones. It should be noted that the problem is still NP-hard the same as other optimal policies due to the need to generate the reachability graph of a Petri net. The future research is thus much needed to overcome the computational inefficiency of all these methods.

Author details

Yen-Liang Pan
Department of Avionic Engineering, R.O.C. Air Force Academy, Taiwan, R.O.C.

Acknowledgement

The author is grateful to Prof. Yi-Sheng Huang and Prof. MengChu Zhou whose comments and suggestions greatly helped me improve the presentation and quality of this work.

7. References

[1]   Fanti MP, Zhou MC. Deadlock control methods in automated manufacturing systems. IEEE Trans Syst Man Cybern A Syst Humans, 2004;34(1):5-22.

[2]   Murata T. Petri nets: Properties, analysis and applications. In Proc IEEE. 1989;77(4):541-580.

[3]   Ezpeleta J, Colom JM, Martinez J. A Petri net based deadlock prevention policy for flexible manufacturing systems. IEEE Trans Robot Autom. 1995;11(2):173-184.

[4]   Jeng MD. A Petri net synthesis theory for modeling flexible manufacturing systems. IEEE Trans Syst Man Cybern B Cybern. 1997;27(2):169-183.

[5]   Huang YS, Jeng MD, Xie XL, Chung SL. Deadlock prevention policy based on Petri nets and siphons Int J Prod Res. 2001;39(2):283-305.

[6]   Li ZW, Hu HS, Wang AR. Design of liveness-enforcing supervisors for flexible manufacturing systems using Petri nets. IEEE Trans Syst Man Cybern C Appl Rev. 2007;37(4):517-526.

[7]   Iordache MV, Moody JO, Antsaklis PJ. A method for the synthesis liveness enforcing supervisors in Petri nets. Procceedings of the 2001 American Control Conference; 2011 Jun 25-27; Arlington, VA, USA. P. 4943-8. (ISBN:0-7803-6495-3)

[8] Park J, Reveliotis SA. Algebraic synthesis of efficient deadlock avoidance policies for sequential resource allocation systems IEEE Trans Autom Control. 2000;16(2):190-195.

[9] Li ZW, Zhou MC. Elementary siphons of Petri nets and their application to deadlock prevention in flexible manufacturing systems. IEEE Trans Syst Man Cybern A Syst Humans. 2004 Jan;34(1):38-51.

[10] Li ZW, Zhou MC. On siphon computation for deadlock control in a class of Petri nets. IEEE Trans Syst Man Cybern A Syst Humans. 2008;38(3):667-679.

[11] Cho H, Kumaran TK, Wysk RA. Graph-theoretic deadlock detection and resolution for flexible manufacturing systems. IEEE Trans Robot Autom. 2000;11(2):190-195.

[12] Uzam M. An optimal deadlock prevention policy for flexible manufacturing systems using Petri net models with resources and the theory of regions. Int J Adv Manuf Technol. 2002;19(3):192-208.

[13] Ghaffari A, Rezg N, Xie XL. Design of a live and maximally permissive Petri net controller using the theory of regions IEEE Trans Robot Autom. 2003;19(1):137-142.

[14] Reveliotis SA, Choi JY. Designing reversibility-enforcing supervisors of polynomial complexity for bounded Petri nets through the theory of regions. Lecture Notes in Computer Science. 2006;4024:322-341.

[15] Badouel E, Darondeau P. Theory of Regions. Third Advance Course on Petri Nets. Springer-Verlag, 1998.

[16] Li ZW, Zhou MC, Jeng MD. A maximally permissive deadlock prevention policy for FMS based on Petri net siphon control and the theory of regions. IEEE Trans Autom Sci Eng. 2008;5(1):183-188.

[17] Uzam M, Zhou MC. An iterative synthesis approach to Petri net-based deadlock prevention policy for flexible manufacturing systems. IEEE Trans Syst Man Cybern A Syst Humans. 2007;37(3):362-371.

[18] Li ZW, Zhou MC, Wu NQ. A survey and comparison of petri net-based deadlock prevention policies for flexible manufacturing systems. IEEE Trans Syst Man Cybern C Appl Rev. 2008 ;38(2):173-188.

[19] Piroddi L, Cordone R, Fumagalli I. Selective siphon control for deadlock prevention in Petri nets. IEEE Trans Syst Man Cybern A Syst Humans. 2008;38(6):1337-1348.

[20] Silva M, Teruel E, Colom JM. Linear algebraic and linear programming techniques for the analysis of P/T net systems. LNCS, 1998;1491:303-373.

[21] Ramadge PJ, Wonham WM. The control of discrete event systems. Proc IEEE. 1989;77(1):81-98.

[22] Viswanadham N, Narahari Y, Johnson TL. Deadlock prevention and deadlock avoidance in flexible manufacturing systems using Petri net models. IEEE Trans Robot Autom. 1990;6(6):713-723.

[23] Abdallah IB, ElMaraghy HA. Deadlock prevention and avoidance in FMS: A Petri net based approach. Int J Adv Manuf Technol. 1998;14(10):704-715.

[24] Li ZW, Wang A, Lin H. A deadlock prevention approach for FMS using siphon and the theory of regions. Proceeding of the IEEE International Conference on Systems, Man and Cybernetics; 2004 Oct 10-13; The Hague, Netherlands. P. 5079-84. (ISBN:0-7803-8566-7)

[25] INA. (Integrated Net Analyzer), A Software Tool for Analysis of Petri Nets. Version 2.2, 31.07. 2003. [Online]. Available: http://www.informatik.hu-berlin.de/~starke/ina.html.

[26] Huang YS, Pan YL. Enhancement of An Efficient Liveness-Enforcing Supervisor for Flexible Manufacture Systems. Int J Adv Manuf Technol. 2010;48:725-737. (DOI: 10.1007/s00170-009-2299-x)

[27] Huang YS, Pan YL. An Improved Maximally Permissive Deadlock Prevention Policy Based on the Theory of Regions and Reduction Approach. IET Control Theory Appl. 2011;5(9):1069-1078. (DOI: 10.1049/iet-cta.2010.0371.)

[28] Pan YL, Huang YS. Solutions for Deadlocked Problem of FMSs Using Theory of Regions. Adv Mat Res. 2011 ;314-346 :535-538. (DOI:10.4028/www.scientific.net/AMR.314-316.535.)

[29] Huang YS, Pan YL, Zhou MC. Computationally Improved Optimal Deadlock Control Policy for Flexible Manufacturing Systems. IEEE Trans Syst Man Cybern A Syst Humans. 2012; 42(2):404-415.

Specifying and Verifying Holonic Multi-Agent Systems Using Stochastic Petri Net and Object-Z: Application to Industrial Maintenance Organizations

Belhassen Mazigh and Abdeljalil Abbas-Turki

Additional information is available at the end of the chapter

1. Introduction

In Industrial Maintenance Company (IMC) a vast number of entities interact and the global behaviour of this system is made of several emergent phenomena resulting from these interactions. The characteristics of this system have increased both in size and complexity and are expected to be distributed, open and highly dynamic. Multi-Agent Systems (MAS) are well adapted to handle this type of systems. Indeed, the agent abstraction facilitates the conception and analysis of distributed microscopic models [9]. Using any holonic perspective, the designer can model a system with entities of different granularities. It is then possible to recursively model subcomponents of a complex system until the requested tasks are manageable by atomic easy-to-implement entities. In multi-agent systems, the vision of holons is someway closer to the one that MAS researchers have of Recursive or Composed agents. A holon constitutes a way to gather local and global, individual and collective points of view. A holon is a self-similar structure composed of holons as sub-structures. A hierarchical structure composed of holons is called a holarchy. A holon can be seen, depending on the level of observation, either as an autonomous atomic entity or as an organisation of holons (this is often called the Janus effect [12]). Holonic systems have already been used to model a wide range of systems, manufacturing systems [15, 16, 33], health organizations [32], transportation [2], etc. The different organisations which make up an IMC must collaborate in order to find and put in place various strategies to maintain different production sites. In order to honour its contracts, the IMC should handle the whole of its resources (human and material), ensure the follow up in real time the equipment in different production sites and plan actions to be executed. A part of the maintenance could be remotely achieved (tele-maintenance and/or tele-assistance [17], e-maintenance [13], etc.). Several constraints should be integrated in the process of strategy search and decision making before mobilizing operation teams. Concretely, the search for an efficient maintenance strategy should be found while taking into account the following constraints: (a) The urgency level of the maintenance task requested by a given production site, (b) A distance between mobile teams and production sites, (c) The estimated intervention duration, (d) The respect of the legal daily working time of maintenance crew, (e) Verification of the availability of the stored spare parts, (f) The reconstitution of new teams in view of the mentioned constraints.

To satisfy some of these constraints, we propose a formal holonic approach for modelling and analysis all the entities that constitutes an IMC. We use Holonic Multi-Agent Systems (HMAS) in which holons are agents that may be composed of agents for developing complex systems. To this end, we use an Agent-oriented Software Process for Engineering Complex Systems called ASPECS [8]. The process is considered by their authors as an evolution of the PASSI [3] process for modelling HMAS and it also collects experiences about holon design coming from the RIO (Role, Interaction and Organization) approach [11]. It is sufficient to say that the definition of the MAS meta-model adopted by the new process has been the first step and from this element all the others (activities, guidelines and workflow) have been built according to this guideline [4, 30, 31]. This meta-model defines the underlying concepts. A step-by-step guide from requirements to code allows the modelling of a system at different levels of details. Going from each level to the next consists in a refinement of the meta-model concepts. The objective of this work consists in consolidating the ASPECS methodology by using a formal specification and analysis of the various organizations and the interactions between them. This phase will facilitate the code production of organizations, roles and holons. In addition, it will be possible to test each organization, their roles and each holons independently. This type of analysis, will allow checking certain qualitative properties such as invariants and deadlock, as well as a quantitative analysis to measure the indicators of performance (cost of maintenances, average duration of the interventions, average time to reach a site of production, etc). In this chapter, our extended approach will be used to model and analyze an Industrial Maintenance Company (IMC). After a brief presentation of the framework, the maintenance activities in a distributed context are presented. ASPECS process and modelling approach will be introduced in section 3. Analysis and conception phase of this process and their associated activities are then described in order to identify the holonic IMC organisation. In section 4, first we present our specification formalism and second we assign an operational semantics to it. Additionally, we illustrate how to use the operational semantics as a basis for verification purposes. The specification formalism we intend to present combines two formal languages: Stochastic Petri Nets and Object-Z. Finally, Section 5 summarises the results of the chapter and describes some future work directions.

2. Industrial maintenance company distributed context

For economic and/or efficacy reasons, many companies are being implanted in geographically wide spread areas. Hence, many IMC are compelled to represent their organisations so as to meet efficiently the demands of their clients. Therefore this activity is among those witnessing a rise on the word market in spite of the economic moroseness (particularly large scale and multiple competence maintenance companies). In this distributed context, the maintenance activities are divided on two following structures: (a) Central Maintenance Teams (CMT) which realizes the process of reparation - corrective maintenance, (b) Mobile Maintenance Teams (MMT) which carries out inspections, replacement and several other actions on the various production sites.

To ensure the maintenance of several production sites, many teams specialized in various competence fields should be mobilized. Those in charge of handling these resources should

Specifying and Verifying Holonic Multi-Agent
Systems Using Stochastic Petri Net and Object-Z: Application to Industrial Maintenance Organizations

53

overcome complex logistical problems thereby the need to develop aiding methods and tools for decision making to efficiently manage this type of organizations. Among the services proposed by an IMC, we can mention: (a) On site intervention, (b) Technical assistance via telephone or distance intervention, (c) The study and improvement of equipment, (d) Organisation and engineering, (e) Formation in industrial maintenance, (f) The search for and the development of new maintenance methods. The focus in this research is to find an efficient maintenance policies taking into account multiples alias. We propose a formal approach, based on the paradigm HMAS, to specify and analyze an efficient and adaptive IMC. As such, a specification approach based on HMAS to be a promising approach to deal with the unpredictable request of maintenance due to their decentralization, autonomy, cooperation features and their hierarchical ability to react to unexpected situation. For this specification, we use ASPECS methodology to identify holonic organization of a steady system and we combine two formal languages: Object-Z and Petri Nets for modeling and analysis specification of an IMC.

3. A holonic specification approach of an IMC

3.1. A quick overview of ASPECS process

The ASPECS process structure is based on the Software Process Engineering Metamodel (SPEM) specification proposed by OMG [25]. This specification is based on the idea that a software development process is collaboration between abstract active entities, called Roles that perform operations, called Activities, on concrete, tangible entities, called Work Products. Such as it was proposed by [4], ASPECS is a step-by-step requirement to code software engineering process based on a metamodel, which defines the main concepts for the proposed HMAS analysis, design and development. The target scope for the proposed approach can be found in complex systems and especially hierarchical complex systems. The main vocation of ASPECS is towards the development of societies of holonic (as well as not-holonic) multi-agent systems. ASPECS has been built by adopting the Model Driven Architecture (MDA) [25]. In [5] they label the three meta-models "domains" thus maintaining the link with the PASSI meta-model. The three definite fields are: (a) The Problem Domain. It provides the organisational description of the problem independently of a specific solution. The concepts introduced in this domain are mainly used during the analysis phase and at the beginning of the design phase, (b) The Agency Domain. It introduces agent-related concepts and provides a description of the holonic, multi-agent solution resulting from a refinement of the Problem Domain elements, (c) The Solution Domain is related to the implementation of the solution on a specific platform. This domain is thus dependent on a particular implementation and deployment platform.

Our contribution will relate to the consolidation of the Problem Domain and the Agency Domain. We propose a formal specification approach for analysis the various organizations and the interactions between them facilitating therefore the *Solution Domain*.

3.2. Requirements analysis

The analysis phase needs to provide a complete description of the problem based on the abstractions defined in the metamodel problem domain CRIO (Capacity, Role, Interaction and Organization). All the activities that make up this first phase and their main products can be identified. Indeed, this phase shows the different steps that can be used for the requirements since the description of the field requirements to capacities identification. It also shows how documents and UML diagrams must be constructed for each step. In the following, we present objective, description and diagrams for each step used in the requirements analysis phase.

3.2.1. Requirements domain description

The aim of this phase is to develop a first description of the application context and its functionalities. This activity aims to identify, classify and organize in hierarchy all functional and non functional requirements of different project actors. It must also provide a first estimated scope of the application as well as its size and complexity. In this work, the analysis approach adopted is based on the use case UML diagrams. To facilitate the analysis and reduce the complexity of the system studied, we decomposed the system studied into three modules: Mobile Maintenance Teams (MMT), Maintenance Policies (MP) and Maintenance Mediation (MM) which plays the role of mediator between the first two as shown in Figure 1. Let us now explain the role of each part of the system. The objective of "Mobile Maintenance

Figure 1. Set parts associated to the IMC

Teams" (MMT) is: (a) Receive maintenance requests from "Mediation Maintenance", (b) Planning for maintenance actions, (c) Execute maintenance tasks, (d) Generate maintenance report. The role of "Mediation Maintenance" (MM) is: (a) Receive maintenance requests of different production sites, (b) Diagnosing problems, (c) Classify problems, (d) Responding to customers, (e) Send request maintenance to MMT or MP, (f) Receive execution plans of maintenance from MT or MP if necessary. The objective of "Maintenance Policies" (MP) is: (a) Receive maintenance requests from "Mediation Maintenance", (b) Scheduling maintenance tasks, (c) Execute maintenance tasks, (d) Generate maintenance report, (e) Send report to maintenance "Mediation service", (f) Develop new maintenance methods, (g) Provide training maintenance.

As an example, we'll just show the use case diagram of different scenarios associated to the MMT (Figure 2.). Similarly, we can use identical approach to describe other roles and establish their use case diagrams.

3.2.2. Problem ontology description

First, problem ontology provides a definition of the application context and specific domain vocabulary. It aims to deeper understanding the problem, completing requirements analysis and use cases, with the description of the concepts that make up the problem domain and their relationships. Ontology plays a crucial role in ASPECS process development. Indeed, its structure will be a determining factor for identifying organizations. The ontology is described here in terms of concepts, actions and predicates. It is represented using a specific profile for UML class diagrams. The ontology of the IMC is described in Figure 3.

This ontology represents the knowledge related to the Mobile Maintenance Teams, Mediation Maintenance, Maintenance Policies, the different concepts that compose and the relationships between these components.

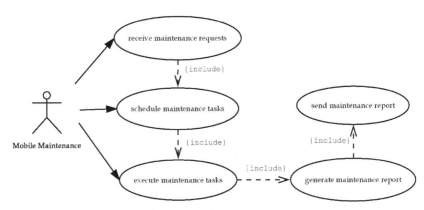

Figure 2. Use case diagram of Mobile Maintenance Teams

3.2.3. Identifying organizations

This action must establish a decomposition of the organizational system and define the objectives of each organization. Every needs identified in the first activity, has an associated organization incarnating the global behavior in charge to satisfy or to realize. Identified organizations are added directly to the use case diagram, in the form of packages including stereotyped use cases diagram that are responsible to satisfy. The Mobile Maintenance Teams organization can be decomposed into three sub-organizations: MMT Forwarding, Tasks Planning and Tasks Execution as shown in Figure 4.

The same process can be used to describe Mediation and Mobile Maintenance Teams organization. According to this decomposition, we can obtain organizational hierarchy of the IMC (Figure 5).

In this hierarchy, MMT Forwarder serves as an intermediary between Mediation Maintenance and Mobile Maintenance Teams. Similarly, CMT Forwarding is directly linked to both organizations Mediation Maintenance and Maintenance Policies.

3.2.4. Identification of roles and interactions

The context and objectives of each organization are now identified. The identification of roles and interactions aims to decompose the global behavior incarnated by an organization into a set of interacting roles. This activity must also describe the responsibilities of each role in satisfying the needs associated with their respective organizations. Each role is associated with a set of concepts in the ontology and generally a subset of those associated with his organization. Roles and interactions that constitute each organization are added to their class diagrams as described in Figure 6. A role is represented by a stereotyped class, and an interaction between two roles is represented by an association between classes of roles. Note also that in this figure, the link "Contributes to" means that an organization contributes in part to the behavior of a role at a higher level of abstraction.

3.2.5. Description of interaction scenarios

The objective of this activity is to specify the interactions between roles to induce higher level behavior. This activity describes the interactions between the roles defined within a given

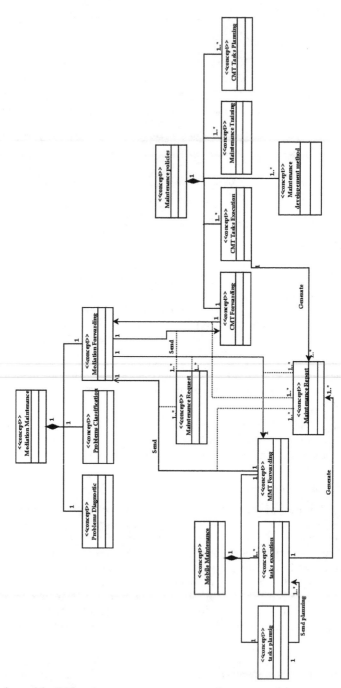

Figure 3. Ontology of the IMC system

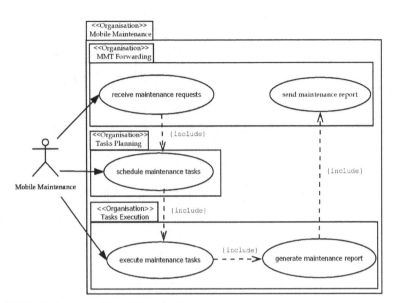

Figure 4. Mobile Maintenance Teams Organization

organization and specifies the means of coordination between them to meet the objectives of their organization. Consequently, each organization is associated with at least one scenario and it may involve defined roles in different organizations. Indeed, an organization usually requires information from other organizations at different level of abstraction. The scenarios detail the sequence of arrival or transfer of such information. Describing interaction scenarios is supported by a set of UML sequence diagrams. An example of interaction scenario associated with the organization IMC system is shown in Figure 7. This diagram above describes possible scenarios within the organization "Mobile Maintenance Teams". For each received request, "Planning Tasks" will schedule maintenance tasks and "Tasks Execution" executes maintenance tasks and finally generates a maintenance report. Scenarios of "Mediation Maintenance" and "Maintenance Policies" organization are not complicated and are not represented here.

3.2.6. Behavioral roles plans of organizations

The description of the behavior plans of roles specify the behavior of each role adapted with the objectives assigned to it and interactions in which it is implicated. Each plan describes the combination of behavior and sequencing of interactions, external events and tasks that make up the behavior of each role. Figure 8 shows the behavior plans of the roles that constitute the IMC organizations.

3.2.7. Identification of capacities

This activity aims to increase the generic behavior of roles by separate clearly the definition of these behaviors of their external dependencies organizations. It is particularly to refine the behavior of roles, to abstract the architecture of the entities that will play them, and ensuring

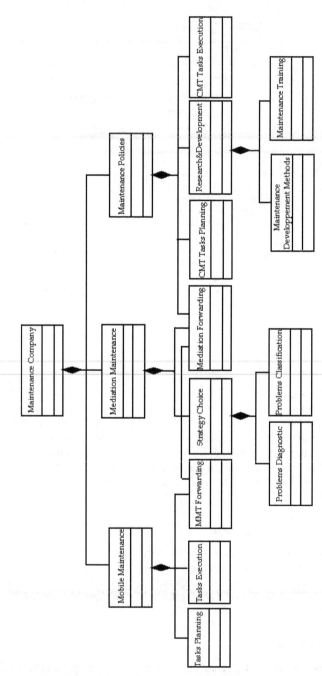

Figure 5. Organizational hierarchy of the IMC

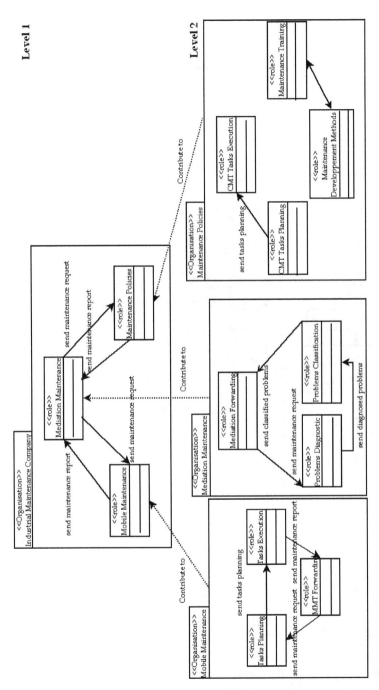

Figure 6. Description of a few roles and interactions of the IMC organization

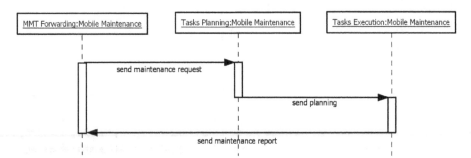

Figure 7. Description of interaction scenarios for MMT

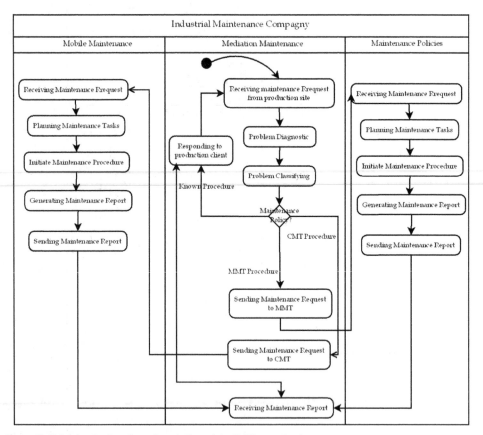

Figure 8. Behavioral roles plans description of the IMC organization

their independence from any external element not associated to them. The identification of capacity needs to determine the competences set required for each role. Capacities are added as stereotyped classes in UML class diagrams of the organizations concerned. In our case, we will identify the capacities required by the roles of the IMC organization (Figure 9).

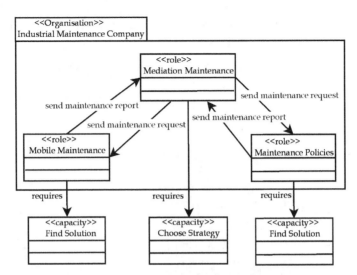

Figure 9. Identification of capacities required by the roles of the IMC organization

3.3. Holarchies design

At this stage of the process, all system organizations, their roles and associated communications are now fully described and specified. Holarchies design is the last activity of the design phase. It performs a global synthesis in which the results of all previous work are summarized and combined in one product. It is devoted to the agentification of the organizational hierarchy and the definition of the entities in charge of running it. Its objective is to define holons system and deduce the holarchy structure. To build the holarchy of the system, the organizations that compose the system are instantiated as groups. A set of holons is then created at each level, each playing one or more roles in one or more groups in the same level. Composition relations between super-holons and sub-holons are then specified in accordance with the contributions from the organizations defined in the organizational hierarchy. The organizational hierarchy is directly associated with the hierarchy of holons (or holarchy). The dynamics governing rules of holons, and the types of governance of each composed holon, are also described. All these elements are then synthesized to describe the structure of the initial holarchy system. To represent static structure of holarchy, the notation used is inspired from the "cheese board" diagrams proposed by [7]. However, it was adapted to better represent the holonic approach. The holonic structure of the IMC is presented in Figure 10.

At level 0 of the holarchy, we find three super-colons H1, H2 and H3, which play respectively Mobile Maintenance, Mediation Maintenance and Maintenance Policies in the group g0: Industrial Maintenance Company. It is reminded that this name means that the group g0 is an instance of the organization Industrial Maintenance Company. The super-holon H1 contains an instance of the Mobile Maintenance organization (g2 group), the super-holon H2 contains an instance of the Maintenance Mediation organization (g4 group) and the super-holon H3 contains an instance of the Maintenance policies (g8 group). The holon H7 of Mediation organization is also a super-holon strategy Choice who plays in the group g4 (Mediation Maintenance). This super-holon contains an instance of the organization strategy Choice (g6 group). Holon H11, of the Maintenance Policies organization, is also a super-holon which acts in the Research & Development group g8.

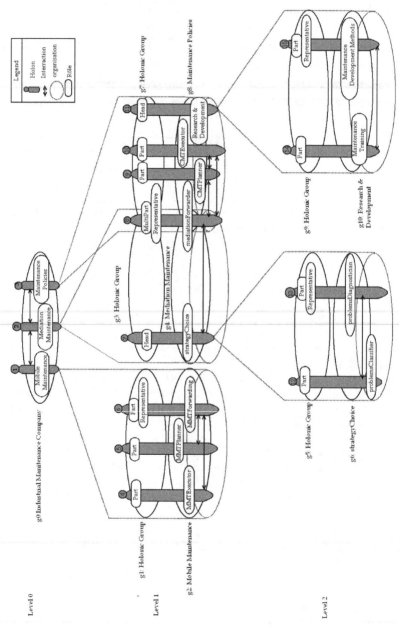

Figure 10. Holonic Structure of the IMC

Specifying and Verifying Holonic Multi-Agent
Systems Using Stochastic Petri Net and Object-Z: Application to Industrial Maintenance Organizations

63

This super-holon contains an instance of the Research & Development organization (g10 group). Holon H8 Playing Mediation role is named Multi-part role since sharing between Maintenance Policies and Maintenance Mediation organizations. In different organizations, interactions between holons are represented by arrows.

4. Heterogeneous formal specification and verification of holonic organisation based on SPN and object-Z language

In this section, we present an integration method of Stochastic Petri Nest (SPN) and Object-Z (OZ) by define coherent formalism called SPNOZ. This formalism is an extension of our formalism which was first defined and based on Z language [14] and GSPN called ZGSPN [19]. Petri nets (PN) are an excellent graphic formal model for describing the control structures and dynamic behaviour of concurrent and distributed systems, but Petri nets lack modelling power and mechanisms for data abstraction and refinement [22, 28].

OZ [6] is a formal notation for specifying the functionality of sequential systems. It is based on typed set theory and first order logic and thus offers rich type definition facility and supports formal reasoning. However, OZ does not support the effective definition of concurrent and distributed systems and OZ specifications often do not have an explicit operational semantics. The benefits of integrating SPN with OZ include: (a) a unified formal model for specifying different aspects of a system (structure, control flow, data types and functionality), (b) a unified formal model for specifying different types of systems (sequential, concurrent and distributed systems), (c) a rich set of complementary specification development and analysis techniques. Our approach consists in giving a syntactic and semantic integration of both languages. Syntactic integration is done by introducing a behaviour schema into OZ schema. The semantic integration is made by translating both languages towards the same semantic domain as shown in (Figure 11). An operational semantics is aimed to the description of how the system evolves along the time.

The semantic entity associated to a given specification can be seen as an abstract machine capable of producing a set of computations. Because of this, we believe that an operational semantics is a suitable representation for verification and simulation purposes. The approach consists in using a pre-existent model checker rather than developing a specific one. Both transition system models of a SPNOZ class can be used for verification purposes by model checking. In this work, the resulting specification is model-checked by using the Symbolic Analysis Laboratory (SAL) [23]. One of the reasons for choosing SAL is that it also includes verification tools and procedures that support from deductive techniques and theorem proving.

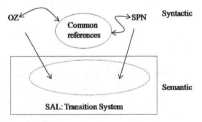

Figure 11. Composition formalisms Approach

4.1. Our syntactic integration method

To be able to build a multi-formalisms specification system, it is necessary to establish a relation of composition between partial specifications. Indeed, any whole of partial specifications must at one moment or another indicates or calls upon part of the system specified by another whole of partial specifications. As the process of composition that we use is based in type integration, the formalism of the Petri Nets is integrated into Object-Z formalism to specify schema with dynamic aspects. This composition can be expressed in several ways: sharing variables with the constraints expressed on the same entity or with translation into a single formalism for all formalisms used. SPN formalism is integrated into the formalism Object-Z to specify classes with behavioral aspects. This integration from the syntactically point of view, is based on a shared syntactic domain which consists of two parts: (a) A set of types and classes Object-Z specifying the main aspects of the SPN, (b) A function that converts a SPN in syntactic elements of the shared domain. This syntactic domain does not share instead of translation of Petri nets to Object-Z but is used to reference within the class Object-Z the elements of the Petri nets included. For instance, the approach presented here assigns to Object-Z the description of data structures and functions, and to the Stochastic Petri Nets the description of behavioral aspects. This section presents a simplified description of the operational semantics of SPNOZ [20] specification models. To express the aspects of SPN in Object-Z, we must have rules to translate a SPN into syntactic elements of the domain. For this, we use a function like relationship between PN and Object-Z scheme.

4.1.1. From PN to SPN

In [19], we proposed some syntactic integration of different classes of Petri Nets with abbreviations and extensions. We remind here that corresponding to SPN after recalling the semantic of ordinary PN. Inherently, the basic components of a Petri net, the concepts of marking and firing. Petri nets (PNs) introduced by C. A. Petri [27] were originally intended as a means for the representation of the interaction, logical sequence and synchronization among activities which are only of a logical nature [26]. A PN is a directed bipartite graph which comprises a set of places P, a set of transitions T, and a set of directed arcs defined by input and output incidence application (Pre and Post). Each place contains an integer (positive or zero) number of tokens or marks. The number of tokens contained in a place P_i will be called either $m(P_i)$ or m_i. The net marking, m, is defined by the vector of these markings, i.e., $m = \{m_1, m_2, \ldots, m_{|P|}\}$. The marking defines the state of the PN, or more precisely the state of the system described by the PN. The evolution of the state thus corresponds to an evolution of the marking, an evolution which is caused by firing of transitions, as we shall see. Generalized PN is a PN in which weights (noted by w, strictly positive integers) are associated with the arcs. When an arc $P_i \rightarrow T_j$ has a weight w, this means that transition T_j will only be enabled (or firable) if place P_i contains at least w tokens. When this transition is fired, w tokens will be removed from place P_i. When an arc $T_i \rightarrow P_j$ has a weight w, this means that when T_j is fired; w tokens will be added to place P_i.

The graph of markings (or reachability graph) is made up of summits which correspond to reachable markings and of arcs corresponding to firing of transitions resulting in the passing from one marking to another. The specification of a PN is completed by the initial marking m0. Since standard Petri nets did not convey any information about the duration of each activity or about the way in which the transition, which will fire next in a given marking, is actually

Specifying and Verifying Holonic Multi-Agent
Systems Using Stochastic Petri Net and Object-Z: Application to Industrial Maintenance Organizations

65

selected among the enabled transitions, a lot of research effort has been made to exploit the modeling power of PNs. Most efforts were concerned with embedding PN models into timed environments. Stochastic Petri Nets (SPN) was introduced independently by [21, 24]. Both efforts shared the common idea of associating an exponentially distributed firing time with each transition in a PN, but differed in delays.

This random variable expresses the delay from the enabling to the firing of the transition. A formal definition of a SPN is given by the following 8-tuple [18]:

$SPN = (P, T, Pre, Post, C, Ih, R, m_0)$; where

$P = \{P_1, P_2, ..., P_n\}$ is a finite, not empty, set of places;

$T = \{T_1, T_2, ..., T_m\}$ is a finite, not empty, set of transitions;

$P \cap T = \emptyset$ is the sets P and T are disjointed;

$Pre : P \times T \longrightarrow N$ is the input incidence application;

$Post : P \times T \longrightarrow N$ is the output incidence application;

$C : P \longrightarrow N^+ \cup \{\infty\}$ is the capacity of places;

$Ih \subset \{P \times T\}$ is the set of k-inhibitor arcs;

$R : T \rightarrow \{\text{firing rate expressions}\}$ associated with timed transitions;

$m_0 = \{m_{01}, m_{02}, ., m_{0n}\}$ is the initial marking , with $m_{0i} = m_0(P_i)$.

Basically, a Stochastic PN may be considered as a timed PN in which the timings have stochastic values. The firing of transition T_j will occur when a time d_j has elapsed after its enabling and this time is a random value. In this basic model, usually called stochastic PN, the random variable d_j follows an exponential law of rate $\lambda_j \in \lambda(\lambda = \{\lambda_1, \lambda_2, ..., \lambda_{|T|}\})$. Noted that firing rates may depend on places markings, and in this case, firing rate expression is used. This means that: $Pr[d_j \leq t + dt | d_j > t] = \lambda_j.dt$. The probability density and the distribution function of this law are, respectively, $h(t) = \lambda_j e^{-\lambda_j t}$ and $H(t) = Pr[d_j \leq t] = 1 - e^{-\lambda_j t}$.

The average value of this law is $1/\lambda_j$ and its variance $1/\lambda_j^2$. It is clear, from the previous equations, that this law is completely defined by the parameter λ_j. A fundamental feature of an exponential law is the memoryless property, i.e.: $Pr[d_j \leq t_0 + t | d_j > t_0] = Pr[(d_j \leq t)$.

This property may be interpreted in the following way: let d_j be a random variable exponentially distributed, representing for example the service time of a customer. The service of this customer begins at time $t = 0$. If at time t_0 the service is not yet completed, the distribution law of the residual service time is exponential with the same rate as the distribution law of d_j. This property is important since it implies the following one.

Property: If transition T_j, whose firing rate is λ_j, is q-enabled at time t and if $q > 0$:

$$q \leq min_{i:P_i \in {}^0T_j} \left(m(P_i) / Pre(P_i, P_j) \right) < q + 1$$

${}^0T_j$ is the set of input places of T_j, then $Pr[\lambda_j$ will be fired between t and $t + dt] = q.\lambda_j.dt$, independently of the times when the q enabling occurred (simultaneously or not). The product $q.\lambda_j = \lambda_j(m)$ is the firing rate associated with T_j for marking m. It results from the previous property, that the marking $m(t)$ of the stochastic PN is an homogeneous Markovian process, and thus an homogeneous Markov chain can be associated with every SPN. From the graph of reachable markings, the Markov chain isomorphic to SPN is obtained. A state of the Markov chain is associated with every reachable marking and the transition rates of the Markov chain are obtained from the previous property. Note that there is no actual conflict in a SPN. For example, the probability that firing transition T_i occurs simultaneously with transition T_j is zero since continuous time is considered. One approach may be used to analyze a SPN consists of analyzing a continuous time, discrete state space Markov process (bounded PN). Let $T(m)$, denote the set of transitions enabled by m. If $T_k \in T(m)$, the conditional firing probability of T_k from m is: $Pr[T_k$ will be fired $|m] = \lambda_k(m) / \sum_{j:T_j \in T(m)} \lambda_j(m)$; the dwelling time $\lambda(m)$ follows an exponential law, and the mean dwelling time in marking m is $1/\lambda(m)$ with $\lambda(m) = \sum_{j:T_j \in T(m)} \lambda_j(m)$.

4.1.2. SPN expressed in OZ

This section discusses aspects of SPN expressed in OZ. These aspects can be obtained by successive refinements starting from formal definition of ordinary PN. Figure 12 shows the specification of a SPN expressed by the OZ syntax. The class schema SPN includes, from top to bottom, an abbreviation declaration and two free types [1] places and transitions. After that, comes an unnamed schema generally called the state schema, including the declaration of all class attributes. Next schema INIT includes a predicate that characterize the initial state of the class. The last schema defines specific operation of the SPN class. The first two lines in the predicates determine the input and output places of a transition. The third and fourth predicate verifies if the transition is firable (enable): input places contain enough tokens and output places have not reached their maximum capacity. The fifth verifies inhibitor arc between P and T authorizes the firing. Finally, the last two predicates express the marking change after firing timed transition. At the end, we specify the invariants of the SPN model. Now that we have expressed aspects of SPN in OZ, we must have rules for translating any PN of syntactic elements. For this we inspired from [11] using a function like relationship between PN and the types and patterns of the OZ domain. This function transforms any PN into OZ specification written with the schemas defined in the previous section. The function we call $\aleph$ is the basis of the mechanism of syntactic integration of our multi-formalisms. This function is defined inductively $\aleph$ as follows: (a) If ψ is an ordinary Petri Nets then $\aleph(\psi)$ is a PN scheme, (b) If ψ is a Stochastic Petri Nets then $\aleph(\psi)$ is a SPN scheme.

4.2. Syntactic integration based in SPNOZ formalism

4.2.1. The case of the IMC organisation

In order to illustrate syntactic integration of our approach, we specify a part of our Industrial Maintenance Company (IMC-Part). We have limited our work to the specification of the Mobile Maintenance Teams Organization which is a part of the holonic structure of the system studied with two MMT. We assume that the choice of the intervening teams depends on the following information: the availability of the MMT, the distance at which the MMT is from the production site and spare parts stock level of MMT. We suppose that our system can be in three different states: Mobile Team(i) Available (MTA(i)), Mobile Team(i) on Production Site (MTPS(i)) and Mobile Team(i) with Critical Level of Stock (MTCLS(i)). For this reason, we use a free or built type to describe the system state:

STATE_IMC-Part ::= MTA I MTPS I MTCLS.

Specifying and Verifying Holonic Multi-Agent
Systems Using Stochastic Petri Net and Object-Z: Application to Industrial Maintenance Organizations

67

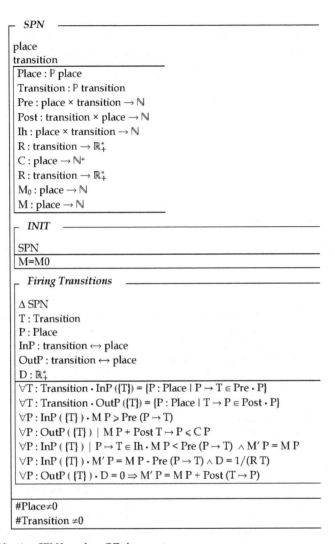

Figure 12. Specification SPN based on OZ class syntax

The system to be specified is described by its state and following average times, estimated by the Maintenance Policies organization, such as: t_{DMMTi} the average time Displacement of Mobile Maintenance Team(i) to reach Production site, associated to transition $T(i)$; $t_{RepMMTi}$ the average time for intervention of Mobile Maintenance Team(i), associated to transition $T'(i)$; t_{SD} the time limit to which Maintenance Team must arrive on a production site; t_{RepCMT} the average time for Repairing the defective parts by Central Maintenance Team, associated to transition $T''(i)$. Other parameters are introduced to supplement the specification such as: Ci the level stock of Mobile Maintenance Team(i); Cmin(i) the minimum level stock of Mobile Maintenance Team(i) (below this value, MMT(i) must re-enters to the IMC); m and n the initial state of stocks. Syntactically, SPNOZ specification IMC-Part is like OZ class, with the addition of a behaviour schema, which includes a SPN. The IMC-Part class on Figure 13 specifies a part of the IMC system. The class IMC-Part includes an abbreviation declaration and the behaviour schema which containing SPN. The state system is presented with class schema IMC-Part. In the initial state, all the MMT are available and the spare parts stock level is at its maximum (m and n). The initial state is presented with Init_IMC-Part schema.

In Figure 13, transitions in dotted lines (T1, T2, T''1 and T''2) are transition that interact with MMT forwarding and Tasks Planning organizations.

4.2.2. SPNOZ syntax

Formally, an SPNOZ class C is defined by giving a triple (V_C, B_C, O_C). The set V_C includes the variables of the class, as named in the state schema. B_C is the behaviour SPN and O_C is the set of operations of the class, the names of the operation schemas of the class. For the IMC-Part class, variables and operations are:

$$V_{IMC-Part} = \{S, t_{DMMT1}, t_{DMMT2}, t_{RepMMT1}, t_{RepMMT2}, t_{RepCMT}, t_{SD}, C1, C2, Cmin1, Cmin2\}$$

$$O_{IMC-Part} = \{SelectTeam1, SelectTeam2\}$$

Operation Select Team1 and Select Team2 can select a mobile team to involve on a production site. This selection will be made according to predefines criteria (availability of MMT, the average time Displacement of MMT and his spare parts stock level). If a team meets the different criteria, it will be chosen and its associated SPN model will be instantiated with different values for the new crossing rates $(\lambda_i, \lambda_i', \lambda_i'')$. Otherwise MMT will not be selected and its associated model will be blocked (Pre(MTAi $\mapsto T_i$)=∞) and second team will be solicited. Finally, Select Team1 and Select Team2 expressions translate the fact that if the level of the inventories of MMTi teams with reached critical level, it will not have the possibility of intervening on any site of production (probably it will turn over to IMC).

4.3. SPNOZ semantics

The semantic integration is made by translating both languages towards the same semantic domain. The semantic entity associated to a given class takes the form of a transition system, in two possible versions, timed or untimed. As the approach proposed in [10], rather thaninsert one language into the other produces their semantic integration by adopting a common semantic domain, i.e., transition systems. The semantic description of a SPNOZ class C consists in representing the set of computations that C can take. Computations are sequences of states subject to causal restrictions imposed by the structure and the elements of C. The state of class C, which we call a situation, is essentially a pair $s = (v, m)$. Symbol $v : V_C \rightarrow D$ denotes a estimation of all the variables of C, with D denoting the super domain where all the variables take values, each one according to its type. Symbol m represents a state configuration of the behavior Stochastic Petri Nets. A state configuration is a state that can be active multiple transitions. The initial situation $s_0 = (v_0, m_0)$, is determined as follows. The initial valuation v_0 is a valuation that satisfies the predicates of the INIT scheme. Variables that do not appear in the INIT scheme usually are given default values m_0 is the initial state configuration. The basic evolution stage is the situation change, called firing, which we describe now. Step $i + 1$ takes the system from situation i to situation $i + 1$ and is noted

Specifying and Verifying Holonic Multi-Agent
Systems Using Stochastic Petri Net and Object-Z: Application to Industrial Maintenance Organizations

69

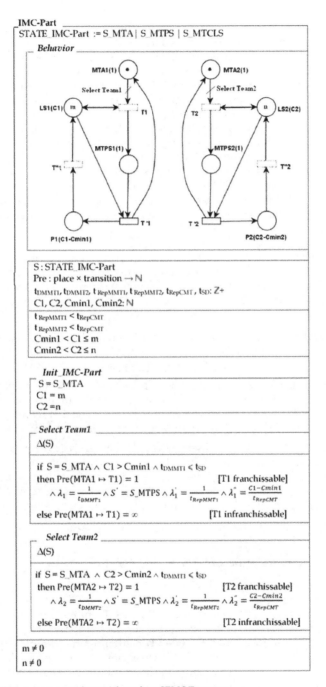

Figure 13. IMC-Part system specification based on SPNOZ syntax

$(v_i, m_i) \overset{T(m_i)}{\rightarrow} (v_{i+1}, m_{i+1})$ where $T(m_i)$ is the set of transitions activated at step i. (marking m_i). The step occurs when at least one of the SPN's transitions is enable. To describe the situation transformation produced by a step, we adopt the formalism of transition systems, particularly the Mana and Pnueli notation style by means of predicates. With class C, we associate the transition system $Tr_{sys} = (V, \phi, T_{sys})$. Symbol $V = V_C \cup \{m\}$ represents the set of variables. Variable m takes value in the graph of markings. The states of the transition system Tr_{sys} are the situations of C, i.e., valuations of the variables in V. If s denote a state of Tr_{sys}, we simplify notation as follows: for all $v \in V$, $s[v]$ denotes the value of v at s. Symbol ϕ represents the initial state predicate. Any valuation of V that satisfies ϕ is an initial state of the system: s is an initial state if $s[\phi] = true$ (where $s[\phi]$ denotes the valuation of formula ϕ from the value of its variables in s). Symbol $T_{sys} = T_{B_C} \cup T_{O_C}$ represents the set of transitions of PNOZ class where T_{B_C} represent the set of PN shown in behavior scheme of the class and T_{O_C} represent the set of transition generated from the operation liste O_C of the class C. A transition $T_i \in T_{sys}$ defines an elementary change of the state of the transition system. Such a change is described by a transition relation: $\rho_i = V \times V' \to \{TRUE, FALSE\}$. To the set V of variable symbols we add the set V' of variable symbols decorated with a prime character ('). For any $x \in V$, an occurrence of symbol x in ρ_i represents the valuation of x in the source state of transition T_i and an occurrence of x' the valuation of x in the destination state of T_i. The couple of states (s, s') can be a couple (source; destination) of transition T_i if $\rho_i(s[V], s'[V']) = true$, where $s[V]$ denotes the valuation of unprimed variables in the state s and $s'[V']$ the valuation of primed variables in state s'.

Concerning Timed transition system (TTS) associated to the SPNOZ class C, from the transition system the transition system $Tr_{sys} = (V, \phi, T_{sys})$ previously defined, we define $TTS_{sys} = (V^t, \phi^t, T^t_{sys})$ obtained as follows: (a) Augment variables set V with time variable t; $V^t = V \cup \{t\}$ which takes value in some totally ordered set with a lowest bound. Typically, $\mathbb{N}$ (the natural integers) is used to model discrete time and $\mathbb{R}^+$ to model dense time, (b) Let $\phi^t = \phi \wedge (t = 0)$, (c) For each transition $T_i \in T^t_{sys}$, add a variable that represents the real-time in the system. Next, we define the set of computations that a timed transition system can yield, which is to be considered as the timed semantics of a SPNOZ classes. We note $m_i \overset{T_i}{\rightarrow} m_{i+1}$ to assert that the transition system goes from state m_i to state m_{i+1} by means of transition T_i and take time $t = 1/\lambda_i$, (with λ_i : firing rate of T_i). We define a finite macro-step to be a finite succession $m_0, m_1, \ldots, m_n$ of state that: (a) $m_0 \models \phi^t$, (b) For every state m_i of TTS_{sys}, there is a transition $T_i \in T^t_{sys}$ such that $m_i \models Pre(T_i)$ and $m_i \models Post(T_i)$ and $t = 1/\lambda_i$.

In [19], more details about the full semantic integration is presented.

4.4. Validation and simulation of SPNOZ specification

SALenv contains a symbolic model checker called sal-smc allows users to specify properties in Linear Temporal Logic (LTL), and Computation Tree Logic (CTL). However, in the current version, SALenv does not print counter examples for CTL properties. When users specify an invalid property in LTL, a counter example is produced. LTL formulas state properties about each linear path induced by a module. For instance, the formula G(p⇒F(q)) states that whenever p holds, q will eventually hold. The formula G(F(p)) states that p often holds infinitely. The example illustrated by Figure 14 shows some properties of the system written in the form of theorems with the LTL and CTL formulas. The SAL language includes the clause theorem for declaring that a property is valid with respect to a modeled system by a

Specifying and Verifying Holonic Multi-Agent
Systems Using Stochastic Petri Net and Object-Z: Application to Industrial Maintenance Organizations

71

```
IMC: CONTEXT =
BEGIN

      Time : Real;
      Vals : TYPE = [0 .. n];
      STATE_IMC-Part : TYPE = {S_MTA, S_MTPS, S_MTCLS};
      IMC-Part : MODULE =
      BEGIN
            INPUT t_{DMMT1}, t_{DMMT2}, t_{RepMMT1}, t_{RepMMT2}, t_{RepCMT1}, t_{RepCMT2}, t_{SD} : Time
            INPUT C1, C2, Cmin1, Cmin2, n, m : INTEGER
            INPUT Select Team1, Select Team2 : BOOLEAN
            OUTPUT S : STATE_IMC-Part
            OUTPUT λ_1, λ_2 : Time
            OUTPUT M : ARRAY[MTA1, LS1, P1, MTPS1, MTCLS1, MTA2,
LS2, P2, MTPS2, MTCLS2] OF Vals
            LOCAL Trans_sys IN {T1, T'1, T''1, T2, T'2, T''2}

INITIALIZATION
      S = S_MTA,
      M0 = {1, m, 0, 0, 1, n, 0, 0},
      C1 = m,
      C2 = n,
      t_{RepMMT1} < t_{RepCMT}, t_{RepMMT2} < t_{RepCMT}, Cmin1 < C1 ≤ m, Cmin2 < C2 ≤ n

      TRANSITION [
        Pre (S : STATE_IMC-Part , T : Trans_sys ) : INTEGER
        t_Select Team1 :
            IF (S = S_MTA   AND   M[MTA1] = 1 AND   C1 > Cmin1 AND
t_{DMMT1} ≤ t_{SD} )
                THEN
                    S' = S_MTPS   AND M[MTPS1] = 1 AND   λ_1 = \frac{1}{t_{DMMT1}}   AND
λ_1' = \frac{1}{t_{RepMMT1}}  AND  λ_1'' = \frac{C1-Cmin1}{t_{RepCMT1}}
                ELSE
                    Pre (S_MTA , T1) = ∞
                ENDIF
        []

      t_Select Team2 :
            IF (S= S_MTA AND   M[MTA2]= 1 AND   C2 > Cmin2  AND t_{DMMT1} ≤
t_{SD} )
                THEN
                    S' = S_MTPS   AND M[MTPS 2]= 1 AND   λ_2 = \frac{1}{t_{DMMT2}}   AND
λ_2' = \frac{1}{t_{RepMMT2}}  AND  λ_2'' = \frac{C2-Cmin2}{t_{RepCMT2}}
                ELSE
                    Pre (S_MTA , T2) = ∞
                ENDIF
      END;

      %%-----------------------
      %% system properties
      %%-----------------------
      th1 : THEOREM IMC-Part |- G(S = S_MTA AND M[LS1] > Cmin1 AND
λ_1 = (1/ t_{DMMT1}) AND t_Select Team1 => F( S' = S_MTPS));
      Liveness : THEOREM IMC-Part |- G(M[LS1] /= 0 AND M[LS2] /=0);
      Boundedness : THEOREM IMC-Part |- G(M[MTA1] + M[MTPS1]=1 AND
M[P1]+M[LS1]= m);

END
```

Figure 14. SAL CONTEXT associated to the SPNOZ IMC

CONTEXT. The first theorem th1 can be interpreted as whenever the system in state S_MTA and Select Team1 is true, transition holds, the system will probably in S_MTPS state. The following command line is used:

./sal-smc IMC th1
proved.

SALenv also contains a Bounded Model Checker called sal-bmc. This model checker only supports LTL formulas, and it is basically used for refutation, although it can produce proofs by induction of safety properties. The following command line is used:

./sal-bmc IMC th1
no counterexample between depths [0, 10]

Remark: The default behavior is to look for counterexample up to depth 10. The option -depth=<num> can be used to control the depth of the search. The option -iterative forces the model checker to use iterative deepening, and it is useful to find the shortest counterexample for a given property. Before proving a liveness property, we must check if the transition relation is total, that is, if every state has at least one successor. The model checker may produce unsound result when the transition relation is not total. The totality property can be verified using the sal-deadlock-checker. The following command line is used:

/sal-deadlock-checker IMC IMC-Part
Ok (module does NOT contain deadlock state).

The liveness theorem can be interpreted as always, the quantity of stock of piece is not null in the two teams. Now, we use sal-smc to check the property liveness with the following command line:

./sal-smc -v 3 IMC-Part liveness
proved.

The Boundedness theorem can be interpreted as always, the state space system is bounded. Now, we use sal-bmc to check the property Boundedness with the following command line:

./sal-bmc IMC Boundedness
no counterexample between depths [0, 10]

5. Conclusion

In this chapter we showed that HMAS is well adapted to analyse and design an IMC holarchy. The meta-model utilized can be exploited in the implantation stage with the advantage of having formally validated its structure and its behaviour by using Heterogeneous formal specification based on Stochastic Petri Nets and Object-Z. For the moment, we are now refining our SPNOZ tool to establish a semantic-based in Markov chain isomorphic to SPN. This semantic seems best adapted to be transformed into Transition systems. Our future works will focus on a finer analysis of this system type and on a formal modelling of the various scenarios associated with the analysis stage. The notion of multi-views should be integrated. Indeed, the search for and the choice of strategy depends on the point of view of the person or the team required to take decisions according not only the constraints linked to the system but also to their environments. At the same time, it will be interesting to use HMAS which proposes multi-view holarchy introduced in [29] and consequently integrate it in the different existing meta-models.

Specifying and Verifying Holonic Multi-Agent
Systems Using Stochastic Petri Net and Object-Z: Application to Industrial Maintenance Organizations

73

Author details

Belhassen Mazigh
Faculty of sciences, Department of Computer Sciences, 5000, Monastir, Tunisia

Abdeljalil Abbas-Turki
Laboratoire SET, Université de Technologie de Belfort Montbéliard, Belfort, France

6. References

[1] Arthan, R.D. (1992) On Free Type Definitions in Z, Published in the Proceedings of the 1991 Z User Meeting, Springer Verlag.

[2] Burckert, H.-J., Fischer, K., Vierke, G. (1998) Transportation scheduling with holonic MAS-the teletruck approach, Proceedings of the Third International Conference on Practical Applications of Intelligent Agents and Multi-agent, pp. 577-590.

[3] Cossentino, M. (2005) From requirements to code with the PASSI methodology, In B. Henderson-Sellers & P. Giorgini (Eds.), Agent-oriented methodologies, Hershey, PA, USA: Idea Group Publishing, Chap. IV, pp. 79-106.

[4] Cossentino, M., Gaglio, S., Garro, A., Seidita, V. (2007) Method fragments for agent design methodologies: From standardization to research, In international Journal on Agent Oriented Software Engineering, 1(1), pp. 91-121.

[5] Cossentino, M., Gaud, N., Hilaire, V., Galland, S., Koukam, A. (2010) ASPECS: an agent-oriented software process for engineering complex systems How to design agent societies under a holonic perspective, Auton Agent Multi-Agent System.

[6] Duke, R., Rose, G., Smith, G. (1995) Object-Z: A specification Language Advocated for Description of Standards, Technical report Software Verification Research Center, Departement of Computer Science, University of Queensland, AUSTRALIA.

[7] Ferber, J., Gutknecht, O., Michel, F. (2004) From agents to organizations: an organizational view of multi-agent systems, In Agent-Oriented Software Engineering 4th International Workshop, volume 2935 of LNCS, Melbourne, Australia, Springer Verlag, pp. 214-230.

[8] Gaud, N. (2007) Systèmes Multi-Agents Holoniques : de l'analyse à l'implantation, Ph.D. thesis, Université de Technologie de Belfort-Montbéliard, France.

[9] Gruer, J.P., Hilaire, V., Koukam, A. (2001) Multi-agent approach to modeling and simulation of urban transportation systems, IEEE International Conference on Systems, Man, and Cybernetics, IEEE 4, 2499-2504.

[10] Gruer, P., Hilaire, V., Koukam, A., Rovarini, P. (2003) Heterogeneous formal specification based on Object-Z and statecharts: semantics and verification, In journal Systems and Software, Elsevier Science.

[11] Hilaire, V., Koukam, A., Gruer, P., Müller, J.-P. (2000) Formal specification and prototyping of multi-agent systems, In A. Omicini, R. Tolksdorf, & F. Zambonelli (Eds.), ESAW, LNAI (No. 1972), Springer Verlag.

[12] Koestler, A. (1967) The Ghost in the Machine, Hutchinson.

[13] Lebold, M., Thurston, M. (2001) Open standards for Condition-Based Maintenance and Prognostic Systems, In Proceedings Of 5th Annual Maintenance and Reliability Conference, Gatlinburg, USA.

[14] Lightfoot, D. (2000) Formal Specification Using Z, Palgrave MacMillan, United Kingdom, 2nd Revised edition.

[15] Maturana, F. (1997) Metamorph: an adaptive multi-agent architecture for advanced manfacturing systems, Ph.D. thesis, The University of Calgary.

[16] Maturana, F., Shen, W., Norrie, D. (1999) Metamorph: An adaptive agent-based architecture for intelligent manufacturing, International Journal of Production Research 37 (10) (1999) 2159-2174.

[17] Mayer, G., Wan Abdullah, Z., Lim Ai, M. (2003) Tele-Maintenance for Remote Online Diagnostic and Evaluation of Problems at Offshore Facilities, Sarawak, SPE Asia Pacific Oil and Gas Conference and Exhibition, Jakarta, Indonesia.

[18] Mazigh, B. (1994) Modeling and Evaluation of Production Systems with GSPN, Ph.D. thesis, Institut Polytechnique de Mulhouse, France.

[19] Mazigh, B. (2006) ZGSPN: Formal specification using Z and GSPN, Technical Report MAZ-SPEc-01-06, Department of Computer Science, University of Monastir, Tunisia.

[20] Mazigh, B., Garoui, M., Koukam, A. (2011) Heterogeneous Formal specification of a Holonic MAS methodology based on Petri Nets and Object-Z, In Proceedings of the Federated Conference on Computer Science and Information Systems, 5th International Workshop on Multi-Agent Systems and Simulation, IEEE Computer Society Press,Pologne, pp. 661-668.

[21] Molloy, M. K. (1981) On the Integration of Delay and Throughput Measures in Distributed Processing Models, Ph.D. thesis, UCLA, Los Angeles, CA, USA.

[22] Natarajan, S. (1989) Petri nets: Properties, analysis and applications, Computer Science Laboratory SRI International, Proceedings of IEEE, 77(4).

[23] Natarajan, S. (2000) Symbolic Analysis of Transition Systems, Computer Science Laboratory SRI International.

[24] Natkin, S. (1980) Réseaux de Petri Stochastiques, Ph.D. thesis, CNAM, Paris.

[25] Object Management Group. (2003) MDA guide, v1.0.1, OMG/2003-06-01.

[26] Peterson, J. L. (1982) Petri Net Theory and the Modeling Systems, Prentice-Hall, Englewood Cliffs, NJ.

[27] Petri, C. A. (1966) Communication with Automata, Ph.D. thesis, Technical Report RADC-TR-65-377, New York.

[28] Reisig, W. (1985) Petri Nets an Introduction, EATCS Monographs on Theoretical Computer Science 4.

[29] Rodriguez, S., Hilaire, V., Koukam, A. (2007) Towards a holonic multiple aspect analysis and modeling approach for complex systems: Application to the simulation of industrial plants, In journal Simulation Modelling Practice and Theory 15, pp. 521-543.

[30] Seidita, V., Cossentino, M., Hilaire, V., Gaud, N., Galland, S., Koukam, A (2009) The metamodel: A starting point for design processes construction, In international Journal of Software Engineering and Knowledge Engineering (IJSEKE).

[31] SPEM. (2007) Software process engineering metamodel specification, v2.0, final adopted specification, ptc/07-03-03, Object Management Group.

[32] Ulieru, M., Geras, A. (2002) Emergent holarchies for e-health applications: a case in glaucoma diagnosis, IECON 02 28th Annual Conference of the Industrial Electronics Society, IEEE, vol. 4, pp. 2957-2961.
URL: people.mech.kuleuven.ac.be/jwyns/phd/order.html

[33] Wyns, J. (1999) Reference architecture for holonic manufacturing systems-the key to support evolution and reconfiguration, Ph.D. thesis, Katholieke Universiteit Leuven.

Chapter 4

Measurement of Work-in-Process and Manufacturing Lead Time by Petri Nets Modeling and Throughput Diagram

Tiago Facchin and Miguel Afonso Sellitto

Additional information is available at the end of the chapter

1. Introduction

A proper planning and the search for better results in the production processes are important for the competitiveness that manufacturing can add to business operations. However, changes in manufacturing involve risks and uncertainties that may affect the company's operations. In this case, modeling and simulation of the production line can assist the decision-making process, avoiding unnecessary expenses and risks before making a decision. A model that can be simulated in the computer is a mechanism that turns input parameters, known and associated requirements of the process, into output parameters and performance metrics that have not yet happened in the real world (Law; Kelton, 1991).

Thereby, a line production model, which can be used in a computer simulation, can be a tool for decision support, because, before the results will crystallize in the real world manufacturing, it can be predicted, with a given reliability, in virtual simulation.

Inventory in process and throughput time that a production plan will generate are quantities that may be useful in decision making in manufacturing and can be predicted by computer simulation. The inventory process (work in process or WIP) consists of materials that have already been released for manufacture (have already left the warehouse or have been received from suppliers), but their orders still not been completed. Lead time is the time between release manufacture order and the product availability for shipment to the customer (Antunes et al., 2007). Some decisions in internal logistics of manufacturing may be related to these quantities: choosing alternatives for compliance with scheduled delivery dates, intermediate storage areas for processing of applications, equipment for internal movement; resources for tool changes and machinery preparation. The most important decision that can be supported by the proposed method is the definition of in-process inventory level that will be allowed in manufacturing. This should not be so low as to generate idle nor so high as to increase the throughput time.

In the first two chapters will be presented basic concepts for modelling the proposed system using Petri Nets and throughput diagram, these methods will be applied in a real manufacturing and the results compared with the real manufacturing outputs.

The aim of this paper is to measure in advance in-process inventory and lead time in manufacturing that a production plan will generate. Knowing the magnitudes of the plan prior to release, a manager can predict and possibly prevent problems, changing the plan. The specific objectives were: i) mapping manufacturing, ii) model building for PN, refining and validated by field data, iii) with the results simulated by throughput diagram, calculate the inventory in process and expected lead time; and iv) discuss the application. Computer simulation is the research method. Delimitation is that made in a single application in shoe manufacturing, in a period of two weeks. The working method includes two operations research techniques, Petri nets (PN) and the throughput diagram and was tested in a production plan already performed, whose results served to refine and validate the model, which can be used in plans not yet released for manufacturing.

The main contribution of this paper is the method of working, replicable to other applications: simulation PN, validated by data field and use the throughput diagram results to calculate the performance metric. The method can be useful in ill-structured problems, as may occur in manufacturing.

2. Petri Nets

The PN describes the system structure as a directed graph and can capture precedence relations and structural links of real systems with graphical expressiveness to model conflicts and queues. Formally, it can be defined as a sixfold (P, T, A, M_0, W, K) in wich: P is a set of states/places, T is a set of transitions, A is a set of arcs subject to the constraint that arcs do not connect directly two positions or transitions, M_0 is the initial state, which tells how many marks/tokens there are in each position to the beginning of the processing, W is a set of arc weights, which tells, for each arc, how many marks are required for a place by the transition or how many are placed in a place after the respective transition; and K is a set of capacity constraints, which reports to each position, the maximum number of marks which may occupy the place (Castrucci; Moraes, 2001). Applying the definition in the PN of Figure 1, P = [p_0, p_1]; T = [t_0]; A = [(p_0, t_0), (t_0, p_1)]; W: w (p_0, t_0) = 1, w (t_0, p_1) = 1 e M_0 = [1; 0]. The token in p_0 enables the transition t_0. After firing, M = [0; 1].

The transitions correspond to changes of states and places correspond to state variables of the system. In the firing of a transition, the tokens move across the network in two phases: enabling and firing transition. A transition $t_j \in$ T is enabled by a token m if $\forall\ p_i \in$ P, m (p_i) $\geq$ w(p_i, t_j), i.e., the token in place p_i is greater than or equal to the arc weight that connects p_i to t_j.

Some variations are allowed in Petri Nets and were used for modeling, for example, the use of inhibitor arcs.

Before Transition   **After Transition**

Figure 1. Symbolic representation of Petri Nets

3. Throughput diagram in manufacturing

In manufacturing, a queue arises when, for variability, at a given instant, the number of orders to be implemented is greater than the available job centers. The manufacturing arrives at the work position (or center), waiting its turn, is processed and proceeds. The sequence is subject to change priorities and interruptions for maintenance or lack of materials (Silva; Morabito, 2007; Papadopoulos et al., 1993).

A work center (machine, production line or manufacturing plant) can be compared to a funnel, in which orders arrive (input), waiting for service (inventory) and leave the system (output). When the work center is observed for a continuous period, the reference period, the cumulative results can be plotted. In Figure 2, it is possible to observe strokes representing the accumulated input and output, measured in amount of work (Wiendahl, 1995). This quantity may be in parts, numbers of hours or another unit value which represents a significant manufacturing effort (Sellitto, 2005).

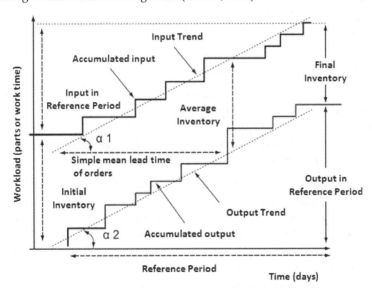

Figure 2. Throughput diagram of a work center

To obtain the line that represents input is necessary knowing the amount of work waiting in the initial inventory at the beginning of the reference period and the output is plotted summing the completed work orders. Wiendahl (1995) presents an analytical development related to the throughput diagram and calculates various quantities of interest to workload control (WLC) such as: lead time, average performance, autonomy, work progress and delays in delivery of orders. For this study case, the funnel formula will be applied:

$$TL_m = I_m / P_m \tag{1}$$

Where, TL_m = simple mean lead time of orders (days); I_m = mean inventory (parts); and P_m = mean performance (parts per day).

For the demonstration, the author uses the figure and considers steady state, i.e., the balance between input and outputs ($\alpha1 = \alpha2$) and $\tan \alpha1 = I_m / TL_m$ e $\tan \alpha2 = P_m$. Wiendahl (1995) suggests that the equation can be used for measurement and control of manufacturing.

4. Research - characterization

The research method was a computer simulation. Simplifications have been admitted, but without losing the replicability. The work method was: i) choice of manufacturing,

process mapping and data collection; ii) model construction by Petri Nets; iii) feeding the model with the initial situation of load in a production plan already executed, run and use the results to fit the model; iv) with the results, calculate the mean lead time of orders; and v) discussing and refining the method, analysis of the implications of its use in manufacturing management.

4.1. Manufacturing process mapping

The production process consists of modeling, cutting, sewing, assembling, packing and delivery (dispatching process). Some works use multitasking labour, that moves between closer stages. The manufacturing was divided in three different process: i) Process 1 (cutting, splitting and chamfer); ii) Process 2 (preparation and sewing); and iii) Process 3 (assembling and dispatching).

Basically, the first process consists in cutting operations of the pre-fabricated (insole and sole) and the upper part of the shoes (leather upper). In pre-fabricated, the model was simplified grouping sequential operations. The input of the system is the place "INPUT – m1", all the orders should be loaded in this place, the transition Separation Table (after place m41) is only enabled when all the parts arrive at the place "Separation Table – m41", and is guaranteed by the auxiliary places (m78, m82, m79, m28, m83, m84, m85). The cutting of leather upper was detailed, this process is sequential because the parts should be cutted in different parts of the leather. The input of this process is the place "m42", observe that some operations are performed by the same operators, which explains the use of inhibitor arcs. The third process includes the assembling and dispatching, after this, the shoe process will be finished and ready to leave the factory. The output of the system is the place "BOX OUTPUT – m16".

4.2. Transition time assignments

To assign time to the transitions, all the processes were timed. With the orientation of the production supervisor, the start/end time of each task was defined. It was considered a confidence level of 95% and used the calculation model suggested by Vaz (1993) and AEP (2003). As an example, for the sole cutting operation the average time was 18.13 seconds and the standard deviation was 2 seconds. The minimum number of samples to ensure the confidence level was 19.5, adopting 20 samples. The time for each transition is the average values collected.

4.3. Simulation, inventory and lead time calculations

To test and refine the model was chosen a plan already done, two weeks and nine production orders. It was informed the load for each place, resulting from earlier orders, at the moment of the first evaluated order will enter the system. A new order is queued of previous processing orders, which explains why the lead time in manufacturing is much higher than the standard manufacturing time. The queuing discipline adopted was FIFO (First-In-First-Out). Table 1 shows data from nine manufacturing orders contained in the production plan (dates are considering working days – 8h40m/day = 3.200s/day). In the last column, there is the order lead time, calculated by simulation, and their average.

Order (pairs)	Real Input Date (days)	Real Output Date (days)	Real Input Date (s)	Real Output Date (s)	Simulated Output Date (s)	Simulated Lead Time of Order (s)
1,000	0	2.5	0	78,000	66,480	66,480
500	1	3.5	31,200	109,200	104,450	73,250
1,500	2	6.5	62,400	202,800	174,860	112,460
800	4	7.5	124,800	234,000	233,872	109,072
800	5	9	156,000	280,800	280,704	124,704
400	7	10	218,400	312,000	313,763	95,363
1,000	10.2	12.5	318,240	390,000	361,404	43,164
500	11.2	13	349,440	405,600	399,304	49,864
500	11.7	14	365,040	436,800	428,504	63,464
TOTAL 7,000 Pairs			AVERAGE 81,980 s = 2,627 days			

Table 1. Information for inventory and mean lead time calculation in manufacturing

Wiendahl (1995) presents a method that considers the size of the order Qi. By this method, TLm = [ΣQi x TLorder I] / ΣQi = 2.73 days, close to the calculated 2.63 days. The correlation between real and simulated outputs (column 5 and 6) is 0.99 and the absolute error I real - simulated I average is 9,821s (2.27% of the largest real value). Figure 3 shows the comparison of information from real and simulated outputs, order to order.

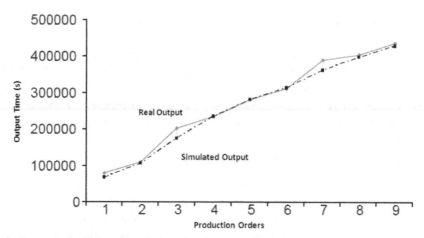

Figure 3. Comparison of information from real and simulated outputs

The simulated mean performance is Pm = 31,200 x [7,000 / (428,504 − 66,480)] = 583 pairs of shoes per day. The calculation basis is: in (428,504 - 66,480) seconds, were delivered 7,000 pairs. The real mean performance is Pm = 31,200 x [7,000 / (428,504 − 78,000)] = 608 pairs of shoes per day.

The time interval between simulated outputs is Δt = [(428,504 − 66,480) / 7,000] = 51.7s and the real is Δt = [(436,800 − 78,000) / 7,000] = 51,25s. The expected mean inventory is Im =Pm.TLm = 583 pairs / day x 2.627 days = 1,531 pairs.

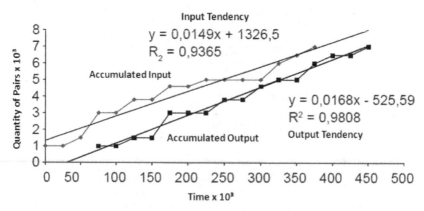

Figure 4. Throughput diagram for real inputs and simulated outputs (at intervals of 25,000s)

The instantaneous numbers of pairs in the system is N(t) = I(t) − O(t). The average, an indicator of mean inventory, calculated by this method is close than the one calculated by the funnel method (1,546 and 1,531 pairs respectively).

Time x 10³ (s)	Accumulated Inputs I(t)	Accumulated Outputs O(t)	Number of Pairs in Manufacturing N(t)
0	1,000	-	-
25	1,000	-	-
50	1,500	-	-
75	3,000	1,000	2,000
100	3,000	1,000	2,000
125	3,800	1,500	2,300
150	3,800	1,500	2,300
175	4,600	3,000	1,600
200	4,600	3,000	1,600
225	5,000	3,000	2,000
250	5,000	3,800	1,200
275	5,000	3,800	1,200
300	5,000	4,600	400
325	6,000	5,000	1,000
350	6,500	5,000	1,500
375	7,000	6,000	1,000
400	-	6,500	-
425	-	6,500	-
450	-	7,000	-
AVERAGE: 1,546 Pairs			

Table 2. Accumulated inputs and outputs of each order presented in Table 1 (at the same interval)

5. Applications in manufacturing management – results discussion

The simulation can generate data for all processes, individually. For instance, Figure 5 shows the results in place INPUT Sewing Process – m44, the operator at this place is overloaded, also observed in the real process. An alternative would be a redistribution of tasks, adopting parallelisms, without overloading the following posts.

A different situation is shown in Figure 6, the time that the operator is idle in this place is low, and there are no accumulations of tasks over time. This represents that, for this place, the tasks are well distributed.

Other screens allow similar analyzes in all manufacturing places. It is important to analyze the changes in the manufacturing and the impacts that an action causes in each process (for instance, allocate more operators to develop a specific task).

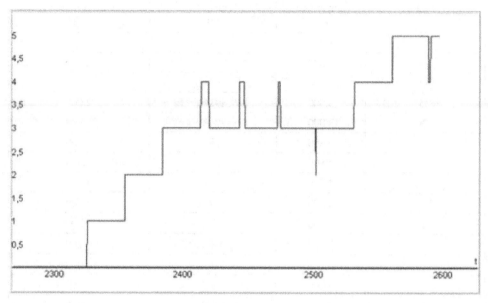

Figure 5. Place: "INPUT Sewing Process – m44"– Results obtained with the simulation

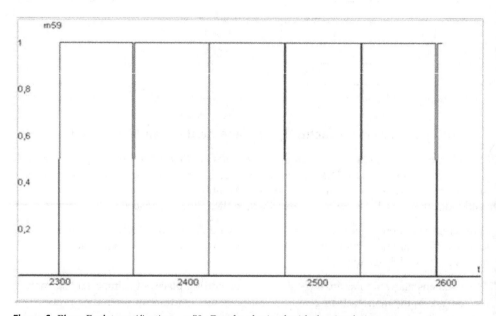

Figure 6. Place: Eyelets verification – m59– Results obtained with the simulation

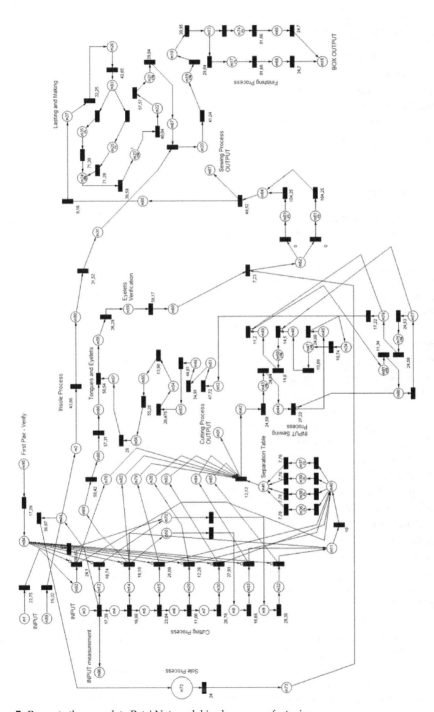

Figure 7. Presents the complete Petri Net model in shoes manufacturing.

6. Final considerations

It was presented and tested a method based on modelling an simulation by Petri Nets and Throughput Diagram for the calculation of two important indicators in manufacturing management: in process inventory and lead time. With the simulation results (provided by the Petri Net model outputs and the throughput diagram) the manufacturing process can be predicted, as well as some modification can be measured and analyzed to optimize the production. As well as save money on alterations that could produce losses in production processes and often, in the real world, are hard to be perceived.

Author details

Tiago Facchin and Miguel Afonso Sellitto
Universidade do Vale do Rio do Sinos - UNISINOS, Brazil

7. References

AEP- Associação Empresarial de Portugal. Métodos e Tempos: Manual Pedagógico. Leça da Palmeira, 2003.

Antunes, J.; Alvarez, R.; Klippel, M.; Bortolotto, P.; Pellegrin, I. Sistemas de Produção. Porto Alegre: Bookman, 2007.

Askin, R.; Krisht, A. Optimal Operation of Manufacturing Systems with Controlled Work-in-Process Levels. International Journal of Production Research, London, v.32, n.7, p.1637-1653, 1994.

Banaszak, Z.; Krogh, B. Deadlock avoidance in flexible manufacturing systems with concurrently competing process flows.

IEEE Transactions on Robotics and Automation, v.6, n.6, p.724-734, 1990.

Bechte, W. Load-oriented manufacturing control just-in-time production for job shops. Production Planning & Control, London, v.5, n.3, p.292-307, 1994.

Breithaupt, J.; Land, M.; Nyhuis, P. The workload control concept: theory and practical extensions of Load Oriented Order Release. Production Planning & Control, London, v.13, n.7, p. 625-638, 2002.

Bitran, G.; Sarkar, D. Throughput Analysis in Manufacturing Networks. European Journal of Operational Research, v.74, n.3, p.448-465, 1994.

Bitran, G.; Morabito, R. Um exame dos modelos de redes de filas abertas aplicados a sistemas de manufatura discretos: Parte I. Gestão & Produção, São Carlos, v. 2, n.2, p.192-219, 1995.

Bitran, G.; Morabito, R. Um exame dos modelos de redes de filas abertas aplicados a sistemas de manufatura discretos: Parte II. Gestão & Produção, São Carlos, v. 2, n.3, p.297-320, 1995A.

Bitran, G.; Dasu, S. A review of open queueing network models of manufacturing systems. Queuing Systems, v.12, n.1-2, p. 95-133, 1992.

Castrucci, P.; Moraes, C. Engenharia de automação industrial. Rio de Janeiro: LTC, 2001.

Boucher, T.; Jafari, M.; Meredith, G. Petri net control of an automated manufacturing cell. Computers and Industrial Engineering, Tarry Town, NY, USA, v. 17, n.1, p.459-463, 1989.

Dallery, Y.; Gershwin, S. Manufacturing flow line systems: a review of models and analytical results. Queuing Systems, v. 12, n.1-2, p. 3-94, 1992.

Dicesare, F.; Harhalakis, G.; PROTH, J. M.; Silva, M.; Vernadat, F. B. Practice of Petri nets in manufacturing. London: Chapman & Hall, 1993.

Drath, R.; Schwuchow, S. Modellierung diskretkontinuierlicher Systeme mit Petri-Netzen. In: Schneider, E. (Org.). Entwurf komplexer Automatisierungssyteme. Braunschweig: Technische Universität Braunschweig, Institut für Regelungs-und-Automatisierungstechnick, 1997.

Fung, R.; Jiang, Z.; Zuo, M.; TU, P. Adaptive production scheduling of virtual production systems using object-oriented Petri nets with changeable structure. International Journal of Production Research, v. 40, n.8, p.1759-1785, 2002.

Govil, M.; FU, M. Queuing theory in manufacturing: a survey. Journal of Manufacturing Systems, v. 18, n.3, p.210-214, 1999.

Jeng, M. A Petri net synthesis theory for modeling flexible manufacturing systems. IEEE Transactions on Systems, Man and Cybernetics Part B, v. 27, n. 2, p.169-183, 1997.

Jeng, M.; Xie, X.; Huang, Y. Manufacturing modeling using process nets with resources. In: IEEE International Conference on Robotics and Automation. April. 2000, San Francisco, USA. Proceedings... San francisco, USA: IEEE, 2000.

Law, A.; Kelton, W. Simulation modeling and analysis. New York: McGraw-Hill, 1991.

Lee, D.; Dicesare, F. Scheduling flexible manufacturing systems using Petri nets and heuristic search. IEEE Transactions on Robotics and Automation, New York, NY, v.10, n.2, p.123-133, 1994.

Maciel, P.; Lins, R.; Cunha, P. Introdução às redes Petri e aplicações. Campinas: Instituto de Computação - UNICAMP, 1996.

Martinez, J.; Muro, P.; Silva, M. Modeling, validation and software implementation of production systems using high level Petri nets. IEEE International Conference on Robotics and Automation. Março – Abril, 1987, Raleigh, North Carolina. Proceedings... Raleigh, North Carolina: I3E Comput. Soc., v.4, p. 1180-1185.

Murata, T. Petri Nets: Properties, Analysis and Applications. Proceedings of the IEEE, Chicago, IL, USA, v. 77, n.4, p.541-580, 1989.

Papadopoulos, H. T.; Heavey, C.; Browne, J. Queuing theory in manufacturing systems analysis and design. London: Chapman & Hall, 1993.

Papadopoulos, H.; Heavey, C. Queuing theory in manufacturing systems analysis and design: a classification of models for production and transfer olines. European Journal of Operational Research, v.92, n.1, p.1-27, 1996.

Peterson, J. Petri Net Theory and the modelling of system. Englewood Cliffs, NJ: Prentice-Hall Editions, 1981.

Proth, J.; Wang, L.; XIE, X. A class of Petri nets for manufacturing system integration. IEEE Transactions on Robotics and Automation, Valbonne, v.13, n.3, p.317-326, 1997.

Reisig, W. Elements of distributed algorithms: modeling and analysis with Petri Nets. Berlim: Springer Verlag, 1998.

Sellitto, M. Medição e controle de desempenho em sistemas de manufatura. Porto Alegre, 2005. Tese – (Doutorado em Engenharia de Produção), UFRGS.

Silva, A. Modelagem de custos em sistemas de manufatura utilizando Redes de Petri. São Carlos, 2002. Dissertação – (Mestrado em Engenharia Mecânica), USP São Carlos.

Silva, C.; Morabito, R. Aplicação de modelos de redes de filas abertas no planejamento do sistema job-shop de uma planta metal-mecânica. Gestão & Produção, São Carlos, v.14, n.2, p.393-410, 2007.

Vaz, A. Cronometragem e a nova realidade. Tecnicouro, Novo Hamburgo, v. 3, n.4, p.34-35, 1993.

Visual Object Net. Software e guia de usuário. Disponível em: http://www.systemtechnik.tu-ilmenau.de/~drath. Acesso em: março 2005.

Xing, K.; Hu, B.; Chen, H. Deadlock avoidance policy for Petri-net modeling of flexible manufacturing systems with shared resources. IEEE Transactions on Automatic Control, New York, NY, USA, v.41, n.2, p.289-295, 1996.

Xiong, H.; Zhou, M. Deadlock-free scheduling of an automated manufacturing system based on Petri nets. IEEE International Conference on Robotics and Automation, Abril 1997, Albuquerque, New Mexico. Proceedings... Albuquerque, New Mexico: IEEE, v.2, p. 945 – 950.

Wiendahl, H. Load-oriented manufacturing control. Berlim: Springer, 1995.

Wiendahl, H.; Breithaupt, J. Automatic production control applying control theory. International Journal of Production Economics, Amsterdam, v. 63, n.1, p.33-46, 2000.

Wu, N.; Zhou, M. Avoiding deadlock and reducing starvation and blocking in automated manufacturing systems. IEEE Transactions on Robotics and Automation, Guang Zhou, v.17, n.5, p.658-669, 2001.

Zhou, M.; Dicesare, F. Parallel and sequential mutual exclusions for Petri net modeling of manufacturing systems with shared resources. IEEE Transactions on Robotics and Automation, Newark, NJ, USA, v.7, n.4, p.515-527, 1991.

Chapter 5

Implementation of Distributed Control Architecture for Multiple Robot Systems Using Petri Nets

Gen'ichi Yasuda

Additional information is available at the end of the chapter

1. Introduction

Because of the generality of the robot's physical structure, control and reprogrammability, it is expected that more and more robots will be introduced into industry to automate various operations. This flexibility can be exploited if the robot control system can be programmed easily. Anyway, it is quite obvious that a single robot cannot perform effective tasks in an industrial environment, unless it is provided with some additional equipment. For example, in building a component, two robots are required to cooperate, one holding some part while the other attaches some other part to it. In other tasks, robots may pursue different goals, making sure that they both don't attempt to use the same resource at the same time. Such synchronization and coordination can only be achieved by getting the robots to talk to each other or to some supervising agent. However, for large-scaled and complicated manufacturing systems, from the viewpoint of cost-performance and reliability appropriate representation and analysis methods of the control system have not sufficiently been established [1]. The lack of adequate programming tools for multiple robots make some tasks impossible to be performed. In other cases, since the control requirements are diversified and often changed, the cost of programming may be a significant fraction of the total cost of an application. Due to these reasons, the development of an effective programming method to integrate a system which includes various robots and other devices that cooperate in the same task is urgently required [2].

In programming by the well-known teaching-playback or teaching by showing, the programmer specifies a single execution for the robot: there are no loops, no conditionals, no data retrieval, nor computations. This method can be implemented without a general-purpose computer, and it is especially adequate for some applications, such as spot welding, painting, and simple materials handling. In other applications such as mechanical assembly and inspection, robot-level languages provide computer programming languages with commands to access sensors and to specify robot motions, enabling the data from external sensors, such as vision and force, to be used in modifying the robot's motion. Many recent methods in robot programming provide the power of robot-level languages without requiring deep programming knowledge, extending the basic philosophy of teaching to include decision-making based on sensing. Another method, known as task-level programming [3], [4], requires specifying goals for the positions of objects, rather than the motions of the robot needed to achieve those goals. A task-level specification is meant to be completely robot-independent; no positions or paths specified by the user depend on the robot geometry or kinematics. This method requires complete geometric models of the environment and of the robot, referred to as world-modeling systems. An object oriented approach has been held for modeling, simulation and control of multiple robot systems and intelligent manufacturing systems [5]-[9]. The main drawback of these methods relative to teaching is that they require the robot programmer to be an expert in computer programming and in the design of sensor-based motion strategies. Hence, this method is not accessible to the typical worker on the factory floor [10], [11].

Robot program development is often ignored in the design of robot control systems and, consequently, complex robot programs can be very difficult to debug. The development of robot programs has several characteristics which need special treatment. Because robot programs have complex side-effects and their execution time is usually long, it is not always feasible to re-initialize the program upon failure. So, robot programming systems should allow programs to be modified on-line and immediately restarted. Sensory information and real-time interactions are crucial and not usually repeatable. The ability to record the sensor outputs, together with program traces should be provided as a real-time debugging tool. Further, because complex geometry and motions are difficult to visualize, 3D graphic simulators can play an important role. Another difficulty comes from the fact that each robot has its own programming system, and it is often undesirable to alter or substitute it with something else. Besides cost considerations, this is because each robot programming language is tailored to the machine it has to control, and it would be simply impossible, for example to obtain a good performance from an articulated robot using a language designed for a Cartesian one. To attend the above requirements, a universal robot programming method with real-time automatic translation from a robot language to another one is required in integrated manufacturing systems.

The decision was then taken to develop a robot programming method for multiple robot systems that would provide the following characteristics. All the activities of the global system should be supervised by the control system, which is the method suitable to the integrated management that is necessary in manufacturing systems. So the integral controller with the strong computational power to do the complex task of the coordination system is needed. According to the parallelism among the subtasks in the multi-robot coordination system, advantage of the parallel architecture of the control system is taken to reach the good control capabilities [12]. To give a prior attention to the requirements about the part flow control, the control algorithm is designed based on the Petri net [13]. The Petri net can describe parallel flows, design and implement real-time robot control tasks [14]-[16], so that the process schedule is easily and effectively laid down, inspected and corrected. Each robot may be programmed in its own language in order to maintain best performance of each machine. Each step of the programming procedure can be verified by graphic simulation in order to improve the interaction between the operator and the robots and to make possible the off-line programming.

In this chapter, the method described in the previous work [17] is applied to program cooperative tasks by multiple robots and to concurrently control real robots. The aim of this chapter is to describe and implement a programming and execution system based on Petri nets that allows easy programming of a control system which includes multiple different robots and a variety of auxiliary devices. The problem how the control and coordination algorithms based on Petri nets are realized in an example of two robots carrying parts cooperatively is resolved.

2. Net models of robotic processes

Because discrete event robotic systems are characterized by the occurrence of events and changing conditions, the type of Petri net considered here is the condition-event net, in which conditions can be modeled by places whilst events can be modeled by transitions. A token is placed in a place to indicate that the condition corresponding to the place is holding. Because a condition-event net should be safe, which means that the number of tokens in each place does not exceed one, all of its arc weights are 1's and it has no self-loops. Condition-event nets can be easily extended and can efficiently model complex robotic processes. By the Petri nets extension, some capabilities which connect the net model to its external environment are employed. A gate arc connects a transition with a signal source, and an output arc connects a place with an external robot to send a command. The marking of a net changes, when a transition, which is enabled, eventually is fired. The place and gate variables involved in transition firing are shown in Figure 1.

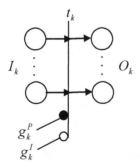

Figure 1. Place and gate variables involved in transition firing test

The firing condition of transition t_k can be written as

$$t_k = (\bigcap_{i \in I_k} p_i \cdot \bigcap_{j \in O_k} \overline{p_j} \cdot g_k^P \cdot \overline{g_k^I}) \tag{1}$$

where $\bigcap$ denotes the logical product operation, and

I_k : set of input places of transition t_k

O_k : set of output places of transition t_k

g_k^P : logical variable of permissive gate condition of transition t_k

g_k^I : logical variable of inhibitive gate condition of transition t_k

The marking change of input and output places of transition t_k can be written as follows:

$$\begin{aligned} For \quad & p_i \in I_k, \quad p_i = \overline{t_k} \cdot p_i \\ For \quad & p_j \in O_k, \quad p_j = t_k + p_j \end{aligned} \tag{2}$$

If a place has two or more input transitions or output transitions, these transitions may be in conflict for firing. When two or more transitions are enabled only one transition should be fired using some arbitration rule. Well-known properties of the condition-event net are as follows. From (1), if the directions of the input and output arcs of a place and the existence of token in the place are reversed, the firing conditions of all the transitions in the net are unchanged. If there is no conflict place in a net, then the net can be transformed into a net with no loop. If there is a loop with no conflict place in a net, the number of tokens in the loop is unchanged. In case that initially there is no token in a net marking, if there are parallel paths between two transitions, the maximum number of tokens in each path is equal to the minimum number of places in each path. So, by addition of a dummy path with a specified number of places, the number of tokens in each path can be controlled.

The dynamic behavior of the system represented by a net model is simulated using the enabling and firing rules. One cycle of the simulation comprises the following steps, which are executed when some gate condition is changed.

1. Calculate the logical variable of the transition associated with the new gate condition using (1).
2. If the transition is fired, calculate the logical variables of its input and output places using (2).
3. Then the marking is changed and a new command is sent to the corresponding robot.

In any initial marking, there must not be more than one token in a place. According to these rules, the number of tokens in a place never exceeds one; the net is essentially a safe graph. A robotic action is modeled by two transitions and one condition as shown in Figure 2. At the "Start" transition the command associated with the transition is sent to the corresponding robot or machine. At the "End" transition the status report is received. When a token is present in the "Action" place, the action is in progressive. The "Completed" place can be omitted, and then the "End" transition is fused with the "Start" transition of the next action. Activities can be assigned an amount of time units to monitor them in time for real performance evaluation. In case of "Waiting" place for a specified timing, after the interval the end signal is sent by the timer. In case of "Waiting" place for a specified signal, the logical function is tested and the resultant signal is sent as a gate condition in place of end signal by the sensing module.

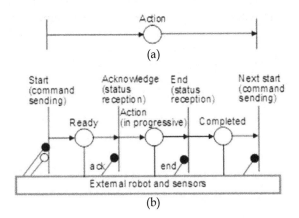

Figure 2. Net representation of robotic action: (a) macro representation, (b) detailed representation

Figure 3 shows the net representation of real-time control of a chucking operation with an external device. Each action place represents a subtask. The "Loading" place represents the macro model of the operation and indicates that, when a token is in the place, only one token exists in the path of places from "Grasp" to "Return".

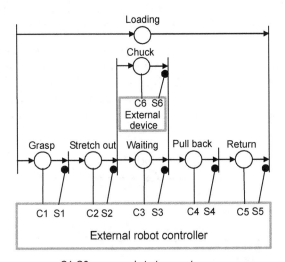

C1-C6: command start request
S1-S6: acknowledgment or end status

Figure 3. Net representation of chucking operation with a robot and an external device

Figure 4 shows the procedure of macro representation of a pick-and-place operation by a single robot. Figure 4 (a) shows the detailed net model, where if the first transition fires it never fires until the last transition fires. So, a dummy place "Robot" can be added as shown in Figure 4 (b) and a token in the place indicates that the state of the robot is "operating", because a real robot may load or unload only one part at a time. Thus, the place represents the macro state of the task without the detailed net as shown in Figure 4 (c).

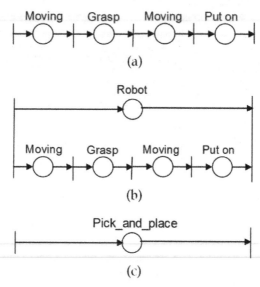

Figure 4. Macro representation of Pick_and_place operation by a robot: (a) detailed representation, (b) parallel representation with dummy place in direct path, (c) macro representation

A dummy place is used to control the maximum number of tokens in the paths parallel to the direct path. In case that the hardware of a robotic system is composed of one or more motion units or axes, the number of tokens in the dummy place indicates the maximum number of processing or parts processed by each motion unit. The overall action is decomposed into detailed actions of constituent motion units by the coordinator.

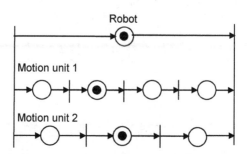

Figure 5. Net representation of robotic system composed of two motion units

A single task executed by a robot or machine is represented as a sequential net model. The places are connected via transitions, each having a Boolean condition or gate condition. This condition is tested while the transition is enabled, i.e., when the preceding place is active. If the condition is true, the succeeding place becomes active, and the preceding place becomes inactive. Places for motion and computational actions have a unique output transition. Decision actions introduce conflict into the net. The choice can either be made non-deterministically or may be controlled by some external signal or command from the upper level controller. Figure 6 shows a basic net structure with task selection. Figure 7 shows a net model with task selection and its corresponding VAL program [18], which is written using direct commands for the hardware robot controller and implies the lowest level detailed representation of the subtasks.

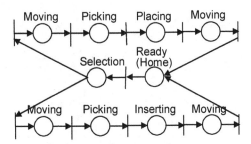

Figure 6. Basic structure of macro net model with task selection

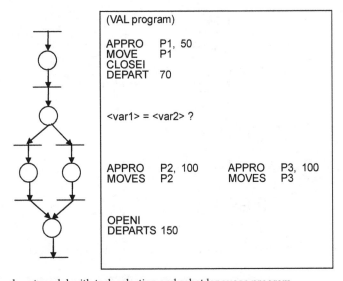

Figure 7. Example net model with task selection and robot language program

Cooperation which requires the sharing of information and resources between the processes, is usefully introduced into the composite net which is simply the union of such sequential nets. Figure 8 shows two equivalent net representations of concurrent tasks with synchronization. In Figure 9, a loop with no token implies that the net falls into a deadlock because of inconsistency with respect to transition firing.

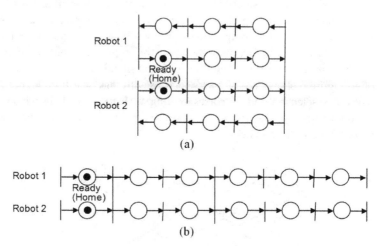

(a)

(b)

Figure 8. Net representations of basic structure of cooperation between two robots: (a) cyclic, (b) parallel

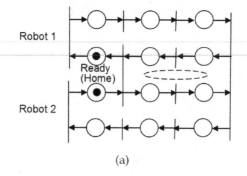

(a)

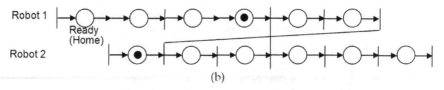

(b)

Figure 9. (a) Example net which has a loop with no token, (b) parallel representation which indicates a deadlock situation

3. Synchronization and coordination

A net representation of cooperative operation using synchronization mechanism with permissive and inhibitive gate arcs is shown in Figure 10, where the shared transition requires mutual synchronization between two tasks [19]. Synchronization of transitions is also employed for decomposition of a complex task into simple tasks cooperatively executed by two robots, as shown in Figure 11.

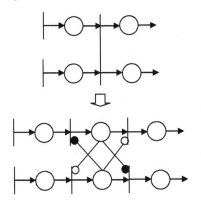

Figure 10. Distributed implementation of synchronization between two machines

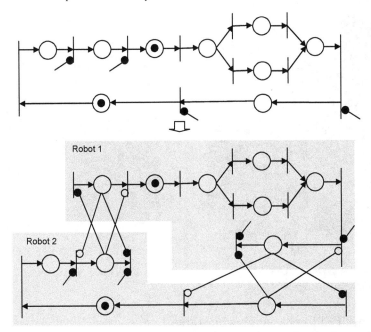

Figure 11. Decomposition of a complex net into two simple nets using synchronization mechanism of transitions

The decomposition procedure of a net is as follows. First, a new place is added in parallel to the input place of the decomposed transition. Then, transitions are added in the input and output of the two places. The input transition of the new place is a source transition. Each place exchanges internal gate signals to input and output transitions with the other place when a token is in the place. The gate arcs are implemented using asynchronous communication between different robots.

4. Net based multiple robot coordination

A coordination task of carrying parts from a machining station to depository is considered as an example application using multiple robots. An arm robot picks up a part from the station and loads it into a mobile robot by which the part is sent to the storehouse. The arm robot is equipped with a visual sensor via which it can recognize the parts as well as their positions and also equipped with a force sensor which is necessary for grasping and loading the parts. On the mobile robot, a radio transceiver is used for its communication sending back feedback information from the sensors and receiving the control information from the main controller. The visual sensor is used for landmark recognition in the environment and infra-red sensors are used for obstacle avoidance. Figure 12 shows the arm robot and the mobile robot.

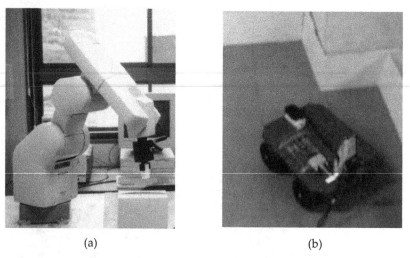

(a)   (b)

Figure 12. View of experimental robot systems: (a) arm robot, (b) autonomous mobile robot with radio transceiver and visual sensor

4.1. Task specification based on work flow

Based on robot task level programming of the specified part flow, the coordination task of carrying parts from a machining station to depository is represented as a work flow graph for a part sequentially processed by the arm robot and the mobile robot · In the work flow graph, each node represents a place where any processing is performed on the part, while an arc represent physical processing such as picking, loading, transfer or machining. The work flow comprises the following three arcs as shown in Figure 13.

1.   picking from the station pallet by the arm robot
2.   loading into the mobile robot by the arm robot
3.   transfer from the station to the depository by the mobile robot

Station $\xrightarrow{\text{Picking}}$ Arm robot $\xrightarrow{\text{Loading}}$ Mobile robot $\xrightarrow{\text{Transfer}}$ Depository

Figure 13. Task specification based on work flow processed on parts

The picking, loading, or transfer is specified using a local path in the neighborhood of the start and end place and a global path from the two places. Mutual exclusive resources or shared workspace such as buffers are also considered to avoid robot collision. The work flow diagram is transformed into a conceptual net model considering machines in charge of each processing. Figure 14 illustrates the net model of the coordination task between the two robots. At this point, associated processing such as object identification, alarm processing, exception handling is added. Then each processing is translated into detailed operations or actions. At each step of detailed specification, places of the net are substituted by a subnet in a manner which maintains the structural property such as liveness and safeness. Hierarchical decomposition assures detailed net models free from deadlock.

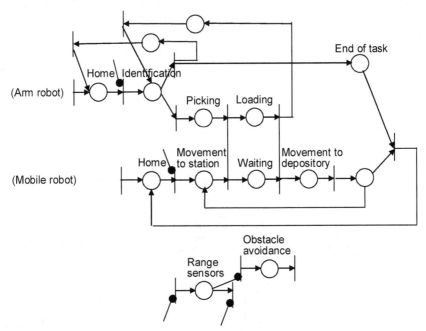

Figure 14. Net model of carrying task by two robots

The conceptual coordination task is specified as follows. First, after the reception of a start command, in "Identification" place, the arm robot judges whether or not there are still parts in the station using the visual sensor. If not, the arm robot informs the mobile robot that the task has been finished with "End of task" place and returns back to its home position. On the contrary, the arm robot starts to get the position of a part and grasp it. The mobile robot moves to the station, and the arm robot, after the completion of the "Grasp" subtask and the "Movement to station" subtask, starts "Loading" subtask while the mobile robot waits at the specified position. After the completion of loading, the mobile robot moves to the depository, and the arm robot executes the "Identification" subtask repeatedly. If the signal of "End of task" is on, the mobile robot returns back to its home position, and if not it moves to the station. From the "Movement to station" and "Movement to depository" places, the gate signal is sent to repeatedly execute the "Obstacle avoidance" subtask using infrared range sensors. In the coordination task, synchronization is represented as a shared transition which is implemented using a sequence of asynchronous communications as shown in Figure 10.

4.2. Subtask control of arm robots

For net based control of the arm robot, unit actions or motions should be defined in a task coordinate system. The trajectories can be free (point to point), straight or circular. The speed of forward movement of a trajectory is specified in the main coordinate of the task coordinate system. The movements in the other coordinates are compensated based on errors. At the end of a trajectory, it can be stopped or continued while turning the direction. When a trajectory is circular, the end-effector can have either of two orientations, that is, to the center of the circle or fixed. In the case of control of the end-effector, there are commands to represent the coordinate frames, open the hand, close the hand, and grasp. The grasp command assumes that the hand has a proximity sensor to autonomously grasp a workpiece in an appropriate direction. Synchronous actions by the arm and the wrist or sequences of unit actions by the arm, the wrist and the fingers are also specified using commands. The reference positions for arm movement are set by a separated teaching method, as well as desired positions of parts known at the programming time. The other positions relative to these positions are computed on-line. In this way, using these commands the final point and the trajectory of the motion can be specified in the task coordinate system. Figure 15 shows the block diagram of the trajectory tracking control in the task coordinate system.

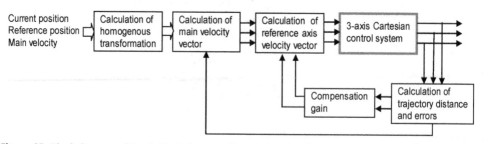

Figure 15. Block diagram of 3-axis Cartesian coordinate arm control system

The command system can be extended to execute actions specified based on information from the external sensors such as visual sensors, proximity sensors or slippage sensors.

Figure 14 shows the hardware structure of the microcontroller-based control system. The visual sensor detects the coordinates of the center of an object and the orientation of an edge of the object. The proximity sensors, which are composed of several LED arrays attached to the fingers can detect the distance and orientation of the object with respect to the planes of the fingers. For the grip command, the grip action raises the grip force till the signal from the slippage sensor becomes zero. When the hand is moving down vertically, if the signal from the slippage sensor rises inversely, then the hand is opened.

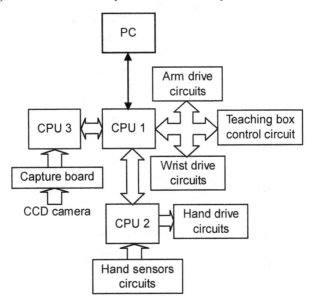

Figure 16. Block diagram of multi-axis arm control system

When programming a specific task, the task is broken down into subtasks through task planning. These subtasks are composed of the position data and the programs that are edited using the robot motion simulator. Each subtask is represented as a place. A place can also represent the internal state of the robot, which is operating or idle, and the state of external devices. The relations of these places are explicitly represented by interconnections of transitions, arcs and gates that are edited with the robot task program editor and simulator. For places that represent subtasks, the following parameters are necessary: 1) the code of the controller such as the vehicle, arm, hand or sensor etc., that executes the subtask, 2) the file name where the subtask such as MOVE, GRASP, RELEASE, or HOLD, etc., is explicitly written with some programming language, and 3) the file name of a set of position data that will be used to execute the subtask. The procedures of editing and simulating of the net model are done interactively until certain specifications are satisfied. At this point, it is expected that problems such as deadlock, conflict resolution, concurrency, synchronization, etc., have been well studied and analyzed. If some error is found, that is if the net model does not satisfy the specification, it can be easily amended by reediting the net model and simulating again.

4.3. Subtask control of mobile robots

The decomposition of "Movement to station" place and the associated control structure are illustrated in Figure 17. In movement control of the mobile robot using state feedback based on pose sensors, the robot's planning task is reduced to setting some intermediate positions (subgoals), with respective control modes, lying on the requested path. The global path planner in the trajectory controller determines a sequence of subgoals to reach the goal. Given a set of subgoal locations, the target tracking controller plans a detailed path to the closest subgoal position only and executes this plan. In the target tracking control, the distance between the robot and the specified target position and the angle between the forward direction and the target is computed based on the current location detected by the internal pose sensors (accelerators and gyros) and the current target. And then, the reference tangent and angular velocities of the mobile robot is determined to meet the target tracking using a state feedback algorithm, and the reference wheel velocities are computed based on inverse kinematics. The new velocity setpoints are sent to the respective wheel velocity controller, which executes proportional plus integral control of its wheel velocity using the rotary encoder.

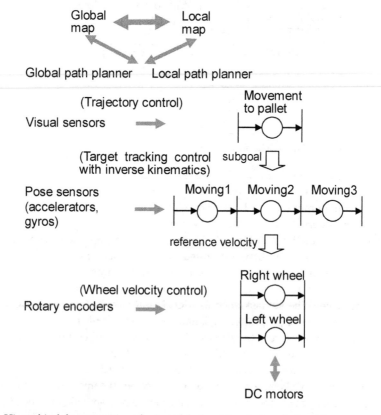

Figure 17. Hierarchical decomposition of net model of mobile robot control system

In case of detection of a blockage on the intended path, the trajectory controller receives a failure notification from the visual sensor, then modifies the subgoals and the short term local knowledge of the robot's surroundings and triggers the target tracking in view of this change to the local environment knowledge. The trajectory controller has the dynamic map with global and local representation that becomes more accurate as the robot moves. Upon reaching this subgoal location, its local map will change based on the perceptual information using the PSD data extracted during motion. Then the target tracking controller triggers the local path planner to generate a path from the new location to the next subgoal location. When the lowest-level wheel velocity control fails to make progress, the target tracking controller attempts to find a way past the obstacle by turning the robot in position and trying again. The trajectory controller decides when and if new information integrated into the local map can be copied into the global map.

The current subgoal and current location are shared by the trajectory controller and the target tracking controller. In the coordinator program, a place is assigned to each shared variable to be protected from concurrent access. Mutual exclusive access to a shared variable is represented by a place, which is identical to the P and V operations on the semaphore, as shown in Figure 18.

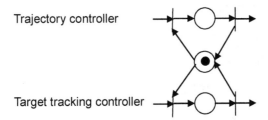

Figure 18. Net representation of mutual exclusive access

If a time-out in real-time control, communication, or sensing data acquisition, is brought about, an alarm signal is sent to the upper controller. When an alarm is processed, a signal is sent to stop any active controller. These signals are implemented by places, as shown in Figure 19. If the final goal is reached, the target tracking controller sends an "End" signal to the trajectory controller, which then sends end signals to the rest of the system.

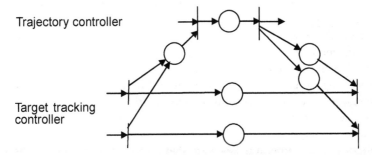

Figure 19. Net representation of signaling between controllers

5. Implementation of net based control system

Based on net models, a programming and execution system is implemented. A whole task is edited with a net based robot task program editor and simulator. In parallel, a robot motion simulator is used to edit the subtask programs. Using these systems, the net program file, the sequence program file, and the position data file are created and used by the multi-robot controller to execute the coordination task. A schematic of the functions of the robot programming system is illustrated in Figure 20. The connections of the robots and devices with PC are shown in Figure 21.

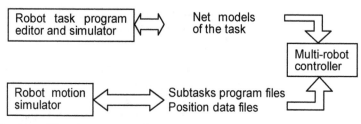

Figure 20. Structure of the robot programming system

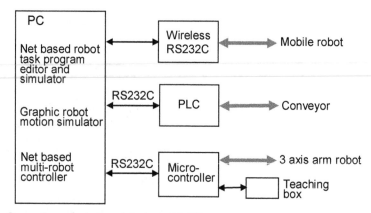

Figure 21. Connections of robots and devices with PC

The geometric data of the robot and workspace are specified using the length of the links of the robot, the geometric parameters of workpiece as well as input and deletion positions, and the form of the end-effector. The simulator constructs the three dimensional model of the robot and the workspace. The numerical data of the joint angles, absolute position and orientation of the robot are displayed on the terminal. The operator inputs the sequence of unit motion commands and position data. Then, the motion data are computed with consideration to the geometric parameters of the robots and workpieces. The net model file, the subtask program files and position data files are simulated with the robot task program editor and simulator and robot motion simulator respectively to test the programs and data that will be used to control the robots. The robot behavior is displayed graphically on a terminal step by step. Then the completed net model is transformed into the tabular form, and these files are loaded into the multi-robot controller that executes the programs. Example views of 3D graphic simulation of the arm robot and the mobile robot are shown in Figure 22. The flow chart of the net based programming method of multi-robot tasks using the separated teaching method is shown in Figure 23.

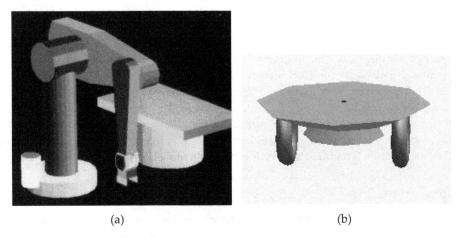

(a)   (b)

Figure 22. View of 3D graphic simulation of (a) arm robot and (b) mobile robot

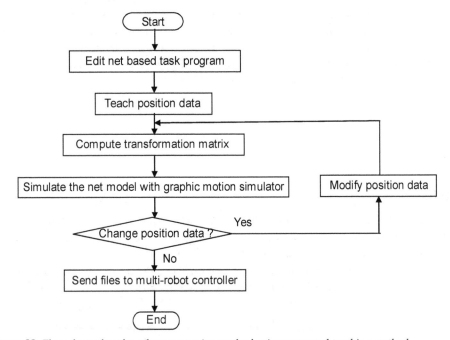

Figure 23. Flow chart of net based programming method using separated teaching method

The multi-robot controller accomplishes the specified task by executing the net model constructed above. Unit actions in a net model used for lowest level controllers are defined in a specified task space, where the action is executed. In the control software the position and orientation in the task space is transformed to the robot coordinate system using the homogeneous transformation matrix. The controller coordinates and supervises the individual controllers based on information explicitly represented by places, place parameters, transitions, arcs, and gates. That is, when a token enters a place that represents a subtask, immediately the controller defined by the control code is informed to execute the subtask with a specified data. Because of the proper nature of the Petri net, the designer can easily create a multi-robot task program which is free of logical errors. The method acts as a programming method on the coordination level and on the organization level [20]. That is, the Petri net is applied as a tool to the operator who plans the multi-robot task, and by executing the net model the individual hardware controllers are regulated and supervised. If, before moving the real robot, the outputs of the robot controller are linked with the graphic robot motion simulator, the whole task programmed can be tested off-line. When the task specification is required to be changed, the net model can be modified on-line.

6. Conclusions

It was confirmed that the multi-robot controller developed based on tasks programmed in the net form controls the equipment according to the programmed net model. The method provides concurrent movement of all robots and machines in the system, and it provides synchronization commands to allow coordination of their movements to accomplish user defined tasks. The commands used by this system are not based on any specific existing robot language. So, the method can be used in any real robot by translating it to the appropriate robot language, and it acts as a programming tool on the coordination level and on the organization level in multiple robot systems.

Author details

Gen'ichi Yasuda
Nagasaki Institute of Applied Science, Japan

7. References

[1] Martinez, J., Muro, P. & Silva, M. (1987). Modeling, Validation and Software Implementation of Production Systems Using High Level Petri Nets, *Proceedings of IEEE International Conference on Robotics and Automation*, pp. 1180-1185

[2] Sakane, S. (1993). Distributed Sensing System with 3D model-based agents, *Proceedings of IEEE/RSJ International Conference on Intelligent Robots and Systems*, pp. 1157-1163

[3] Bonner, J. & Shin, K. G. (1982). A Comparative Study of Robot Languages. *Computer Magazine*, IEEE, Vol. 14, No. 12, pp. 82-96

[4] Lozano-Perez, T. (1983). Robot Programming. *Proceedings of the IEEE*, Vol. 71, No. 7, pp. 821-841

[5] Yasuda, G. (1996). An Object-oriented Network Environment for Computer Vision Based Multirobot System Architectures, *Proceedings of 20th International Conference on Computers & Industrial Engineering*, pp. 1199-1202

[6] Yasuda, G. & Tachibana, K. (1996). An Integrated Object-oriented Expert System for Welding Procedure Selection and Process Control, *CRITICAL TECHNOLOGY: Proceedings of the Third World Congress on Expert Systems*, pp. 186-193

[7] Yasuda, G. (1997). Intelligent Manufacturing and Engineering, In: Jay Liebowitz Ed. *The Handbook of Applied Expert Systems*, CRC Press, Chapter 22, pp. 22.1-22.14

[8] Bussmann, S. (1998). Agent-Oriented Programming of Manufacturing Control Tasks, *Proceedings of the 3rd International Conference on Multi-Agent Systems*, pp. 57 - 63

[9] Yasuda, G. (1999). A Multiagent Architecture for Sensor-Based Control of Intelligent Autonomous Mobile Robots, *ACTA IMEKO 1999 (Proceedings of the 15th World Congress of the International Measurement Confederation (IMEKO))*, Vol. X (TC-17), pp. 145-152

[10] Cassinis, R. (1983). Hierarchical Control of Integrated Manufacturing Systems, *Proceedings of the 13th International Symposium on Industrial Robots and Robots 7*, pp. 12-9 - 12-20

[11] Wood, B. O. & Fugelso, M. A. (1983). MCL, The Manufacturing Control Language, *Proceedings of the 13th International Symposium on Industrial Robots and Robots 7*, pp. 12-84 - 12-96

[12] Yasuda, G., Takai, H. & Tachibana, K. (1994). Performance Evaluation of a Multimicrocomputer-Based Software Servo System for Real-Time Distributed Robot Control, *AUTOMATIC CONTROL 1994 (Proceedings of the 12th Triennial World Congress of IFAC)*, Pergamon, Vol. 2, pp. 673-678

[13] Murata, T. (1989). Petri Nets: Properties, Analysis and Applications. *Proceedings of the IEEE*, Vol. 77, No. 4, pp. 541-580

[14] Simon, D., Espiau, B., Kapellos, K. & Pissard-Gibolette, R. (1997). Orccad: Software Engineering for Real-Time Robotics. A Technical Insight. *Robotica*, Vol. 15, pp. 111-115

[15] Caloini, A., Magnani, G. & Pesse, M. (1998). A Technique for Designing Robotic Control Systems Based on Petri Nets. *IEEE Transactions on Control Systems Technology*, Vol. 6, No. 1, pp. 72-87

[16] Oliveira, P., Pascoal, A., Silva, V. & Silvestre, C. (1998). Mission Control of the Autonomous Underwater Vehicle: System Design, Implementation and Sea Trials. *International Journal of Systems Science*, Vol. 29, No. 4, pp. 1065-1080

[17] Yasuda, G. (2010). Design and Implementation of Hierarchical and Distributed Control for Robotic Manufacturing Systems using Petri Nets. In: Pawel Pawlewski Ed. *Petri Nets: Applications*, InTech Education and Publishing, Chapter 19, pp. 379-392

[18] Unimation Inc. (1979). *User Guide to VAL – A Robot Programming and Control System Version II*

[19] Yasuda, G. & Tachibana, K. (1991). A Parallel Processing Control Approach to the Design of Autonomous Robotic Manufacturing Systems, *Proceedings of the XIth International Conference on Production Research*, pp. 445-449

[20] Graham, J. H. & Saridis, G. N. (1982). Linguistic Decision Structures for Hierarchical Systems. *IEEE Transaction on Systems, Man, and Cybernetics*, Vo. 12, No. 3, pp. 325-329

Chapter 6

Workflow Modelling Based on Synchrony

Chongyi Yuan

Additional information is available at the end of the chapter

1. Introduction

Prof. Carl Adam Petri wrote: "In order to apply net theory with success, a user of net theory can just rely on the fact that every net which he can specify explicitly (draw on paper) can be connected by a short (≤ 4) chain of net morphisms to the physical real word; your net is, in a very precise sense, physically implementable." (Status Report On Net Theory, 1989, a forward for my book Petri Nets in Chinese[1]).

Why a net is physically implementable? The reason is, every concept in net theory is carefully chosen based on nature laws, and well defined in terms of precise mathematics and logic. For example, the concept of global time does not belong to net theory. Time measured with real numbers exists only in theories like theoretical physics. Logical time does not exist in the real world. For net theory, time is just "clock reading", a measurement of physical changes. Global time is not realistic for systems in which a shared clock is not available.

On the other hand however, it is easy to find in the literature, that many an author introduces new concepts into his or her Petri net with implementation totally forgotten. "Timed Petri Net" is just one of such examples.

As one of the chapters in this book on Petri nets, implementable concepts and only implementable concepts will be introduced.

We start with the definition of a directed net, which is the most fundamental concept in net theory. The next two sections serve to keep this chapter self-reliant.

This chapter is organized as below:

Sections 2 and 3 recall basic definitions of Petri Nets: The concept of directed net deserves a separate section since it is the foundation of the whole net theory. Section 3 is mainly about Place/Transition-systems, based on which workflow models are to be constructed.

Section 4 is an introduction of synchrony, a branch in net theory on transition synchronization that provides theoretical support to workflow modelling.

Section 5 talks about business processes, the subject of workflow research. A full understanding of the concept of business processes makes a good start.

Section 6 proposes the concepts of synchronizers and workflow logic. A synchronizer connects transitions in two consecutive steps in a business process, and workflow logic is obtained when all transitions in a business process are so connected. Properties and analysis methods of workflow logic are defined and proposed. A transition in workflow logic represents a business task while a synchronizer represents a task in workflow management. Workflow logic specifies all possible routes a business case may take when it is processed. An individual business case corresponds to a unique route among all routes given by workflow logic. This route is considered as the semantics of that case. Section 7 defines the concept of case semantics.

Section 8 is about business process management, or automatic management. The dual net of workflow logic is exactly the logic of management, based on which workflow engine conducts the process of individual cases.

Section 9 concludes this chapter with acknowledgement, and the last section is a list of references.

This chapter is about Petri nets and workflow modelling.

There are many ways in the literature to define nets and net systems. For example, the concept of flow relation, namely F, has been made implicit by many researchers. It is often combined with weight function W. Without the flow relation, the concept of directed nets would disappear; and without the concept of directed nets, the whole theoretical part of Petri nets would be without a foundation. Thus, this chapter starts from the definition of directed nets given by C. A. Petri himself.

Petri net systems have been considered as one of the adequate and promising candidates for workflow modelling. The concept of WF-nets proposed by Prof. Aalst from Holland has become popular in the last 10 to 20 years. A team in the Software Development Company of Peking University tried to use WF-nets as a formal model to develop software for a government organization at a time around the year 2000. The WF-nets didn't work, and they didn't know why. The author joint them, and we found problems of WF-nets, leading to failure. The concept of WF-nets was proposed without theoretical foundation. These problems were discussed in our paper titled "A Three Layer Model for Business process" [7]. The concepts of synchronizers, workflow logic and case semantics etc were defined in this paper for the first time. After so many years since then, people interested in workflow modelling remain sticking to WF-nets. Many people do not even know our work, it seems. The reason is, the author guess, General Net Theory (theoretical part of Petri nets) is not popular yet. This chapter shows how important "Synchrony" is to a successful application of Petri nets in the area of workflow modelling.

2. Directed net

Definition 1

A triple N=(S,T;F) is a directed net if $S \cup T \neq \emptyset \wedge S \cap T = \emptyset \wedge F \subseteq (S \times T \cup T \times S) \wedge dom(F) \cup cod(F) = S \cup T$ Where dom(F)={x | $\exists$y: (x,y) $\in$ F} and cod (F)={y | $\exists$x: (x,y) $\in$ F}.◆

A directed net used to be called "Petri net". We keep the term "Petri net" to mean "net theory", a term Carl Adam Petri used in *Status Report*. "Net" is often used to mean "directed net" if it causes no ambiguity.

$S \cup T \neq \emptyset \wedge S \cap T = \emptyset$ demands that a net consists of at least one element, and its elements are clearly classified.

$F \subseteq S \times T \cup T \times S$ indicates that direct dependence does not exist between elements in the same class. $dom(F) \cup cod(F) = S \cup T$ excludes isolated elements from a net.

A directed net has a graphical presentation as shown in Figure 1, in which elements in S and T appear as circles and boxes respectively while elements in F appear as arrows (arcs). The arrow from x to y represents (x,y) in F.

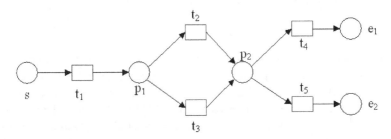

Figure 1. A Directed Net

Petri net (net theory) consists of Special Net Theory and General Net Theory. Special Net Theory focuses on system modelling and General Net Theory focuses on theories supporting system modelling. The concept of directed nets is their common foundation.

Definition 2

Let N=(S,T;F) be a directed net and X=S$\cup$T, For x in X, $\cdot$x={y|(y,x)$\in$ F} is the pre-set of x, x$\cdot$={y|(x,y)$\in$ F} is the post-set of x. For t$\in$ T, $\cdot$t$\cup$t$\cdot$ is the extension of t.◆

Special Net Theory (SNT for short) and General Net Theory (GNT for short) are derived from Directed Net based on pre-sets and post-sets of elements as described below.

The concept of extensions of transitions leads to the principle of local determinism.

The S-complementation operation on a net leads to the removal of contact. The T-complementation operation on a net leads to the removal of differences between forward and backward flow of tokens (SNT).

The S-completion operation on a net leads to Synchrony while the T-completion operation on a net leads to Enlogy(GNT).

A directed net implies a unique undirected net that leads to Net Topology (GNT).

A special class of directed nets is the occurrence nets that lead to Concurrency (GNT).

Synchrony will be briefly introduced in Section 3, since it provides guidance to workflow modelling. It is impossible in this chapter to go any further on SNT and GNT. The point is, successful applications of Petri nets rely on both SNT and GNT, not only SNT.

3. Net system

Definition 3

A 6-tuple $\Sigma = (S,T;F,K,W,M_0)$ is a net system if $(S,T;F)$ is a directed net and:

$K: S \rightarrow \{1,2,\cdots\} \cup \{\infty\} \wedge W: F \rightarrow \{1,2,\cdots\} \wedge M_0: \rightarrow \{0,1,2,\cdots\}$ such that $\forall s \in S: M_0(s) \le K(s)$, where $K,W,M0$ are respectively the capacity function, the weight function and the initial marking. ◆

A mapping $M : \rightarrow \{0,1,2,\cdots\}$ is a marking if it satisfies

$$\forall s \in S: M(s) \le K(s).$$

Conventionally, elements in S are called places and elements in T are transitions. A place is capable to hold certain kind of resources, with an allowance given by K. Infinite capacity does not mean infinite space for resources. It is just an indication that the capacity of that place is not a factor for a transition to become enabled (see definition below). A transition resembles a change of resource quantities (consumed or produced) and a change in kind. The precise change is given by transition rules. In the rest of this chapter, Σ is always assumed finite, i.e. Σ has a finite number of places and transitions.

Definition 4

1. Transition t is enabled by marking M if $\forall s \in \, ^{\cdot}t: W(s,t) \le M(s) \wedge \forall s \in t^{\cdot}: M(s)+W(t,s) \le K(s)$. This fact is denoted by M[t>.
2. Transition t may fire, if M[t>, to yield a successor marking M′ given by
   $M'(s)= M(s) - W(s,t)$ for s in $\,^{\cdot}t - t^{\cdot}$, $M'(s) = M(s)+W(t,s)$ for s in $t^{\cdot} - \,^{\cdot}t$, and $M'(s) = M(s)+W(t,s)-W(s,t)$ for s in $\,^{\cdot}t \cap t^{\cdot}$, and $M'(s) = M(s)$ otherwise. This fact is denoted by M[t>M′.◆

It is easy to prove that the successor M′ is indeed a marking.

A marking represents a resource distribution on S. A transition firing causes the flow of resources along arcs in F, and thus F is called the flow relation of Σ.

It is easy to see that M[t> is determined by $\,^{\cdot}t \cup t^{\cdot}$, the extension of t, and the change from M to M′ is confined to $\,^{\cdot}t \cup t^{\cdot}$. This is the principle of local determinism. A marking is a global state, but the transition rules refer to only the extension of a single transition, not the complete marking. Many system models take global states as a means of system control. But this is not always implementable, since a global state is not always instantly known. It takes time to know the current global state, and this delay may be significant to an effective real time control.

Figure 2 illustrates how to represent a net system graphically. The black dot inside place s is a token, denoting $M_0(s) = 1$. Empty places have no token (resource). Conventionally, $M(s)=0$, $W(x,y) =1$ and $K(s) = \infty$ are shown by default.

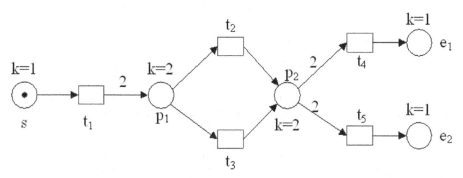

Figure 2. A Net System

Definition 5

Let $\Sigma =(S,T;F,K,W,M0)$ be a net system, M is a marking and t1, t2 are transitions.

1. If $M[t_1>M'\wedge M'[t_2>\wedge {}^{\neg}M[t_2>$, then t_1 and t_2 are in sequential relation at M, denoted by $M[t_1,t_2>$.
2. If $M[t_1>\wedge M[t_2>$, and $\forall s \in {}^{\cdot}t_1 \cap {}^{\cdot}t_2: M(s) \geq W(s,t_1) + W(s,t_2)$ and $\forall s \in t_1{}^{\cdot} \cap t_2{}^{\cdot}: M(s) + W(t_1,s)$ $+ W(t_2,s)\leq K(s)$,then t_1 and t_2 are in concurrent relation at M, denoted by $M[\{t_1,t_2\}>$.
3. If $M[t_1>\wedge M[t_2>\wedge \neg M[\{t_1, t_2\}>$, then t_1,t_2 are in conflict at M, denoted by $cf(t_1,t_2,M)$.
4. If there is a transition t and a place b such that $\forall s \in {}^{\cdot}t_1: M(s)\geq W(s,t)\wedge M(b) + W(t,b)>K(b)$, then t leads to a contact in b at M, denoted by $ct(t,b,M)$. ◆

Two concurrently enabled transitions can fire either concurrently or one after another.

Theorem 1

The marking reached by concurrently fired transitions can also be reached by the transitions fired one after another.◆

This theorem guarantees that the next definition includes markings reached by concurrent transition firings.

Definition 6

The set of markings reachable from M_0 by consecutive transition firings is usually denoted by $[M_0>$.◆

The set [M$_0$> may be infinite for a finite system. The algorithm for computing [M$_0$> produces a finite tree, denoted by T(Σ), and this tree can be re-structured to become a graph, denoted by G(Σ). G(Σ) will be used for the computing of synchronous distances later on. All these concepts and algorithms are in the category of techniques, we will go no further here.

So far we have not said a word about how to relate a net to the real world. This reflects an important aspect of Petri net, that is, a net is unexplained. This nature of nets has its good point and bad point. The good point is: the same net or net system may be explained in different application areas to solve different problems; the bad point is: unexplained transition firings lead to general analysis methods that are bound to be of low efficiency, since they cannot make use of application specific properties.

A net is "physically implementable" when every element in S $\cup$ T has an explanation for a fixed application problem, and every transition firing describes real changes in that application area. A net describes how real changes relate with each other. This chapter aims to show how to build, with the guidance of GNT, net systems for workflow modelling and how to find efficient analysis methods.

Some transitions are defined as "instant transitions" in Timed Petri Nets, for they fire instantly when they become enabled. What would happen when two instant transitions are in conflict? Conflict resolution takes time since it needs to be detected and it requires a decision from the system environment. Generally speaking, an enabled transition may be disabled (by others) without firing.

4. Synchrony

Careful observation reveals that sequential relation, concurrent relation and conflict relation are not relations between two transitions, but rather, they are relations between transition firings, i.e. two transitions may fall into one relation at a marking and fall into a different relation at another marking. Thus, a more precise way to denote these relations is: sq(M[t1>, M[t2>), cn(M[t1>, M[t2>), and cf(M[t1>, M[t2>) respectively. Note that sq(M[t1>, M[t2>) is asymmetry.

Synchrony is about how transitions themselves are synchronized. It describes laws exhibited in the course of transition firings. For example, the sunrise and the sunset are alternating "transitions" while a hand-clapping "transition" consists of simultaneous actions of the two hands. One may observe one more sunrise or one more sunset, depending on the times the observation starts and ends, but one always counts the same number of actions of the two hands for hand clapping. The laws exhibited by alternating transitions and simultaneous transitions are given by "the synchronous distance is 1" and "the synchronous distance is 0" respectively.

The concept of synchronous distance was originally defined in terms of events in a C/E-system, which is a model describing changes in the nature, like the changes of 4 seasons. A C/E-system has no initial marking. Instead, it has a current marking. This chapter is about artificial systems. We have to redefine this concept of synchronous distance to serve our need.

4.1. Synchronous distance in a P/T-system

A net system as defined by Definition 3 and 4 is conventionally called a Place/Transition-system, P/T-system for short.

Definition 7

Let Σ = (S,T;F,K,W,M_0) be a P/T-system. A sequence of transitions δ= $t_1t_2\cdots t_n$ is called a transition sequence if they can fire one after another in the given order, starting from the initial marking. The length of δ is n.

An infinite sequence of transitions is a transition sequence if any of its finite prefix is a transition sequence. ◆

In what follows ρ denotes the set of all transition sequences of Σ.

Definition 8

Let Σ=(S,T;F,K,W,M_0) be a P/T-system and T_1, T_2 be subsets of T, $T_1\neq \emptyset$, $T_2\neq \emptyset$. Let δ be a finite transition sequence, i.e. $\delta \in \rho$. Let $\#(\delta, T_1)$, $\#(\delta, T_2)$ denote the numbers of firings of transitions in T_1,T_2 respectively, and $\#(\delta, T_1,T_2)$ = $\#(\delta, T_1)$ - $\#(\delta, T_2)$. The synchronous distance between T_1 and T_2, denoted by $\sigma(T_1,T_2)$, is defined by

$\sigma(T_1,T_2)$ = max$\{\#(\delta, T_1,T_2)\ |\ \delta\in \rho\}$ - min$\{\#(\delta, T_1,T_2)\ |\ \delta\in \rho\ \}$if exists, other wise $\sigma(T_1,T_2)$ = ∞. ◆

Figure 3 (a) is P/T-system $\Sigma 1$ and its set of transition sequences is {a, ab, b, ba}. We have, for T_1 = {a} and T2 ={b}, max$\{\#(\delta, T_1,T_2)\ |\ \delta\in \rho\}$ = 1 and min$\{\#(\delta, T_1,T_2)\ |\ \delta\in \rho\ \}$ = -1, so $\sigma(T_1,T_2)$ = 2.

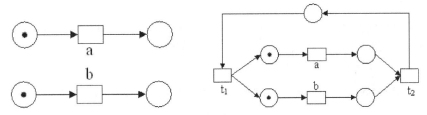

(a) Σ_1, (b) Σ_2

Figure 3. $\sigma(a,b)$ =2

Note that we write $\sigma(a,b)$ =2 instead of $\sigma(T_1,T_2)$ =2 in figure 3 by convention when both T_1,T_2 are singletons.

The set of transition sequences of Σ_2 is infinite and it contains infinite sequences. It is easy to check that any repeatable portion in a finite or infinite transition sequence contains the same number of firings of transition b and transition a. This is why σ(a,b) is finite. The consecutive firings of transition a count at most to 2, so do the consecutive firings of transition b. This is the physical meaning of σ(a,b) =2 for Σ_2.

The distance (i.e. synchronous distance from now on) between left hand action and right hand action is 0, since it is impossible to see only an action of either hand in the course of hand clapping.

Figure 4 (a) shows another situation of σ(a,b) =2, where transitions a and b are in conflict at the initial marking. Figure 4 (b) is still another case of σ(a,b) =2.

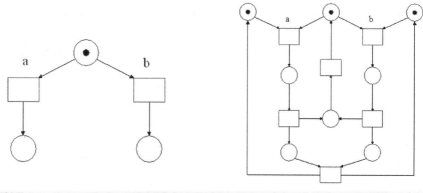

(a) Σ_3 (b) Σ_4

Figure 4. σ(a,b) =2: a and b in conflict

Theorem 2

The synchronous distance defined by Definition 8 satisfies distance axioms:

$\sigma(T_1,T_2) = 0$ if and only if $T_1 = T_2$; $\sigma(T_1,T_2) \geq 0$; $\sigma(T_1,T_2) = \sigma(T_2,T_1)$; $\sigma(T_1,T_2) + \sigma(T_2,T_3) \geq \sigma(T_1,T_3)$.
◆

This theorem explains why the concept is called distance. It is assumed that $T_1 \cap T_2 = \emptyset$ when $\sigma(T_1,T_2) > 0$, since $\sigma(T_1,T_2) = \sigma(T_1-T_2, T_2 - T_1)$ by definition.

Theorem 3

$\sigma(T_1,T_2) < \infty$ if and on ly if for any repeatable portion δ of any sequence in ρ, $\#(\delta, T_1,T_2) = 0$. ◆

It is easy to prove the above two theorems, so omitted here.

4.2. Transition synchronization and place synchronization

People would think, based on experiences in daily life, that synchronization is something participated by different parties like hand clapping, or some events occurring at the same time like a live casting on TV with an on-going game. Such synchronization is characterized by distance 0, since one cannot see one hand clapping or see the TV show without the game.

We have said that hand clapping is a single transition consisting of actions of two hands; A live show and the on-going game would appear in a net as one transition as well since if they were separated as different transitions in parallel, ordered firings would produce the same effect , but this cannot be true. Synchronization characterized by distance 0 is "transition synchronization". Synchronization with $\sigma(T_1,T_2) > 0$ is "place synchronization" since such synchronization is achieved via places and it can be observed by taking an added place as an observation window.

System Σ_5 in Figure 5 (a) is the same system as shown in Figure 3 (b) with an added place p denoted by a dotted circle and connected to transitions by dotted arrows. This added place does not belong to Σ_5, it is to be used for observations.

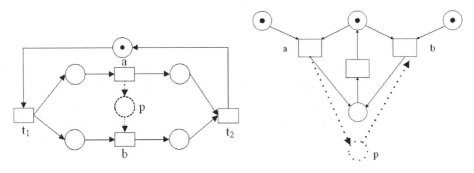

(a) Σ_5 (b) Σ_6

Figure 5. Added Place as Observation Window

An observer records what he finds through the window by putting a token into p when transition a fires and removing a token from p when transition b fires. It is assumed that place p has enough tokens, say n tokens, to start with, so the recording would not be interrupted. The maximum number of tokens in p is n+1 while the minimum is n-1. So the difference is 2 between transition b and transition a. The same observation applies to Σ_6 to get the same distance.

The observation window p for disjoint transition sets T_1 and T_2 is an added place whose input arcs are from T_1 and output arcs are pointing to T_2. Place p gets a token whenever a transition in T_1 fires and loses a token whenever a transition in T2 fires. Place p has enough tokens to start with to ensure a smooth observation. In case the number of tokens in p is not bounded, the distance between T_1 and T_2 is ∞. Otherwise, the difference between the maximum and the minimum is the distance.

It is easy to find that $\sigma(a,b) = \infty$ for the P/T-system in Figure 6 (a), since the repeatable sequence t_1abat_2 contains two firings of a and only one firing of b. The added place p as shown in Figure 6 (b) has weight 2 on the arc from p to transition b, it would have n+1 tokens after the first firing of a and n-1 tokens after the firing of b. The difference is 2.This is a weighted distance between b and a: $\sigma(a,2b) = 2$, the weight for a is 1 while the weight for b is 2. The concept of weighted synchronous distances makes a distinction when infinite distance is encountered. For simplicity, the formal definition of weighted synchronous distances is omitted here.

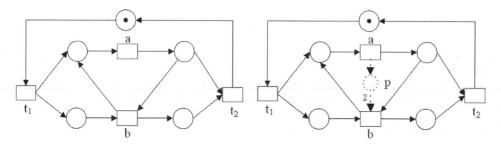

(a) Σ_7 (b)Σ_8

Figure 6. Weighted Synchronous Distance

Generally speaking, T_1 and T_2 may have more than one transition. It is possible that all transitions in the same set share the same weight, it is also possible that different transitions need different weights. It is assumed that the weights, if exist, would take the smallest possible values. For simplicity, we write $\sigma'(T_1,T_2)$ for weighted distance between T_1 and T_2 when the weights for individual transitions are known. The restriction on weights to be smallest leads to uniqueness of the distance.

Theorem 4

For an arbitrary place s in S in P/T-system Σ, as long as s has disjoint pre-set and post-set, $\sigma'(T_1,T_2) = \max\{\ M(s)\ |\ M\in[M_0>\} - \min\{\ M(s)\ |\ M\in[M_0>\}$ if exists, otherwise $\sigma'(T_1,T_2) = \infty$, where T_1 and T_2 are respectively the pre-set and post-set of s and $\sigma'(T_1,T_2)$ denotes a weighted distance with $W(s,t)$ as the weight of transition t in T_2 and $W(t,s)$ as the weight of transition t in T_1.◆

This theorem is true since what the added place records is exactly what happens in s.

In case there are no weights that yield a finite distance between T_1 and T_2, T_1 and T_2 are asynchronous.

4.3. Computing synchronous distance

All transition sequences can be found on the graph $G(\Sigma)$. Synchronous distances, weighted or not, are defined in terms of transition sequences. Thus, it is possible to design algorithms for the computing of distances. Firstly, if a ring exists on $G(\Sigma)$ that contains different numbers of firings of T_1 transitions and T_2 transitions, the distance is ∞. All algorithms are designed for computing finite distances only. The book in Chinese entitled *Petri Net Applications* by the author will soon appear, in which an algorithm for the computing of synchronous distances in P/T-systems can be found. It is easy to design an algorithm for computing weighted distances based on this algorithm.

We go no further on synchronous distances in this chapter since what concerns us is workflow modelling and what has been said about synchronous distances is already sufficient.

5. Business process

A successful application of Petri nets requires a full understanding of the application problem.

The term "workflow" was used as a synonym for "business process" in the book *Workflow Management* by W. Aalst and K. Hee. The terminology was developed by the Workflow Management Coalition (WFMC), an organization dedicated to develop standard terminology and standard interfaces for workflow management systems components.

As the first step towards workflow modelling, we make a clear distinction between "workflow" and "business process".

5.1. Business process vs. workflow

A business process is a pre-designed process in an enterprise or an organization for conducting the manipulation of individual cases of a business. It existed even before the birth of computers. The manipulation of individual business cases consists of business tasks and management tasks. The concept of "workflow" aims at "computerized facilitation or automation of a business process, in whole or part" (WFMC). To this end, the separation of business tasks and management tasks is of first importance. In a way, this is similar to the separation of data processing from a program, leading to the concepts of databases and database management systems.

A single business task may be carried out by a computer program. But "computerized automation of a business process" focuses on management automation rather than task automation. Management automation relies on clearly specified management rules. Most of the rules apply to all cases while some of the rules apply to individual cases. The former is "workflow logic" and the latter is "case semantics". The purpose of workflow modelling is nothing but to establish a formal specification of management rules to serve as a guide in the design, implementation and execution of a computer system called "workflow engine". It is the execution of the engine that conducts the processing of business cases. Figure 7 illustrates how workflow is related to business process.

The workflow logic specifies how business tasks are ordered (for causally dependent tasks) and/or synchronized. But, ordering is also a way of synchronization. Thus, workflow logic specifies how business tasks are synchronized for all conceivable cases in a business. In other words, workflow logic specifies all possible routes that a business case may take when being processed. What workflow logic cares about a single business task is not what data it requires or what data it will produce, let along what exact values are inputted or outputted. In this sense, workflow logic is concerned with abstract business tasks only.

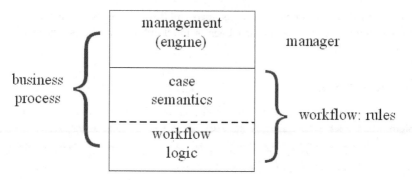

Figure 7. Business Process vs. Workflow

A selection is required at a crossing point of different routes. Concrete data of a given case determine the selection. The so selected route is the "semantics" of the given case. Thus, case semantics is concerned with those data that are used to decide whether a business task is on the route to be selected. These data are called explicit data since they should appear explicitly in the model of case semantics.

5.2. Management task vs. business task

A business must have a pre-designed form (paper form or electronic form) to record how an individual case is initiated and processed. Such a form is called a business form, B-form for short.

A business task can be characterized by

1. It requires professional knowledge, skill and/or experience related to the business.
2. It fills in at least one blank assigned to it on the B-form to tell what has been done.

A management task, on the other hand, requires knowledge on management rules. If it fills in blanks on the B-form at all, the written content is for management need only, e.g. a serial number for sorting and searching B-forms later on.

In the book *Workflow Management*, 16 tasks have been listed for "insurance claim" business in a (fictional) insurance company, among them, the first two tasks are:

1. Recording the receipt of the claim;
2. Establishing the type of claim (for example, fire, motor vehicle, travel, professional).

The first task may assign a serial number to the claim. Otherwise, it would leave no trace on a B-form. In fact, it is even not concerned with what B-form to be used. The second task must fill in the blank "type of claim" at least. Thus, the first task is a management task (may be shared by all businesses in a company) while the second task is a business task. In other words, the first task should be excluded from the workflow logic for "insurance claim", but the second task must be included.

5.3. Iteration vs. no iteration

The author of *Workflow Management* wrote: "This example of a process (i.e. insurance claim) also includes iteration or repetition — namely, the repeated assessment of an objection or the revision of the amount to be paid. In theory, this could go on forever."

As a management rule, an objection to a claim may need to be assessed more than once, but it must be a fixed number of times and by different persons; furthermore, the conclusion of each assessment must be recorded on the B-form. In other words, reassessment is a different task rather than a repetition of assessment.

Mathematically or logically, repetition could go on forever, but not for a theory of management. Endless repetition is not even thinkable in a management theory.

Iteration or repetition implies "redo" of the same task, i.e. what has been written on the B-form should be erased. "Redo" caused by wrong doings could, in theory, occur for every single task since human beings are erroneous by nature. No one would suggest a repetition for every task in a workflow model. "Redo" is nothing but a management measure to heal wrong doings, not a normal portion in a business process. Besides, workflow logic is about abstract tasks, but iteration is case dependent.

Endless redo could not occur since it is under control of the engine.

The execution of a single business task may include iteration. For example, when the amount of goods exceeds the truck load, the truck(s) would have to return after unloading. Such iteration is the detail of task execution, not a measure of management. Besides, it is case dependent. Iteration has nothing to do with workflow logic. What case semantics is concerned with is whether a task is on the route, not how a task is executed.

5.4. Set of tasks vs. set of blanks on B-form

Let $T = \{t_1, t_2, \cdots, t_n\}$ and $B = \{b_1, b_2, \cdots, b_m\}$ be the set of business tasks and respectively the set of blanks on the B-form for a give business process. The investigation here aims at properties of T and B for a well-defined business process.

There must be a correspondence between T and B, telling which blank(s) each task is responsible for. This correspondence should guarantee that no more than one task is responsible for the same blank in the course of processing a single case, and no blank is left empty upon termination of the case processing (those blanks that are not in relation with a given case are assumed to have been crossed out by the engine). Such correspondence has become common sense today. We will say no more about it.

Causal dependence among tasks in T leads to a combinatorial acyclic partial order on T: $<$ $\subseteq T \times T$, and a sub-relation $<\cdot$ of $<$: $x <\cdot y \equiv x < y \land \forall z \in T: \neg(x < z \land z < y)$. $<\cdot$ is the "immediate successor" relation: y is the immediate successor of x. Since the ordering relation $<$ is derivable from $<\cdot$ by transitivity of $<$, we will talk about $(T, <\cdot)$ instead of $(T, <)$. No iteration among tasks in T leads to acyclic partial order.

Let u be a task in T, u is a start task if it is before every other task, i.e. $\forall t \in T: \neg(t <\cdot u)$; u is an end task if u has no immediate successor. It is assumed that there is a unique start task, i.e. all cases share a unique beginning to recognize and to accept a case.

Let T_1, T_2 be nonempty subsets of T. T_2 is called an immediate successor set of T_1, denoted by $T_1 <\cdot T_2$, if $\forall u \in T1 \forall v \in T2: u <\cdot v$. It is easy to prove that T_1 and T_2 are disjoint, and tasks in T_1 (T_2) are not ordered. Synchronization for management need can only be introduced between T_1 and T_2. Here, the synchronization between T_1 and T_2 must be place synchronization since they are different transitions. In case T_1 and T_2 are both singletons, the synchronization can only be the immediate successor relation. As an example, let be $T_1 = \{a, b\}$ and $T_2 = \{c, d\}$, $\sigma(T_1,T_2)=2$ and $\sigma(T_1,2T_2)=2$ are two different ways of synchronization. Taking into account the fact that every task, if it is included on a route, can only be (effectively, redo is not counted) executed once, $\sigma(T_1,T_2)=2$ requires that tasks a ,b being executed in parallel followed by tasks c, d being executed in parallel; $\sigma(T_1,2T_2)=2$ requires that tasks a, b being executed in parallel followed by either task c or task d being executed alone. Data from a given case will be used for the selection between task c and task d. It is clear that synchronous distances would be of no use if redo is taken into account.

Now the processing of a given case goes like this: it begins from the unique start task, each task on the route carries out its duty and fills in blank(s) it is responsible for on the B-form, and passes it to its immediate successor(s) via the engine. The engine takes care of quality checking, successor selection and appointing executer(s) for selected task(s); and finally, the engine passes the B-form to appointed executer(s).

6. Synchronizer and workflow logic

P/T-systems will be used for the modelling of workflow logic. A synchronizer is a special place to connect transitions (tasks) with immediate successor relation ($<\cdot$).

To capture the fact that every task (transition) is executed (effectively) at most once for a single business case and workflow logic contains no iteration, a concept of restricted P/T-systems, RP/T-systems for short, is proposed.

Definition 9

A P/T-system $\Sigma =(S,T;F,K,W,M_0)$ is a RP/T-system if it is acyclic ($F^+\cap(F^{-1})^+) =\emptyset$) and any transition is restricted to fire at most once. ◆

The P/T-system in Figure 2 is a good example: as a normal P/T-system, transition t_2 can fire twice when p_1 has 2 tokens; but as a RP/T-system, t_2 can fire only once at the same marking. In fact, transitions t_2 and t_3 would fire when p_1 has 2 tokens for a RP/T-system, though t_2 remains enabled after its first firing.

Note that RP/T-systems are not a new class of net systems. If we introduce a control place c for every transition t such that c has an empty pre-set and {t} is its post-set, and initially it has one token. Apparently, with an added control place for every transition, every transition can fire at most once by conventional transition rules.

6.1. Synchronizer

Definition 10

A place p in a RP/T-system is a synchronizer if T_1 and T_2 are the pre-set and post-set of p and they are not empty; and $\forall t \in T_1$: $W(t, p) = b$ and $\forall t \in T_2$: $W(p, t) = a$ where b and a are integers such that $0 \leq a \leq n$ and $0 \leq b \leq m$; n, m are respectively the numbers of transitions in T_1 and T_2; and $K(p) = ab.\blacklozenge$

The RP/T-system in Figure 2 has two synchronizers p_1 and p_2 since $K(p_1) = 2$ and $K(p_2) = 2$.

The synchronizer defined by Definition 10 is usually denoted by $p = (T_1, T_2, (a, b))$ or $p = (\dot{p}, p\dot{}, (a, b))$. Figure 8 (a) is the graphical presentation of a synchronizer p and (b) is the detail of p, explaining how synchronization is achieved. Theorem 4 concludes that $\sigma(bT_1, aT_2) = ab$, i.e. the weighted synchronous distance between T_1 and T_2 are ab where b is the weight for all transitions in T_1 and a is the weight for all transitions in T_2.

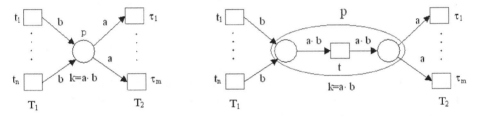

Figure 8. A Synchronizer and its Detail

Definition 11

Let $p = (T_1, T_2, (a, b))$ be a synchronizer and n, m be the numbers of transitions in T_1 and T_2. P can be classified as below:

n=m=1, p is sequential synchronizer,
m>1, p is a split,
n>1, p is a join,
a>1 and a=n, p is an ALL-join,
1<a<n, p is an OR-join,
a=1 and a<n, p is a XOR-join,
b>1 and b=n, p is an ALL-split,
1<b<m, p is an OR-split,
b=1 and b<m, p is a XOR-split.

Here we have deliberately chosen terms used by Prof. Aalst for WF-net. The difference is, our synchronizers are places while synchronization is achieved via transitions in WF-net. Synchrony in Section 3 has made it clear that synchronization with a distance greater than zero is place synchronization. We will see what advantages the concept of synchronizers brings with it when we approach to management logic.

Figure 9 shows how to achieve mixed synchronization where p_1 is an XOR-split and p_2 is an ALL-split. What follows task t would be one of t_1 and t_2 plus both t_3 and t_4.

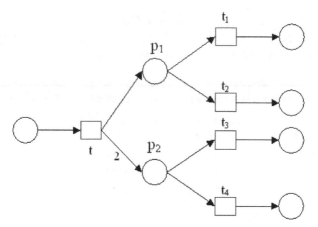

Figure 9. ALL-split and XOR-split mixture

Definition 12

Let x, y be variables of integer type. The place $p_1 = (T_1, T_2, (a, y))$, $p_2 = (T_1, T_2, (x, b))$ and $p_3 = (T_1, T_2, (x, y))$ are variations of synchronizer $p = (T_1, T_2, (a, b))$ as long as $0 < x \leq n$ and $0 < y \leq m$. p_1, p_2 and p_3 are flexible synchronizers, since x and y can take different values.◆

Figure 10 explains how flexible synchronizers work: x may take 1 or 2 as its value to achieve different synchronization.

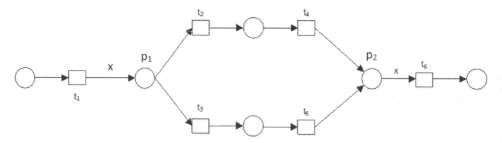

Figure 10. Flexible Synchronizers p_1 and p_2

We have not found a way to express flexible synchronization in terms of WF-net since an OR-split or OR-join transition in WF-net does not tell the exact number "OR" represents.

6.2. Workflow logic

RP/T-systems are candidates for modelling workflow logic, but not every RP/T-system is suitable.

Definition 13

For RP/T-system $\Sigma = (S,T;F,K,W,M_0)$, relation next$\subseteq$ TxT is given by next = $\{(t, t') \mid t \cap t' \neq \emptyset\}$. We write next(t, t') for (t, t') $\in$ next. Σ is well ordered if, for any t, t' in T, next(t, t') implies $\forall u \in T: \neg(next(t,u) \wedge next(u, t'))$.

The system in Figure 11 is not well-ordered, since we have next(t_1, t_3) and next(t_1, t_2)$\wedge$ next(t_2, t_3).

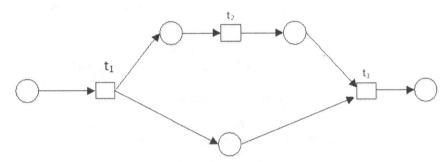

Figure 11. A System not Well-ordered

Remember that we are seeking for net systems that are suitable for modelling workflow logic. If t_1, t_2 and t_3 are tasks, then the B-form would be passed from t_1 to t_3 twice: one directly and one via t_2. This redundancy leads to structure complexity and analytical difficulty. Besides, there might be semantic inconsistency for this or that reason.

Definition 14

A well-ordered RP/T-system $\Sigma = (S,T;F,K,W,M_0)$ is a workflow logic if :

Every transition has nonempty pre- and post- sets; there is a unique place s_0 such that it has an empty pre-set and its post-set is a singleton $\{t_0\}$ and $K(s_0) = 1$, $W(s_0, t_0) = 1$; every intermediate place p is a synchronizer; every end-place, i.e. a place with an empty post-set, has a capacity 1 and its input arc(s) has 1 as its weight; The initial marking has a unique token in s_0. $\blacklozenge$

A task is initiated upon receiving a B-form, and passes it over to its successor upon termination. Thus, its pre-set and post-set are nonempty. The unique place s_0 is the place to receive initiated B-forms one by one and one at a time. Transition t_0 is the unique start task. An end-place is to receive completed B-forms, one by one and one at a time. All tasks must be well synchronized, so intermediate places are synchronizers. The weight on an input arc (t, p) of synchronizer p represents that $W(t, p)$ immediate successors need the B-form completed by t, and the weight on an output arc of p represents that B-forms completed by $W(p, t)$ different immediate predecessors of t are needed by t. The unique token in s_0 represents an abstract single case. It is an abstract case since no data is needed. An abstract case resembles all conceivable cases.

The system in Figure 2 is workflow logic. The conventional transition rules would apply to a workflow logic if a control place is added to each of the transitions (so, no transition can fire for the second time for one case) and the detail of every synchronizer as given in Figure 8 is also made explicit. But, this would make workflow logic too complicated for practical use. The following is the transition rules for workflow logic.

Definition 15

Let $\Sigma = (S,T;F,K,W, M_0)$ be a workflow logic, t in T is a transition and M is a marking (i.e. the initial marking M_0 or reachable from M_0 by rules given here).

1. t is enabled by M (or at M), denoted by M[t», if $\forall s \in t:M(s)=K(s)$,
2. Once M[t» is true, it remains true until either t occurs or t is not enabled according to conventional transition rule.
3. The successor marking, when t fires, is computed according to the conventional rule.◆

It is recommendable to compute the set of reachable markings for the workflow logic given in Figure 2. We denote with [M_0 » the set of reachable markings.

Redundancy is always closely connected to complexity. The property of being well-ordered has removed certain redundancy. The next definition reveals different redundancy.

Definition 16

A workflow logic is well-structured if for every synchronizer p and a reachable marking M, $M(p) = K(p)$ implies the fact that either all transitions in the post-set of p are enabled, or none of them is enabled.◆

Figure 12 illustrates this definition: the workflow logic in (a) is not well- structured, since t_3 is enabled but t_4 is not when p_2 has a token (the capacity of a synchronizer is known without saying). On the other hand, transitions t_3, t_4 and t_5 are all enabled when p_2 has 2 tokens in the system in (b).

Careful readers may have noticed that p_2 in (b) is not a synchronizer. No, it is not. It is a variation of a synchronizer. The two transitions t_3 and t_5 in (b) are viewed as twins: either both of them to be on a route, or none of them to be selected since t_4 requires 2 tokens. Thus, as far as route selection is concerned (workflow logic aims at the description of all possible routes), twin transitions could and should be combined as shown in Figure 13. Variations of synchronizers may be allowed in practice for convenience. But for the analysis of workflow logic, combined twins are preferred.

If the system in Figure 12 (b) is taken as workflow logic with a synchronizer variation, it reveals another problem: there would be two tokens upon the completion of one case when t_3 and t_5 are on its route. This is inconsistent with common knowledge: A single case cannot have two separated conclusions. This observation raises a question: what properties a well-defined workflow logic should have, in addition to being well-ordered and well-structured?

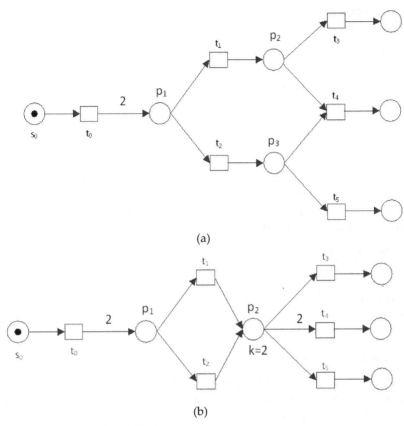

(a)

(b)

Figure 12. Not well- structured workflow logic

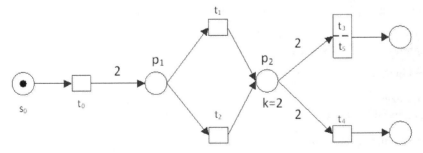

Figure 13. Combined Twins

Soundness! This is the answer from WF-net. Soundness requires:

"A process contains no unnecessary tasks and every case submitted to the process must be completed in full and with no references to it (that is case tokens) remaining in the process."

What we propose is throughness: the token in s_0 (an abstract case) will be passed over by transition firings (tasks) via the engine, to a unique end-place. All properties required by soundness are covered by being through.

In what follows, workflow logic is always assumed well-structured.

6.3. Throughness and reduction rules

Let Σ = (S,T; F, K, W, M_0) be a well-structured workflow logic, and M is a reachable marking.

Definition 17

1. M is a termination marking if it enables no transition; M is an end-marking if there is a unique end-place e such that $M(e) = 1$ and $M(s) = 0$ for all places s other than e.
2. Σ is through if every termination marking is an end-marking and every end-marking is also a termination marking. ◆

The workflow logic in Figure 2 is through.

Theorem 5

If workflow logic Σ is through, then for every transition t, there is a reachable marking M that enables t and there is a route to which t belongs.◆

From the fact that Σ is acyclic and s_0 is unique, we know that there is a directed path from s_0 to t. By mathematical reduction on the length of this path, this theorem is easy to prove.

Soundness of a WF-net is proved via computing T-invariant by adding an extra transition between its unique place o and its unique initial place i. This method applies to workflow logic as well. But we do it differently.

Keep in mind the principle of local determinism. Our attention focuses on local structures of workflow logic rather than global properties like T-invariants.

Characteristics of local structures bring up the following reduction rules for proving throughness of workflow logic.

Reduction Rule 1

Synchronizer p_1 = ($T_1,T_0,(a_1, a_2)$) and p_2 = ($T_0,T_2,(b_1,b_2)$) can be reduced to synchronizer p = ($T_1,T_2,(a_1,b_2)$) if $a_2 = b_1$. ◆

Figure 14 illustrates this rule.

Let Σ be the workflow logic to which rule 1 is applied and Σ' is resulted by replacing p_1, T_0, p_2 with p in Σ. We have

Theorem 6

Σ is through if and only if Σ' is through.◆

Synchronizer p_1 requires that a_2 transitions from T_0 to fire after the firings of a_1 transitions from T_1 while synchronizer p_2 requires that b_1 transitions from T_0 to be fired before any transition firing from T_2. Given $a_2 = b_1$, p_1 and p_2 are consistent with each other on T_0: a_1 transitions from T_1 followed by b_2 transitions from T_2. Thus, the theorem is true. (p_1, T_0, p_2) is in fact the detail of p. This reduction of omitting consistent detail is a net morphism in net topology. No wonder the property of being through is reserved. All reduction rules are in fact to conceal   local details, and as such, they reserve throughness. But there will be no more theorems and proofs to be given below for simplicity.

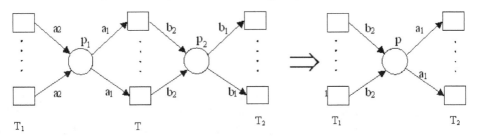

Figure 14. Reduction Rule 1

Reduction Rule 2

For synchronizer $p = (\{t_1\}, \{t_2\}, (1,1))$, if $t_1 \cdot \cap \cdot t_2 = \{p\}$, then (t_1, p, t_2) can be replaced by a single transition t with $\cdot t = \cdot t_1 \cup \cdot t_2 - \{p\}$ and $t \cdot = t_1 \cdot \cup t_2 \cdot - \{p\}$. All weights on remaining arcs remain. ◆

Figure 15 illustrates this rule.

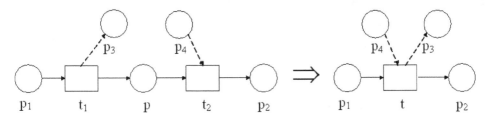

Figure 15. Reduction Rule 2

It is easy to see that the combined effect of t_1 and t_2 on all places other than p is the same as the effect of t. The dotted circles and arcs may exist, but not necessarily.

Reduction Rule 3

For transition t and places p_1, p_2, if $p_1 \cdot \cap \cdot p_2 = \{t\}$ and $W(p_1, t) = W(t, p_2) = 1$, then (p_1, t, p_2) can be replaced by p, $\cdot p = \cdot p_1 \cup \cdot p_2 - \{t\}$ and $p \cdot = p_1 \cdot \cup p_2 \cdot - \{t\}$. All weights on remaining arcs remain. ◆

Note that places p_1 and p_2 are not necessarily synchronizers, i.e. it is possible $\cdot p_1 = \emptyset$ and/or $p_2 \cdot = \emptyset$.

Figure 16 (a) illustrates this rule.

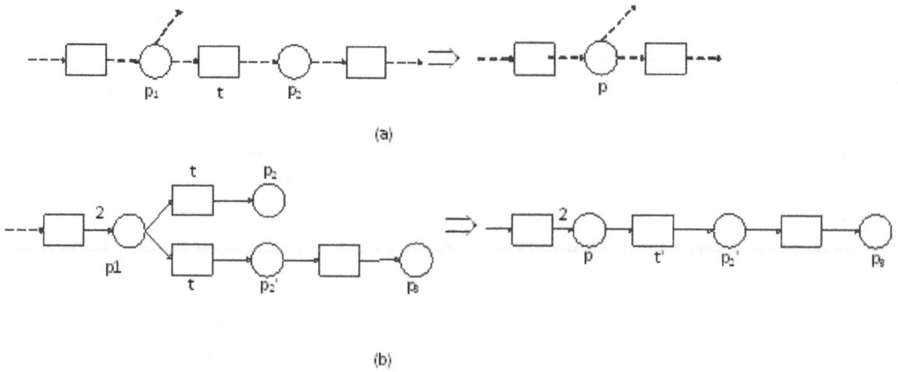

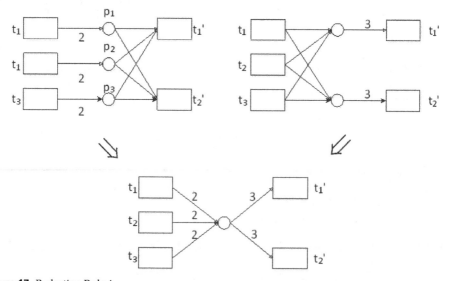

(a)

(b)

Figure 16. Reduction Rule 3

The workflow logic in Figure 16 (b) is not through since the termination marking would have two tokens at two different end-places. Rule 3 can be applied to reduce it in size, but the resulted place p turns out to be inconsistent between its pre-set and its post-set.

Reduction Rule 4

For $T_1 = \{t_1, t_2, \cdots, t_a\}$ and $T_2 = \{t_1', t_2', \cdots, t_b'\}$, if $p_i = (\{t_i\}, T_2, (1, b))$ is a synchronizer, $i = 1, 2, \cdots, a$, then $p_1, p_2, \cdots p_a$ can be reduced to a single synchronizer $p = (T_1, T_2, (a, b))$; If $p_i' = (T_1, \{t_i'\}, (a,1))$ is a synchronizer $i = 1, 2, \cdots, b$, then $p_1', p_2', \cdots p_b'$ can be reduced to the same single synchronizer $p = (T_1, T_2, (a, b))$.◆

Figure 17 illustrates this rule where a = 3 and b = 2.

Figure 17. Redaction Rule 4

We will see the significance of this rule and the rule next when management logic is discussed, since separated managements before the rule is applied become centralized management after it.

Reduction Rule 5

If p_i = ({t}, {t$_i$}, (1, 1)) is a synchronizer for every i, i = 1, 2, $\cdots$, a, then these synchronizers can be reduced to a single synchronizer p = ({t}, {t$_1$, t$_2$,$\cdots$, t$_a$}, (1, a)).

If p_j = ({t$_j$}, {t}, (1, 1)) is a synchronizer for every j, j = 1, 2, $\cdots$, b, then these synchronizers can be reduced to a single synchronizer p = ({t$_1$, t$_2$,$\cdots$, t$_b$}, {t}, (b, 1)).◆

Figure 18 illustrates this rule, where a = b = 3. .

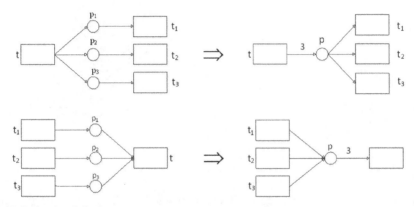

Figure 18. Reduction Rule 5

The next reduction rule reserves throughness, but a place element rather than a synchronizer is used for reduction.

Reduction Rule 6

In this rule, i = 1, 2, $\cdots$, a and j = 1, 2, $\cdots$, b. For transition sets T = {t$_1$, t$_2$,$\cdots$, t$_a$} and T$_i$ = {t$_{i1}$, t$_{i2}$, $\cdots$, t$_{ib}$}, if p_i = ({t$_i$}, T$_i$, (1, b)) is a synchronizer for every i, then these synchronizers can be reduced to the place p: p = T, p$^\cdot$ = $\bigcup_{i=1}^{a}$ T$_i$, K(p) = ab, W(t$_i$, p) = b and W(p, t$_{ij}$) = 1, If $p_{i'}$ = (T$_i$, {t$_i$}, (b, 1)) is a synchronizer for every i, then these synchronizers can be reduced to the place q: $\cdot$q = $\bigcup_{i=1}^{a}$ T$_i$, q$^\cdot$ = T, K(q) = ab, W(t$_{ij}$, q) = 1, W(q, t$_i$) = b.◆

Figure 19 illustrates this rule, where a = 3 and b = 2.

A noticeable fact is: places p and q are different from a synchronizer at two aspects. Firstly, their capacities are both ab instead of the product of the input weight and the output weight. Secondly, transitions in T$_i$ and T$_j$, i ≠ j, maybe enabled at different times before reduction, but they will be enabled at the same time by p; similarly, transitions in T will be enabled at the same time by q, but maybe not before reduction. The important point is, the number of transitions to be selected for a route remain unchanged (real selection is to be determined by concrete data from a practical case later by case semantics.) due to the fact that all synchronizers in question are either ALL-split or ALL-join. This means that the property of being through is reserved.

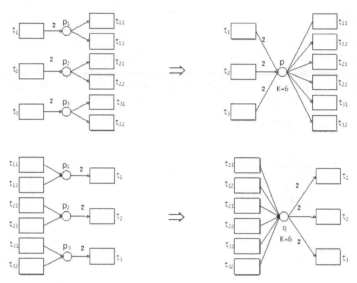

Figure 19. Reduction Rule 6

Definition 18

A place p with $\cdot p = T_1$ and $p \cdot = T_2$, $T_1 \neq \emptyset$, $T_2 \neq \emptyset$, is called a virtual synchronizer if there exist integers a and b such that $\forall t \in T_1 : W(t,p) = b, \forall t \in T_2 : W(p, t) = a$, $K(p) \neq ab$, but $K(p)/b = n$, $K(p)/a = m$, where n, m are respectively the numbers of transitions in T_1 and T_2. For virtual synchronizer p, we also write $p = (\cdot p, p \cdot, (a,b))$.◆

The two places p and q in Figure 19 are virtual synchronizers. It is easy to check that the two places used for reduction by Rule 6 are virtual synchronizers in general.

For further reduction when a virtual synchronizer is involved, we have the revised version of Reduction Tule 1:

Reduction Rule 1':

Let each of $p_1 = (T_1, T_0, (a_1, a_2))$ and $p_2 = (T_0, T_2, (b_1, b_2))$ be a synchronizer or a virtual synchronizer. As long as $K(p_1)/a_1 = K(p_2)/b_2$, (p_1, T_0, p_2) can be reduced to $p = (T_1, T_2, (a, b))$, where $a = K(p_1)/b_1$ and $b = K(p_2)/a_2$, and $K(p) = ab$, $\forall t \in T_2 : W(t, p) = b$ and $\forall t \in T_2 : W(t, p) = a$. ◆

This rule is applicable when the involved virtual synchronizer is of ALL-join and ALL-split nature. Otherwise, local consistence should be checked since a virtual synchronizer is more flexible than a synchronizer. Figure 20 explains: the workflow logic on top is not through since just one of p_2 and p_3 may have 2 tokens while p_4 requires the two of them to have two tokens each. As shown in the figure, a virtual synchronizer p_5 is obtained when rule 6 is applied. The resulted system after rule 6 remains being not through. If rule 1' is further applied to p_5 and p_4, we get a system that is through. Inconsistence between p_1 and p_4 is concealed. The virtual synchronizer p_5 does not tell whether it is ALL-split or OR-split. It inherits property of being ALL-split or OR-split from p_1.

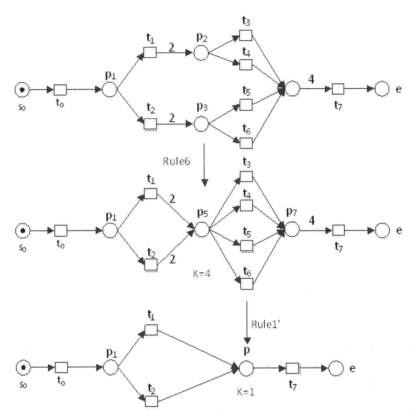

Figure 20. Reduction Rule 1' leads to Error

Figure 21 illustrates Reduction Rule 1', in which the workflow logic on top is apparently through. After twice applications of rule 6, the resulted p_6 and p_7 are virtual synchronizers both. By reduction rule 1', these two virtual synchronizers are replaced by p, which is a synchronizer. This time the property of being through is reserved.

Reduction Rule 6 is suggested not to be used as long as there is a different reduction rule applicable.

Theorem 7

A well-structured workflow logic has the property of being through if it can be reduced to a single isolated place, i.e. a place whose pre-set and post-set are both empty.◆

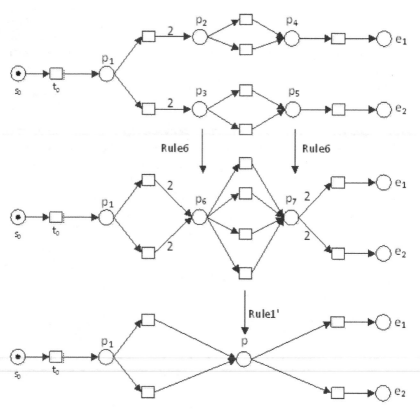

Figure 21. Reduction Rule 1'

This theorem is true since all reduction rules (including carefully used rule 1') reserve throughness . The isolated place is the start-place and the end place at the same time, thus the concealed detail has the property of being through.

This isolated place represents "harmony" as far as workflow logic is concerned. An interesting fact is, the isolated transition represents "contradiction" when it is resulted by applying the Resolution Rule and the Expansion Rule in Enlogy (a branch in GNT, net logic) for logical reasoning. A pair of dual elements, i.e. a place and a transition, lead to opposite concepts in philosophy, could this happen by chance? In fact as we will see soon, the dual of workflow logic is exactly the logic for workflow management.

We do not claim the completeness of this set of reduction rules. Whenever a user finds workflow logic not reducible to "harmony" though it is indeed through, please try to figure out new reduction rules and to let us know. Reduction rules would be enriched this way, we hope.

Figure 22 shows how to reduce to harmony the workflow logic for insurance claim where t_0, t_1, t_2, t_3 and t_4 are respectively the tasks "accept", "check policy", "check claim", "send letter" and "pay" (See *Workflow Management*).

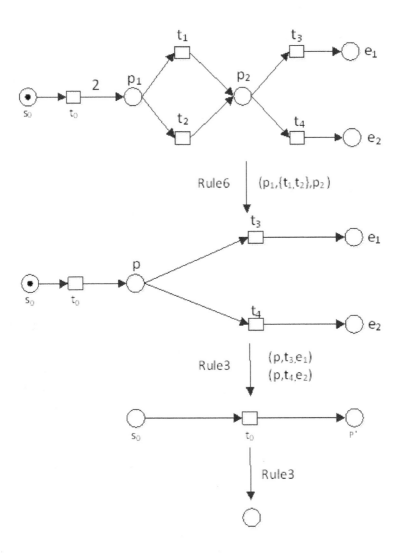

Figure 22. Reducing Workflow to Harmony

Figure 23 is a more complicated net from Dr. Aalst during his visit to Tsinghua University (Beijing, China) in 2004, where (a) is the original net in which every place has the capacity 1 and all weights on arcs are also 1, i.e. a WF-net. The author would suggest to take (b) as the workflow logic for whatever business in mind. Note that (c) contains virtual synchronizers.

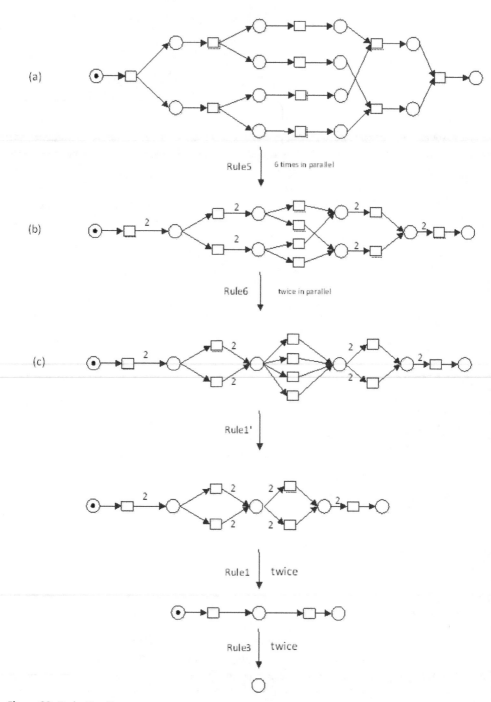

Figure 23. Reduction Process

6.4. Develop a workflow logic for a given business

Let $T = \{t_1, t_2, \cdots t_n\}$ and $B = \{b_1, b_2, \cdots b_m\}$ be respectively the set of business tasks with $< \cdot$ as its immediate successor relation, and the set of blanks on the B-form for a well-designed business. There should be a fixed correspondence between T and B to make clear responsibilities for each of the tasks in T. This correspondence will not be mentioned any more.

Let $\Sigma = (S,T;F,K,W,M_0)$ be the net system such that T is the task set and $S = \{p_1, p_2, \cdots p_k\} \cup \{s_0\}$ $\cup E$ where for each i, $i = 1, 2, \cdots, k$, k is the number of non-end tasks $t_1, t_2, \cdots t_k$ in T, $\cdot p_i = \{t_i\}$, p_i. is the set of immediate successors of t_i. Let a_i be the number of tasks in this immediate successor set, a_i' is the intended number of tasks to be executed after t_i, then $K(p_i) = a_i'$, and $W(t_i, p_i) = a_i$ for every immediate successor t of t_i, $W(p_i, t) = 1$. It is easy to see that p_i is a synchronizer: $p_i = (\{t_i\}, p_i' (1, a_i'))$.

The place named s_0 is the unique start place: it has an empty pre-set and its post-set contains the unique start task with arc weight 1.

For every end-task in T, there is a unique end place e in E with 1 as the arc weight between them. E contains nothing else.

$M_0(s_0) = 1$ and all other elements in S have no token.

As a workflow logic of a business process, transition rules for RP/T-systems are assumed for Σ.

Σ must be well-ordered since $<\cdot$ is exactly its next relation among transitions.

Σ may be not well-structured as shown by Figure 12 (a). In this case, measures must be taken as suggested from Figure 12 (a) to (b), then to Figure 13.

Redundant synchronizers may be removed by Reduction Rule 3.

As an example, Let $T = \{t_1, t_2, t_3, t_4, t_5\}$ and $<\cdot= \{(t_1, t_2), (t_1, t_3), (t_2, t_4), (t_2, t_5), (t_3, t_4), (t_3, t_5)\}$. There are 3 non-end tasks in T, namely t_1, t_2 and t_3. So there 3 synchronizers: p_1, p_2 and p_3. Figure 24 shows the developed workflow logic.

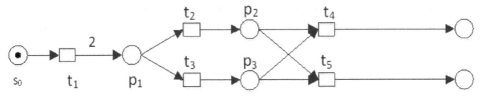

Figure 24. A developed Workflow Logic

There is redundancy in the developed system at p_2 and p_3. By Reduction Rule 3, these two synchronizers are reduced to a single synchronizer $p = (\{t_2, t_3\}, \{t_4, t_5\}, (2, 1))$. This is the workflow logic for insurance claim, as shown in Figure 22, there it was reduced to harmony.

7. Case semantics

Let $\Sigma = (S,T;F,K,W,M_0)$ be the workflow logic developed for a business process. Case semantics is to select a route for the processing of a given case.

A healthy enterprise should have new cases arrive every day. It is impossible to have different routes for different cases. Cases must be classified so that one route for one case class.

Let $C = \{c_1, c_2, \cdots c_k\}$ be the set of conditions for case classification. For example, let Boolean variable x, y be used to record conclusions given by tasks "check policy" and "check claim" respectively for insurance claim i.e. x and y are blanks on the B-form. One way to specify case classes is: $c_1 = x \wedge y$, $c_2 = \neg x \vee \neg y$. This classification is consistent with the workflow logic developed in Figure 24. Another way of case classification is to have 4 classes: $c_1 = x \wedge y$, $c_2 = \neg x \wedge y$, $c_3 = x \wedge \neg y$, $c_4 = \neg x \wedge \neg y$. This classification leads to a different task set: there have to be 4 end tasks. Thus the workflow logic is also different. The B-form should as well be changed accordingly.

Before going on from conditions to routes, a definition of routes is needed.

Definition 19

A route on a workflow logic $\Sigma = (S,T;F,K,W,M_0)$ is a RP/T-system $\Sigma' = (S',T';F',K',W',M_0')$ such that S',T', and F' are subsets of S,T and F respectively:

S 'contains the start place s, a unique end place e, and all synchronizers in S that have a directed path to e

T' consists of the start transition (task), the transition in the pre-set of e, and for every synchronizer $p = (\cdot p, p \cdot (a, b))$ in S', a transitions from $\cdot p$ and b transitions from $p \cdot$.

$F' = \{(x,y) \mid x,y \in S' \cup T' \wedge (x,y) \in F\}$.

For $x \in S'$, $K'(x) = K(x)$; For $(x, y) \in F'$, $W'(x, y) = W(x, y)$; $M_0'(x) = M_0(x)$ for all x in S' .◆

The difference between $\Sigma = (S,T;F,K,W,M_0)$ and $\Sigma' = (S',T';F',K',W',M_0')$ appears when a synchronizer p is an OR-join and/or OR-split. Conditions $c_1, c_2, \cdots c_k$ will be used to select a transitions from $\cdot p$ and b transitions from $p \cdot$. Thus, variables (blanks in B) used in these conditions are explicit variables, since they will appear explicitly in the system model for case semantics.

7.1. C-net: Net with variables [5,8]

C-net was originally defined for programming, i.e. for computation and communication. Variables are essentially different from conventional place elements of directed nets. A conflict between transitions in a net system is caused by either the lack of tokens in a shared place, or by the limited capacity of a shared place; a conflict between operations on a variable is read-write conflict: simultaneous read-write on the same variable is impossible by nature regardless of the exact value of that variable. Besides, there is a rich variety of data types and operations for data types. Conditions for case classification cannot be formally expressed without variables and operations on variables. The example of insurance claim explains: $c_1 = x \wedge y$, $c_2 = (\neg x \wedge y) \vee (x \wedge \neg y)$, $c_3 = \neg x \wedge \neg y$ provide a third way of case classification.

When variables are introduced into a net as another kind of state elements, a net becomes a C-net. A simplified version of C-net is introduced next, just to serve the need of modeling case semantics.

Definition 20

$\Sigma = (S, V, T; F, K, W, R, Wr, M_T, M_0)$ is a C-net system if

S,V,T are the sets of places, variables and transitions respectively; F,R,Wr are respectively the flow relation, the read relation and the write relation; K,W are the capacity function and the arc weight function; M_T is a marking on T and M_0 is a marking (initial marking) on S.◆

A transition may read and/or write a variable, but not must. The marking on a transition has a Boolean expression as its guard and assignments as its body when it writes. The guard and the body must be consistent in relation to read and write. For example, the guard can only refer to variables that are to be read by the transition.

If a transition has nothing to do with variables, conventional transition rules apply. If a transition has nothing to do with places, it is enabled when its guard is true. If a transition is related with places as well as variables, it is enabled if it is enabled by places and its guard is true.

Isolated transitions are excluded in a C-net.

An enabled transition may fire to produce a successor marking on S, the marking on T remains like the weight function and the capacity function; variables in write relation with this transition are assigned values by the assignments.

A c-net transition in general has a figure called "status" as part of M_T. Transition firings may change "status". But this does not concern us.

To save space, detailed formal definitions are avoided. Figure 25 illustrates them, including graphical presentation of C-nets.

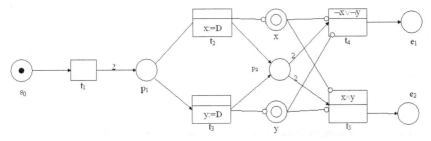

Figure 25. A C-net System: Case Semantics for Insurance Claim

The case semantics of insurance claim given in Figure 25 divides conceivable cases into 2 classes. Variables like x and y are drawn as double circles, write relation is represented by a zero-headed arc from transition to variable, reversed zero-headed arc represents read relation. For example, t_2 writes x and t_4, t_5 read x.

The start transition t_1 is in no relation with x and y, it has no guard, no body. The guards of both t_2 and t_3 are "true", denoted by default. The write operations of these two transitions are to be performed by their executers, denoted as x:= D where D is the abbreviation of "default". Transitions t_4 and t_5 have conditions for case classification as their guards. They have empty body since they write no variables.

Apparently, the case semantic contains two routes: one for each class. As long as the classification of cases is complete and consistent (every case falls into exactly one class), there would be a unique route for each case.

7.2. Workflow logic and its case semantics

Let $(T,<\cdot)$, $B =\{b_1, b_2, \cdots b_m\}$ and $C = \{c_1, c_2, \cdots c_k\}$ be the main constituents of a business process. There is a precise correspondence between tasks in T and blanks (on B-form) in B; Condition set C is complete and consistent; the immediate successor relation $<\cdot$ is implied by a combinatorial acyclic partial order on T. With all these requirements satisfied, $((T,<\cdot), B ,C)$ is a well-designed business process. We will not put all these into formal definitions since that would be cumbersome and uninteresting.

Definition 21

The C-net system $\Sigma'=(S,V,T;F,K,W,R,Wr,M_T,M_0)$ is a case semantics of the workflow logic $\Sigma = (S,T;F,K,W,M_0)$ developed for well-designed business process $((T,<\cdot), B , C)$, if the marking M_T (which is constant) satisfies that for those t in T that have a guard, the guard is a condition in C, and every condition in C is the guard of some transition.◆

Definition 22

Let C-net system $\Sigma'=(S,V,T;F,K,W,R,Wr,M_T,M_0)$ be a case semantics of the workflow logic $\Sigma = (S,T;F,K,W,M_0)$ developed for well-designed business process $((T,<\cdot), B , C)$. If Σ is through, and for every OR-split synchronizer $p = (\cdot p, p^\cdot (a, b))$, $b<|p^\cdot |$, for every condition c_i in C, i = $1,2, \cdots k$, $|\{t | t \in p \wedge$ guard $(t) = c_i\}|=b$, then Σ' is consistent with Σ.◆

Theorem 8

If Σ is a through workflow logic and Σ' is a case semantics consistent with Σ, then there is a unique route for every conceivable case. ◆

For a case in class c_i, the route it will take is obtained by deleting from Σ all transitions whose guard is not c_i together with their successor elements.

Figure 26 shows another case semantics of the insurance claim business process where cases are divided into 3 classes by conditions $c_1 = x \wedge y$, $c_2 = (x \wedge \neg y) \vee (\neg x \wedge y)$ and $c_3 = \neg x \wedge \neg y$. The task set has one more end-task for this classification.

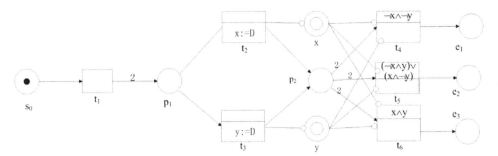

Figure 26. Another Case Semantics for Insurance Claim

The only OR-split synchronizer in Figure 26 is p_2. It has 3 tasks in its post-set and each of which bears a different condition as its guard. This is consistent with p_2: p_2 is a XOR-split synchronizer.

8. Business process management

So far we have proposed a formal model as workflow logic and a formal model as case semantics for a well-designed business process. Case semantics in embedded in a Workflow logic when they are consistent with each other. There is a unique route for every conceivable case as the semantics of that case. Thus, a firm foundation has been laid for management automation. The computer system that conducts the processing of each given case based its semantics is the workflow engine.

8.1. Management logic

As suggested by Figure 8 (b), every synchronizer $p = (\cdot p, p\cdot, (a, b))$ requires management (transition t in the detail of the synchronizer) to keep tasks in $\cdot p$ well synchronized with transitions in $p\cdot$. The start-place requires management, so do all end-places. At the start-place, the engine must recognize the proper business process when a case (B-form) arrives, and to have the corresponding workflow logic ready, and to appoint an executer for the start-task and passes the B-form to the executer. At an end-place, the engine must check whether the case is well processed and to put the completed B-form in place.

All in all, places and synchronizers are exactly where the engine does its duty. In other words, the dual of workflow logic is the management logic, and the dual of case semantics with given condition c_i in C produces the route for all cases classified by c_i.

Definition 22

1. The directed net $N' = (T,S;F)$ is the dual net of directed net $N = (S,T;F)$.
2. $\Sigma' = (T, S; F,K',W', M_0)$ is the workflow management logic for workflow logic $\Sigma = (S, T; F,K,W, M_0)$, where $K'(t) = \sum W(p,t)$ for every t in T, i.e. the capacity of t is the sum of all weights on its input arcs; $W'(x, y) = W(x, y)$ for all (x, y) in F; $M_0(t) = 0$ for t in T.
3. (Σ,Σ') is the logic pair for the business process in question.◆

Figure 27 is the logic pair for insurance claim with two case classes.

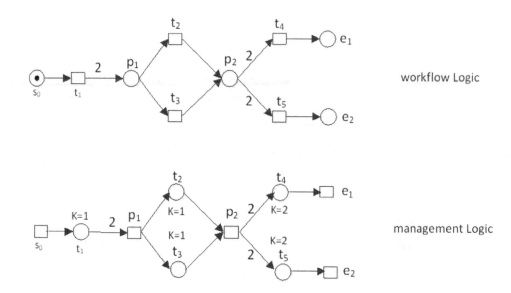

Figure 27. Logic Pair

Management tasks (transitions in Σ') and business tasks (transitions in Σ) are executed in turn: whenever a place (including synchronizers) in Σ has a full capacity of tokens, the transition with the same name in Σ' is enabled. The enabled transition fires to put tokens into its output places in Σ', whenever a place in Σ' has a full capacity of tokens, the transition with the same name in Σ is enabled. This interactive transition firings continue till a transition named with an end-place is fired to move the case token out of the pair. This is the way how management tasks and business tasks interact with each other.

8.2. Route for cases in the same class

A logic pair specifies, for a given business process, how individual cases are processed under the conduction of the engine (the manager). Figure 28 shows a case semantics and its dual, that is a semantic pair, a pair of C-net systems. The guard on a transition (task) will be used by the engine (transitions named after a synchronizer) for the selection of routes. We will not give a formal definition of this pair, since it is clearly specified by the figure. The interaction between this pair is the same with the logic pair, except details given by guards.

Figure 27 and Figure 28 serve as the main part of a formal specification for a workflow engine. The rest of the engine is enterprise specific (personal, organizational division etc.).

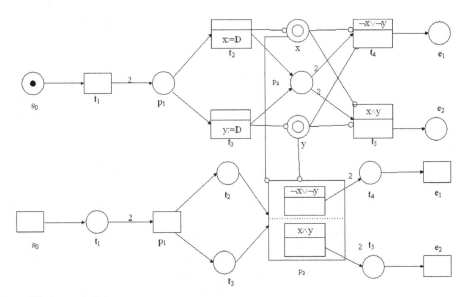

Figure 28. Semantic Pair

8.3. Duty of the engine

The main duty of the engine is to conduct the manipulation of individual cases based on the logic pair (before the class to which the case belongs is known) and the semantic pair (transitions named after an OR-split synchronizer), including appointing executers for selected tasks.

In addition to this major duty, other duties include (not exclusive):

- Set a time upper bound for each task to be executed next, and to remind before expiration, check whether it is done on time;
- Check whether a task is properly done (e.g. whether the content filled in a blank matches its type);
- Decide, based on given rules, what to do when an expiration or quality failure is detected (e.g. redo for quality failure, bad record on the due person for expiration);
- Other thinkable duties, especially enterprise specific ones.

An engine carries out its duty properly if and only if it has predefined management rules to follow. In addition to global rules specified by the logic pair and the semantic pair, local rules are also necessary, i.e. rules for every management task (every place in workflow logic). Remember that all places in workflow logic are where the engine can and must put a hand on.

Some management rules are closely related to individual enterprises, some are even secrete to outsiders. Current and historical business data, business partners data, conventions or traditions etc. All rules related to these must be carefully established and checked together with a well-designed business process, a well-structured workflow logic of the process, a case semantics consistent with the logic. The two pairs are derivable from the logic and semantics. We go no further here in this chapter.

9. Conclusions and acknowledgement

Prof. Carl Adam Petri wrote: "In order to apply net theory with success, a user of net theory can just rely on the fact that every net which he can specify explicitly (draw on paper) can be connected by a short (≤ 4) chain of net morphisms to the physical real world; your net is, in a very precise sense, physically implementable".

We have seen this quotation at the very beginning of this chapter. This chapter tries to make clear how to specify a net that is "in a very precise sense physically implementable". A successful application of net theory starts from a full understanding of the application problem. A well designed business process $((T,<\cdot), B ,C)$ leads to the discovery of workflow logic, case semantics and management pairs, a tree-layer model for workflow modeling.

Without theory, full understanding of application problems becomes hard. Well-structured business process $((T,<\cdot), B , C)$ starts from a clear distinction between business process and workflow, a clear distinction between business tasks and management tasks, and a clear distinction between transition synchronizations and place synchronizations. Business process and workflow are not synonym of each other.

A full understanding of application problems and a good grasp of theories in Petri nets that build a road to success.

The author is grateful to the editors of this book. It is a great honor to me as well as a good chance for me to exchange ideas on Petri nets with friends outside my country.

Author details

Chongyi Yuan
School of Electronics Engineering and Computer Science, Peking University, Beijing, China

10. References

[1]   C.Y. Yuan: *Petri Nets* in Chinese, Southeast University Press,(1989).

[2]   W. Brauer (editor): Net Theory and Applications, Springe LNCS Vol.84.

[3]   C. A. Petri: Nonsequential Processes GMD-ISF Report 77, (1977).

[4]   C.A. Petri: Concurrency incl. in 2 (in Theoretical Computer Science).

[5]   C.Y. Yuan: Principles and applications of Petri Net. Beijing, China: Publishing house of electronics industry, 2005.

[6]   W. Aalst, K. Hee: *Workflow Management*, The MIT Press (2000).

[7]   C.Y. Yuan, W. Zhao, S.K. Zhang, Y. Huang: A Three Layer Model for Business Process —Process Logic, Case Semantics and Workflow Management, Journal of Computer Science & Technology, Vol.22 No.3, 410-425 (2007).

[8]   C.Y. Yuan: *Petri Net Application*, to appear .

Chapter 7

Control Interpreted Petri Nets –
Model Checking and Synthesis

Iwona Grobelna

Additional information is available at the end of the chapter

1. Introduction

The chapter presents a novel approach to formal verification of logic controller programs [2], focusing especially on reconfigurable logic controllers (RLCs). Control Interpreted Petri Nets [8] are used as formal specification of logic controller behavior. The approach proposes to use an abstract rule-based logical model presented at RTL-level. A Control Interpreted Petri Net is written as a logical model, and then processed further. Proposed logical model (Figure 1) is suitable both for formal verification [14] (model checking in the NuSMV tool [19]) and for logical synthesis (using hardware description language VHDL).

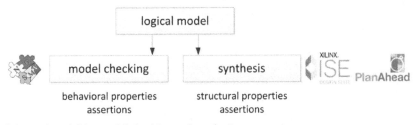

Figure 1. Logical model for model checking and synthesis purposes

Model checking [7, 10] of prepared logical model allows to validate the primary specification of logic controller. It is possible to verify some user-defined properties, which are supposed to be satisfied in designed system.

Logical model derived from a Control Interpreted Petri Nets presented at RTL-level (*Register Transfer Level*) in such a way, that it is easily synthesizable as reconfigurable logic controller or PLC (*Programmable Logic Controller*) without additional changes.

Design methodology at RTL-level allows to convert an algorithm into hardware realization and to use the conception of variables and sequential operation performing. Project description in VHDL language is a specification accepted by synthesis tools at RTL-level [23]. Therefore, logical model is transformed into synthesizable code in VHDL language.

Presented approach to formal verification of reconfigurable logic controllers was tested on several examples of industrial specifications by means of Control Interpreted Petri Nets. Specifications were firstly written as logical models, then transformed into appropriate formats, and finally formally verified (with some properties added) and synthesized.

As a support for testing, a tool has been developed, which allows automatic transformation of logical model into model description in the NuSMV format and into synthesizable code in hardware description language VHDL.

Rules for definition of rule-based logical model and model description in the NuSMV tool are described in section 3, while rules for synthesizable model definition in VHDL are given in section 4.

2. Description and illustration of proposed RLCs design system

Logic controller development process usually starts with specification, further goes through verification [16] and simulation, finally ending with implementation. Schema of proposed system for designing of logic controllers is presented in Figure 2.

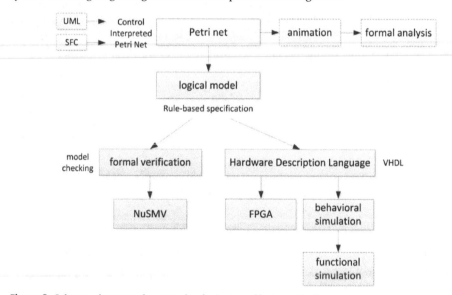

Figure 2. Schema of proposed system for designing of logic controllers

Formal specification is prepared by means of Control Interpreted Petri Nets [8]. They specify and model the behaviour of concurrent logic controllers and take into account properties of controlled objects. Local states, as in typical P/T Petri nets, may change after firing of transitions, if some events occur. Additionally, transition guards are associated with input signals of controller, while places are associated with its output signals.

Formally, a Control Interpreted Petri Net can be defined as a six-tuple:

$$CIPN = (PN, X, Y, \varrho, \lambda, \gamma) \tag{1}$$

where:

- PN is an alive and safe Petri net,
- X is a set of input states,
- Y is a set of output states,
- ρ is a function $T \rightarrow 2^X$, that each transition assigns the subset of input states $X(T)$; 2^X states for the set of all possible subsets of X,
- λ is a function of Moore outputs $M \rightarrow Y$, that each marking M assigns the subset of output states $Y(M)$,
- γ is a function of Mealy outputs $(M \times X) \rightarrow Y$, that each marking M and input states X assigns the subset of output states Y.

3. Novel approach to formal verification of logic controller specification

Control Interpreted Petri Net is first written as an abstract rule-based logical model. Then, basing on that model two other models are built – a verifiable model for the NuSMV model checker (described in details in section 3.2, together with requirements list definition expressed in temporal logic) and a synthesizable model in VHDL (for reconfigurable logic controllers, discussed in section 4). Thanks to proposed methodology, synthesized model is formally verified before the implementation and the two models are fully consistent with each other.

3.1. Rule-based logical model of a Control Interpreted Petri Net

Proposed rule-based logical model used for synthesis and verification purposes is an intermediate format describing desired behaviour of designed logic controller [13, 14]. Model includes variables definition and their initial values, rules describing net functionality, changes of logic controller output and input signal values.

Proposed logical model reflects the behaviour of Moore digital automaton with inputs register (optionally) and outputs register (Figure 3). Combinational circuit (CC) controls system behaviour and operates on internal system states.

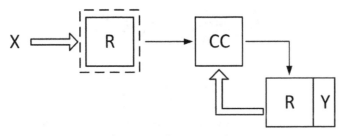

Figure 3. Moore digital automaton with inputs and outputs register

Formally, rule-based logical model can be defined as a seven-tuple:

$$LM = \{P, X, Y, S, T, O, I\} \tag{2}$$

where:

- P stands for places of a Control Interpreted Petri Net (internal local states),
- X stands for inputs of a Control Interpreted Petri Net (input signals to logic controller),
- Y stands for outputs of a Control Interpreted Petri Net (output signals to logic controller),
- S stands for initial values of places, inputs and outputs,
- T stands for rules describing transitions (indicating changes of local states),
- O stands for active outputs corresponding to appropriate places,
- I stands for inputs supposed to be active in appropriate places (for formal verification simplification).

As an example to demonstrate proposed solution a sample control process was chosen, described by means of Control Interpreted Petri Nets, then formally verified for behavioral properties and synthesized. Control process example was taken from. It was verified using CTL temporal logic and the NuSMV model checker in 2.5.2 version [19].

A simple embedded system for drink production is considered (Figure 4).

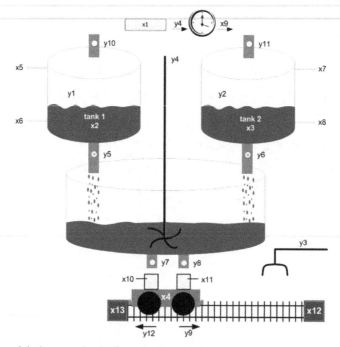

Figure 4. Real model of process for drink production

Logic controller schema with input and output signals (Table 1) is presented in Figure 5. A Control Interpreted Petri Net for drink production process is presented in Figure 6. It has 20 local states and initial marking involves two places – *P1* and *P14*.

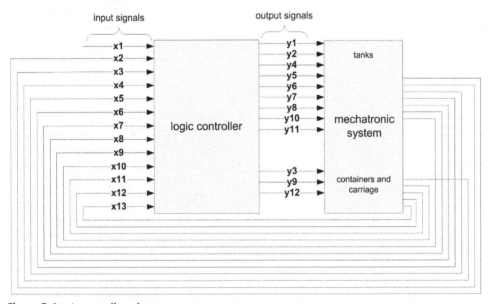

Figure 5. Logic controller schema

Initially, both tanks are empty and process can be started. After pressing the *x1* button, drink production process starts. Valves *y10* and *y11* are opened and target containers are loaded on the carriage (*y3*). Filling tanks process (active signals *y1* and *y2*) is a concurrent process. When a tank is already full (signalized by sensor *x5* or *x7* respectively), the appropriate valve for filling tank is closed. Meanwhile, loaded containers and transported (*y12*) to a proper location (sensor *x13*). When the ingredients are ready, it is signalized by sensors *x2*, *x3* and *x4*. Then, ingredients from both tanks are dropped into the main tank (signals *y5* and *y6*), where they are mixed (signal *y4*). Emptying of small tanks is signalized by sensors *x6* and *x8*. When the drink is well mixed, it is indicated by sensor *x9*. Then, ready drink is filled into containers (*y7*, *y8*). When containers filling process ends (sensors *x10*, *x11*), they are transported (signal *y9*) to their starting location (sensor *x12*).

A Control Interpreted Petri Net is written formally using temporal logic [15]. Logic representation well corresponds to net structure and behavior, and at the same time is easy to formally verify and to synthesize.

Logical model includes variables definition and their initial values. The following elements of Control Interpreted Petri Net are interpreted as model variables: places, input and output signals. Logical model involves also set of rules, which describe how defined variables change over time. Set of rules influences the system behaviour. Each rule (transition) is presented in a separate row and starts with transition name (a label for particular rule).

	Signal	Description
Inputs	x1	Signal to start the process
	x2	Ingredients preparation in the first tank is finished
	x3	Ingredients preparation in the second tank is finished
	x4	Containers preparation is finished
	x5	Maximal fluid level in the first tank
	x6	Minimal fluid level in the first tank
	x7	Maximal fluid level in the second tank
	x8	Minimal fluid level in the second tank
	x9	Drink preparation is finished
	x10	Filling of the first container is finished
	x11	Filling of the second container is finished
	x12	The carriage is in its starting location (the right side)
	x13	The carriage is in its target location (the left side)
Outputs	y1	Preparation of the first ingredient
	y2	Preparation of the second ingredient
	y3	Loading containers
	y4	Mixing ingredients
	y5	Valve for emptying the first tank
	y6	Valve for emptying the second tank
	y7	Valve for filling the first container
	y8	Valve for filling the second container
	y9	Carriage movement to the right
	y10	Valve for filling the first tank
	y11	Valve for filling the second tank
	y12	Carriage movement to the left

Table 1. Logic controller input and output signals

A rule consists of two separated parts. The first part contains conditions for transition firing, namely names of active places and input signals (if required) needed to fire the transition. If the condition involves more than one variable, variables are usually connected with a logical operator *and* (written as &). It is also possible to connect the variables with logical operator *or* (written as |), what can be used by transition activation with one of many input signals. Similar as by initial values of variables, a variable can take the *TRUE* value (active place / input signal) or the *FALSE* value (inactive input signal). The second part describes marking changing of Petri net places. Usage of a temporal logic operator X indicates that marking changing will take place in the next system state. Analogously to previous possible variable values, after transition firing some places can become active (transition output places) or inactive (transition input places, names of these variables are preceded by an exclamation mark). Proposed solution is focused on transitions. Here, transition input places, firing conditions (corresponding to appropriate combinations of input signals) and transition output places are taken into account.

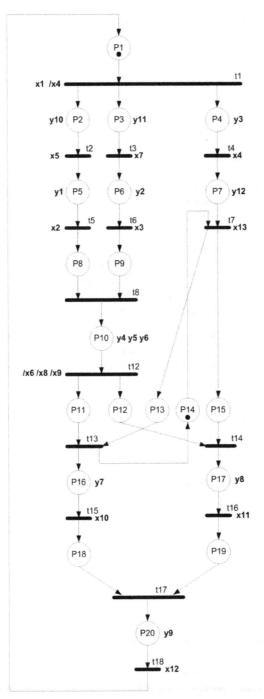

Figure 6. Control Interpreted Petri Net

Transitions from net from Figure 6 are described as separate rules (Figure 7). Firing of each transition changes marking of its input and output places. For example, firing of the *t1* transition removes token from the *p1* place (expressed by *!p1*) and adds a token into three places staring three concurrent processes: *p2*, *p3* and *p4* (expressed by *p2 & p3 & p4*).

```
t1: p1 & x1 & !x4 -> X (!p1 & p2 & p3 & p4);
t2: p2 & x5 -> X (!p2 & p5);
t3: p3 & x7 -> X (!p3 & p6);
...
```

Figure 7. Set of rules in logical model

Places not mentioned in particular rule do not change marking after firing of the (considered) transition. It means that the particular rule does not change marking of not mentioned places. Rules correspond therefore to Petri net transitions firings, and ipso facto marking changing of places. Situations, when a transition cannot be realized are not considered, supposing that active places hold then their marking. Proposed approach is an inertial description oriented on transitions (based on publications [1]. In the paper [11], because of the presence of Mealy outputs (where output signals values depend on input signal values and current internal system state), additionally output signals connected with particular transition firing are taken into account, besides places and input signals.

Output signals are considered for successive Petri net places. If the activity of particular output signal is connected with more than one place, this signal occurs multiple times on the right side of an arrow, by different places. Proposed notation concerns Moore outputs, where output state depends only from internal state of the system.

Output signals from the net in Figure 6 are therefore assigned to places, in which they are active (Figure 8). For example, the *y10* output signal is active only by active marking of the *p2* place, and active marking of the *p10* place implies the activity of output signals *y4*, *y5* and *y6*. The other output signals, which are not present on the right side of particular rule (for particular places) remain default inactive. It is also possible to evidently indicate the activity or inactivity of output signal, as in [1], proposed solutions seems however to be intuitive and does not enforce additional information, which could negative influence its readability.

```
p2 -> y10;
p3 -> y11;
p4 -> y3;
...
p10 -> y4 & y5 & y6;
...
```

Figure 8. Output signals in logical model

Input signals changes are also defined in logical model. However, the definition is only used by model checking process (model description preparation). In the HDL (*Hardware Description Language*) file, input signals are not concerned as they are inputs to the logic controller. Input signals coming from different objects, supervising system or system operator are considered analogously like output signals for successive Petri net places.

Input signals from the net in Figure 6 are assigned to places, where they are essential and may become active (Figure 9). In each other state, the signals remains by default inactive. For example, input signal $x5$ can be activated, when Petri net marking involves the place $p2$.

```
p1 -> (!x1 | x1) & (!x4 | x4);
p2 -> !x5 | x5;
p3 -> !x7 | x7;
. . .
```

Figure 9. Input signals in logical model

3.2. Model checking of rule-based logical model

Model checking technique [7, 10] is one of formal verification methods among others like e.g. *theorem proving* or *equivalence checking* and is currently used in the industry in software and hardware production [12]. System model is compared with defined properties and an answer whether they are satisfied or not is given. In case of any detected errors, appropriate counterexamples are generated which allow to localize error source.

Model checking process can be performed on the whole system or just on a part of it (so-called *partial verification*), what has an important meaning especially by complex systems which can be divided into subsystems.

Logical model derived from Control Interpreted Petri Net is transformed into format of the NuSMV model checker according to some strictly specified rules [13, 14]:

a. Each place $p \epsilon P$ is a variable of Boolean type,
b. Each input signal $x \epsilon X$ is a variable of Boolean type,
c. Each output signal $y \epsilon Y$ is a variable of Boolean type,
d. Defined variable take some initial values. Each variable takes any of two values (*TRUE* or *FALSE*),
e. Each place changes according to the rules defined in the transitions T and the function $\rho: T \rightarrow 2^X$; conditions of changes between places (token flow) occur in pairs (groups) – in the previous place(s) and in the next place(s),
f. Each output signal changes according to the rules defined in the function $\lambda: M \rightarrow Y$,
g. Each input signal changes randomly, but can take the expected values connected with Petri net places or change adequately to the situation.

Logical model into NuSMV model description translation is done automatically using implemented software application.

Similar like in logical model, model description for verification starts with variables definition, which correspond to places, input and output signals. Then, initial values are assigned to the variables. Rules describing net behaviour and token flow correspond to values changes of appropriate places (active/inactive marking of places, Figure 10). Input signals change their value only in expected situations (Figure 11). Output signals are in turn active when appropriate places include token (Figure 12).

```
next(p1) := case
    p1 & x1 & !x4    : FALSE;
    p20 & x12        : TRUE;
    TRUE             : p1;
esac;
next(p2) := case
    p2 & x5          : FALSE;
    p1 & x1 & !x4    : TRUE;
    TRUE             : p2;
esac;
    . . .
```

Figure 10. Rules in verifiable model (assignment of next values to places)

```
next(x1) := case
    p1    : {FALSE, TRUE};
    TRUE  : FALSE;
esac;
next(x2) := case
    p5    : {FALSE, TRUE};
    TRUE  : FALSE;
esac;
    . . .
```

Figure 11. Assignment of next values to input signals in verifiable model

```
next(y1) := case
    p5    : TRUE;
    TRUE  : FALSE;
esac;
next(y2) := case
    p6    : TRUE;
    TRUE  : FALSE;
esac;
    . . .
```

Figure 12. Assignment of next values to output signals in verifiable model

Model description is the first part needed for model checking. Additionally, it is necessary to specify some requirements, which are supposed (expected) to be true in defined model. Structural properties can also be checked on the Petri net level (and do not require model checking technique). However, the most important are here behavioural properties, which describe system functionality, impact of input signals and output signals activity.

Properties to be checked are defined using temporal logic [6, 15, 20] – either LTL (*Linear Temporal Logic*) or CTL (*Computation Tree Logic*). Properties describe safety requirements (*something bad will never happen*), as well as liveness requirements (*something good will eventually happen*). Safety and liveness requirements are the most frequently specified requirements to be verified.

The requirements list should include as much desired properties as possible, as only they will be checked. It is often written basing on an informal specification. In the best practices, it is specified by customer (in textual form) or by engineers not involved in design process (in more or less formalized way).

Using CTL temporal logic the requirements list for considered case study was defined (properties are listed in Figure 13 and described in details in Table 2). All specified requirements are satisfied in the corresponding model description. Some properties concern Petri net structure itself (properties 1 – 20). It is checked, whether particular places are reachable. Next properties describe output signals, which cannot be active at the same time (properties 21 – 23). The last part of properties regards the correlation of input and output signals.

```
CTLSPEC EF p1;                --1
...                           ...
CTLSPEC EF p20;               --20
CTLSPEC AG !(y5 & y10);       --21
CTLSPEC AG !(y6 & y11);       --22
CTLSPEC AG !(y9 & y12);       --23
CTLSPEC AG (x5 -> AF !y10);   --24
CTLSPEC AG (x7 -> AF !y11);   --25
CTLSPEC AG (x13 -> AF !y12);  --26
CTLSPEC AG (x12 -> AF !y9);   --27
```

Figure 13. Requirements list

Property	Description
1	It is possible to reach the $p1$ place
...	...
20	It is possible to reach the $p20$ place
21	The $y5$ and $y10$ output signals can never be active at the same time
22	The $y6$ and $y11$ output signals can never be active at the same time
23	The $y9$ and $y12$ output signals can never be active at the same time
24	Always, when the $x5$ input signal is active (maximal fluid level in the first tank), finally the $y10$ output signal (controlling valve for filling the first tank) becomes inactive
25	Always, when the $x7$ input signal is active (maximal fluid level in the second tank), finally the $y11$ output signal (controlling valve for filling the second tank) becomes inactive
26	Always, when the $x13$ input signal is active (carriage location on the left), finally the $y12$ output signal (carriage movement to the left) becomes inactive
27	Always, when the $x12$ input signal is active (carriage location on the right), finally the $y9$ output signal (carriage movement to the right) becomes inactive

Table 2. Requirements list description

By introducing a subtle modification into Control Interpreted Petri Net, which regards initial marking removing from place *p14* (initial marking involves then only the *p1* place), the corresponding part of logical model and NuSMV model description is also changed. However, such a subtle change dramatically changes net behavior, and thereby designed logic controller behavior. Model checking of the same properties shows now another results. User receives multiple generated counterexamples indicating unsatisfied requirements. Places *p1* to *p12* are reachable, but it is not possible to reach active marking of further places. Next to last requirement is also not satisfied (*CTLSPEC AG (x13 -> AF !y12)*). Summarizing the report – an error occurs starting from transitions *t7* and *t13*, what confirms the fact, that it is indeed correlated with additional initial marking (and actually the lack of it) of Control Interpreted Petri Net.

When model checking process does not indicate any errors, it is then possible and advisable to focus on synthesizable code. Basing on logical model, model in hardware description language VHDL is built. The model is fully synthesizable and may be then implemented in FPGA for a reconfigurable logic controller.

4. Synthesis of rule-based logical model

Combining FPGA [18] as a target hardware platform with hardware description language VHDL ensures high reliability, speed and safety. Additionally, it is possible to modify anytime the already running system, what has a practical sense. Direct implementation of concurrent logic controllers in FPGA is similar to rule-based realization based on classical sequence diagrams. Transition firings are synchronized with clock rising edge.

Control Interpreted Petri Net, which is the core for logical model, is a safe net. Places can be then implemented using simple flip-flops, as their marking is expressed by a binary value. Flip-flops amount (for places) using one-hot encoding is equal to the amount of places (and so to the amount of local states).

Logical model can be easy synthesized as reconfigurable logic controller. Logical model, derived from Control Interpreted Petri Net, is transformed into VHDL language according to some strictly defined rules [13]:

a. Each place is an internal signal of *std_logic* type,
b. Each input signal is an input port of *std_logic* type,
c. Each output signal is an output port of *std_logic* type,
d. Each defined internal signal (Petri net place) takes an initial value, set by clock rising edge and active reset signal,
e. Each place changes its marking according to defined rules; fired transition changes marking of its input and output places,
f. Input signals are not considered, as they are inputs to the logic controller,
g. Each output signal changes its value according to active places; output signals are active by active marking of corresponding places.

Model in VHDL is oriented on places and transitions. It can be simulated and synthesized. Synthesis is performed in form of rapid prototyping [5], what in modern methodology for digital circuits design allows for frequent verification (simulation, analysis) of developed system. Its main goal is to check, whether designed system works at all, but the circuit might be not optimized. Circuit optimization and minimization of resources usage are here out of scope, however they may be important in some fields [9, 18].

Logical model into VHDL model translation is done automatically using implemented software application. Generated VHDL file for considered drink production process is fully synthesizable.

Model for synthesis starts with input and output signals definition. Petri net places are defined as internal signals. By clock rising edge and active reset signal, some initial values are assigned to places, which correspond to initial marking of a Control Interpreted Petri Net. Additionally, by each clock rising edge places hold their heretofore marking.

For places the one-hot encoding was used (called also *isomorphic places encoding*), which is the most accurate (and the simplest) representation of logical model, however it can cause bigger resources usage. For each place one flip-flop is generated, which label corresponds to particular place etiquette. Flip-flop sets the *1* value, if a place contains token, otherwise it holds the *0* value. Additionally, one-hot encoding is recommended by implementation in FPGA circuits, and even seen as the most effective method for states encoding [23], i.e. in FPGA circuits of Xilinx [21], especially for small automata. It is also possible to extend the work to any other encoding.

Places marking can change after transitions firing. Conditions connected with transitions correspond to values of input signals and active marking of particular places. If a condition is satisfied, Petri net transition is realized, and thereby its input and output places change their marking (Figure 14).

```
if p1 = '1' and x1 = '1' and x4 = '0' then
    p1 <= '0';
    p2 <= '1';
    p3 <= '1';
    p4 <= '1';
end if;
```

Figure 14. The *t1* transition firing in VHDL model

Output signals are active by active marking of appropriate places, what is denoted as shown in Figure 15.

```
y1 <= p5;
y2 <= p6;
y3 <= p4;
    . . .
```

Figure 15. Outputs assignment in VHDL model

Input signals value changes come from outside and are not modified inside VHDL model file. Their values are just read out by conditions related to transition firings.

VHDL file can also be simulated i.e. in *Active-HDL* environment [4]. Simulation confirms the proper functionality of designed logic controller (simulation results are presented in Figure 16).

It is then possible to perform logic synthesis and implementation, i.e. in *Xilinx PlanAhead* environment, in version *13.1* [21]. Sample resources usage for the *xa6slx4csg225-2* circuit from *Spartan6* family of *XILINX* [22] is listed in Table 3.

Resource	Utilization	Available	Utilization
Register	18	4800	1%
LUT	18	2400	1%
Slice	6	600	1%
IO	27	132	20%
Global Clock Buffer	1	16	6%

Table 3. Resources usage

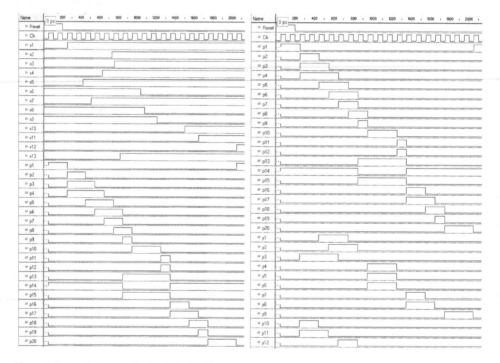

Figure 16. Simulation results in *Active-HDL*

It is also possible to transform logical model into synthesizable code in Verilog language [9, 17], this aspect is however not discussed further in this chapter.

5. Summary and conclusions

Proposed novel approach to verification of reconfigurable logic controller programs and specification by means of Control Interpreted Petri Nets allows to detect even subtle errors on an early stage of system development. Rule-based representation of Control Interpreted Petri Nets in temporal logic is presented at RTL-level and is easy to formally verify using model checking technique and to synthesize using hardware description languages.

Results of the work include the assurance that verified behavioural specification in temporal logic will be an abstract program of matrix reconfigurable logic controller. Hence, logic controller program (its implementation) will be valid according to its primary specification. This may shorten the duration time of logic controllers development process (as early discovered errors are faster corrected) and, consequently, save money (as project budgets will not be exceeded).

Furthermore, formal verification can improve the quality of final products, making them work more reliable. And even if a logic controller, already delivered to customer, will not work properly (it can always happen that some subtle error was overseen or that the specification was incomplete), it is possible to find error source using available techniques (verification, simulation, etc.). Then, some part of corrected system (or the whole system) may be one more time formally verified using extended requirements list and modified logical model.

Future research directions include i.e. (but are not limited to) model checking of other forms of logic controllers specification and mechanisms for behavioural properties specification.

Author details

Iwona Grobelna
University of Zielona Góra, Poland

6. Acknowledgement

The author is a scholar within Sub-measure 8.2.2 Regional Innovation Strategies, Measure 8.2 Transfer of knowledge, Priority VIII Regional human resources for the economy Human Capital Operational Programme co-financed by European Social Fund and state budget.

7. References

[1] Adamski, M & Monteiro, J. L., From Interpreted Petri net specification to Reprogrammable Logic Controller Design, In: *Proceedings of the IEEE International Symposium on Industrial Electronics*, 2000, Vol. 1, pp. 13 – 19.

[2] Adamski, M.A.; Karatkevich, A. & Węgrzyn, M.. *Design of embedded control systems*, Springer Verlag ; 2005.

[3] Adamski, M.; Kołopieńczyk, M. & Mielcarek, K.. Perfect Petri Net in parallel control circuits (in Polish), *Measurement Automation and Monitoring*, 2011, Vol. 57, No. 6, pp. 656 – 660.

[4] Aldec home page. The producer of Active-HLD environment. http://www.aldec.com/ (access 15.04.2012)

[5] Andreu, D.; Souquet, G. & Gil, T.. Petri Net based rapid prototyping of digital complex system, *IEEE Computer Society Annual Symposium on VLSI 2008*, pp. 405 – 410.

[6] Ben-Ari, M., *Mathematical logic for computer science*, Springer Verlag ; 2001.

[7] Clarke, E.M.; Grumberg, O. &Peled, D.A., Model checking, The MIT Press ; 1999.

[8] David, R. & Alla, H., *Discrete, Continuous, and Hybrid Petri Nets*, Springer Verlag ; 2010.

[9] De Micheli, G., *Synthesis and Optimization of Digital Circuits*, McGraw-Hill Higher Education; 1994.

[10] Emerson, E.A., The Beginning of Model Checking: A Personal Perspective, In: *25 Years of Model Checking: History, Achievements, Perspectives*, O. Grumberg, H. Veith (Ed.), Springer Verlag ; 2008, pp. 27 – 45.

[11] Fernandes, J.M. ; Adamski, M. & Proenca, A.J., VHDL generation from hierarchical Petri net specifications of parallel controllers, *IEE Proceedings – Computers and Digital Techniques*, 1997, Vol. 144, No. 2, pp. 127 – 137.

[12] Fix, L., Fifteen years of formal property verification in Intel, In: O. Grumberg, H. Veith (Ed.), *25 Years of Model Checking: History, Achievements, Perspectives*, Springer Verlag ; 2008, pp. 139 – 144.

[13] Grobelna, I., Formal verification of embedded logic controller specification with computer deduction in temporal logic, Electrical Review, 2011, nr 12a, 2011, pp. 47 – 50.

[14] Grobelna, I. & Adamski, M., Model Checking of Control Interpreted Petri Nets, *Proceedings of the 18th International Conference Mixed Design of Integrated Circuits and Systems 2011*, pp. 621 – 626 (available in IEEE Xplore).

[15] Huth, M. & Ryan, M., *Logic in Computer Science. Modelling and Reasoning about Systems*, Cambridge University Press ; 2004.

[16] Kropf, T., *Introduction to Formal Hardware Verification*, Springer Verlag ; 1999.

[17] Minns, P. & Elliott, I., *FSM based Digital Design using Verilog HDL*, Wiley ; 2008.

[18] Nemec, J., Stoke the fires of FPGA design, *Electronic design*, 1994, Vol. 42, Issue 22, pp. 97 – 105.

[19] NuSMV model checker homepage: http://nusmv.fbk.eu/ (access 15.04.2012)

[20] Rice, M.V. & Vardi, M.Y., *Branching vs. Linear Time: Final Showdown*, Proceedings of the 2001 Conference on Tools and Algorithms for the Construction and Analysis of Systems, Lecture Notes in Computer Science, Vol. 2031, Springer Verlag; 2001, pp. 1 – 22.

[21] Xilinx homepage. The producer of XILINX ISE and XILINX PlanAhead software. http://www.xilinx.com (access 15.04.2012)

[22] Xilinx FPGA Spartan6 family home page. http://www.xilinx.com/products/silicon-devices/fpga/spartan-6/index.htm(access 15.04.2012)

[23] Zwoliński, M., *Digital System Design with VHDL*, Prentice Hall; 2004.

Chapter 8

Construction and Application of Learning Petri Net

Liangbing Feng, Masanao Obayashi,
Takashi Kuremoto and Kunikazu Kobayashi

Additional information is available at the end of the chapter

1. Introduction

Petri nets are excellent networks which have great characteristics of combining a well-defined mathematical theory with a graphical representation of the dynamic behavior of systems. The theoretical aspect of Petri nets allows precise modeling and analysis of system behavior, at the same time, the graphical representation of Petri nets enable visualization of state changes of the modeled system [32]. Therefore, Petri nets are recognized as one of the most adequate and sound tool for description and analysis of concurrent, asynchronous and distributed dynamical system. However, the traditional Petri nets do not have learning capability. Therefore, all the parameters which describe the characteristics of the system need to be set individually and empirically when the dynamic system is modeled. Fuzzy Petri net (FPN) combined Petri nets approach with fuzzy theory is a powerful modeling tool for fuzzy production rules-based knowledge systems. However, it is lack of learning mechanism. That is the significant weakness while modeling uncertain knowledge systems.

At the same time, intelligent computing is taken to achieve the development and application of artificial intelligence (AI) methods, i.e. tools that exhibit characteristics associated with intelligence in human behaviour. Reinforcement Learning (RL) and artificial neural networks have been widely used in pattern recognition, decision making, data clustering, and so on. Thus, if intelligent computing methods are introduced into Petri nets, this may make Petri nets have the learning capability, and also performance and the applicable areas of Petri nets models will be widely expanded. The dynamic system can be modeled by Petri nets with the learning capability and then the parameters of the system can be adjusted by online (data-driven) learning. At the same way, if the generalized FPNs are expanded by adding neural networks and their leaning capability, then FPNs are able to realize self-adapting and self-learning functions. Consequently, it achieves automatic knowledge reasoning and fuzzy production rules learning.

Recently, there are some researches for making the Petri net have learning capability and making it optimize itself. The global variables are used to record all state of colored Petri net when it is running [22]. The global variables are optimized and colored Petri net is updated according to these global variables. A learning Petri net model which combines Petri net with a neural network is proposed by Hirasawa et al., and it was applied to nonlinear system control [10]. In our former work [5, 6], a learning Petri net model has been proposed based on reinforcement learning (RL). RL is applied to optimize the parameters of Petri net. And, this learning Petri net model has been applied to robot system control. Konar gave an algorithm to adjust thresholds of a FPN through training instances [1]. In [1], the FPN architecture is built on the connectionism, just like a neural network, and the model provides semantic justification of its hidden layer. It is capable of approximate reasoning and learning from noisy training instances. A generalized FPN model was proposed by Pedrycz et al., which can be transformed into neural networks with OR/AND logic neuron, thus, parameters of the corresponding neural networks can be learned (trained) [24]. Victor and Shen have developed a reinforcement learning algorithm for the high-level fuzzy Petri net models [23].

This chapter focuses on combining the Petri net and fuzzy Petri net with intelligent learning method for construction of learning Petri net and learning fuzzy Petri net (LFPN), respectively. These are applied to dynamic system controls and a system optimization. The rest of this paper is organized as follow. Section 2 elaborates on the Learning Petri net construction and Learning algorithm. Section 3 describes how to use the Learning Petri net model in the robots systems. Section 4 constructs a LFPN. Section 5 shows the LFPN is used in Web service discovery problem. Section 6 summarizes the models of Petri net described in the chapter and results of their applications and demonstrates the future trends concerned with Learning Petri nets.

2. The learning Petri net model

The Learning Petri net (LPN) model is constructed based on high-level time Petri net (HLTPN). The definition of HLTPN is given firstly.

2.1. Definition of HLTPN

HLTPN is one of expanded Petri nets.

Definition 1: HLTPN has a 5-tuple structure, $HLTPN= (NG, C, W, DT, M_0)$ [9], where

i. $NG= (P, Tr, F)$ is called "net graph" with P which called "Places". P is a finite set of nodes. $ID: P \rightarrow N$ is a function marking P, $N = (1, 2, \ldots)$ is the set of natural number. p_1, $p_2, \ldots, p_n$ represents the elements of P and n is the cardinality of set P;

Tr is a finite set of nodes, called "Transitions", which disjoints from P, $P \cap Tr = \varnothing$; $ID: Tr \rightarrow N$ is a function marking Tr. tr_1, tr_2, ..., tr_m represents the elements of Tr, m is the cardinality of set Tr;

$F \subseteq (P \times Tr) \cup (Tr \times P)$ is a finite set of directional arcs, known as the flow relation;

ii. C is a finite and non-empty color set for describing different type of data;

iii. $W: F \rightarrow C$ is a weight function on F. If $F \subseteq (P \times Tr)$, the weight function W is W_{in} that decides which colored Token can go through the arc and enable T fire. This color tokens will be consumed when transition is fired. If $F \subseteq (Tr \times P)$, the weight function W is W_{out} that decides which colored Token will be generated by T and be input to P.

iv. $DT: Tr \rightarrow R$ is a delay time function of a transition which has a *Time* delay for an enable transition fired or the fire of a transition lasting time.

v. $M_0: P \rightarrow U_{p \in P} \mu C(p)$ such that $\forall p \in P$, $M_0(p) \in \mu C(p)$ is the initial marking function which associates a multi-set of tokens of correct type with each place.

2.2. Definition of LPN

In HLTPN, the weight functions of input and output arc for a transition decide the input and output token of a transition. These weight functions express the input-output mapping of transitions. If these weight functions are able to be updated according to the change of system, modeling ability of Petri net will be expanded. The delay time of HLTPN expresses the pre-state lasting time. If the delay time is able to be learnt while system is running, representing ability of Petri net will be enhanced. RL is a learning method interacting with a complex, uncertain environment to achieve an optimal policy for the selection of actions of the learner. RL suits to update dynamic system parameters through interaction with environment [18]. Hence, we consider using the RL to update the weight function and transition's delay time of Petri net for constructing the LPN. In another word, LPN is an expanded HLTPN, in which some transition's input arc weight function and transition delay time have a value item which records the reward from the environment.

Definition 2: LPN has a 3-tuple structure, $LPN = (HLTPN, VW, VT)$, where

i. $HLTPN = (NG, C, W, DT, M_0)$ is a High-Level Time Petri Net and $NG = (P, Tr, F)$.

ii. VW (value of weight function): $W_{in} \rightarrow R$, is a function marking on W_{in}. An arc $F \subseteq (P \times Tr)$ has a set of weight function W_{in} and each W_{in} has a reward value item $VW \in$ real number.

iii. VT (value of delay time): $DT \rightarrow R$, is a function marking on DT. A transition has a set of DT and each DT has a reward value item $VT \in$ real number.

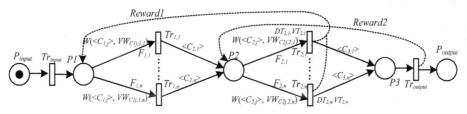

Figure 1. An example of LPN model

An example of LPN model is shown in Figure 1 Using LPN, a mapping of input-output tokens is gotten. For example, in Figure 1, colored tokens C_{ij} ($i=1;j=1, 2, ..., n$) are input to P_1 by Tr_{input}. There are n weight functions $W(<C_{1j}>, VW_{C1j,1,j})$ on a same arc $F_{1,j}$. it is according to the value $VW_{Cij,i,j}$ that token C_{1j} obeys what weight functions in $W(<C_{ij}>, VW_{Cij,i,j})$ to fire a transition. After token C_{1j} passed through arc $F_{i,j}$ ($i=1$; $j=1, 2, ..., n$), one of $Tr_{i,j}$ ($i=1$; $j=1, 2, ..., n$) fires and generates Tokens C_{ij} ($i=2; j=1, 2, ..., n$) in P_2. After P_2 has color Token C_{ij} ($i=2; j=1, 2, ..., n$), $Tr_{i,j}$ ($i=2; j=1, 2, ..., n$) fires and different colored Token C_{ij} ($i=3; j=1, 2, ..., n$) is generated. Then, a mapping of $C_{1j} - C_{3j}$ is gotten. At the same time, a reward will be gotten from environment according to whether it accords with system rule that C_{3j} generated by C_{1j}. These rewards are propagated to every $VW_{Cij,i,j}$ and adjust the $VW_{Cij,i,j}$. After training, the LPN is able to express a correct mapping of input-output tokens.

Using LPN to model a dynamic system, the system state is modeled as Petri net marking which is marked for a set of colored token in all places of Petri net, and the change of the system state (i.e. the system action) is modeled as fired of transitions. Some parameters of system can be expressed as token number and color, arc weight function, transition delay time, and so on. For example, different system signals are expressed as different colored of token. When the system is modeled, some parameters are unknown or uncertain. So, these parameters are set randomly. When system runs, the system parameters are gotten gradually and appropriately through system acting with environment and the effect of RL.

2.3. Learning algorithm for LPN

In LPN, there are two kinds of parameters. One is discrete parameter — the arc's weight function which describes the input and output colored tokens for transition. The other is continuous parameter — the delay time for the transition firing. Now, we will discuss two kinds of parameters which are learnt using RL.

2.3.1. Discrete parameter learning

In LPN, RL is used to adjust VW and VT through interacting with environment. RL could learn the optimal policy of the dynamic system through environment state observation and improvement of its behavior through trial and error with the environment. RL agent senses the environment and takes actions. It receives numeric award and punishments from some reward function. The agent learns to choose actions to maximize a long term sum or average of the future reward it will receive.

The arc weight function learning algorithm is based on Q-learning – a kind of RL [18]. In arc weight function learning algorithm, $VW_{Cij,i,j}$ is randomly set firstly. So, the weight function on the arc is arbitrary. When the system runs, formula (1) is used to update $VW_{Cij,i,j}$.

$$VW_{Cij,i,j} = VW_{Cij,i,jj} + \alpha[r + \gamma(\overline{VW_{ci+1j,i+1,j}}) - VW_{Cij,i,j}] \tag{1}$$

where,

i. $\acute{a}$ is the step-size, is a discount rate.

ii. r is reward which $W(<C_{ij}>, VW_{Cij,i,j})$ gets when $Tr_{i,j}$ is fired by $<C_{ij}>$. Here, because environment gives system reward at only last step, so a feedback learning method is used. If $W(<C_{ij}>, VW_{Cij,i,j})$ through $Tr_{i,j}$ generates Token $<C_{i+1,j}>$ and $W(<C_{i+1,j}>, VW_{Ci+1j,i+1,j})$ through $Tr_{i+1,j}$ generates Token $<C_{i+2,j}>$, $VW_{Ci+1j,i+1,j}$ gets an update value, and this value is feedback as $W(<C_{ij}>, VW_{Cij,i,j})$ next time reward r.

iii. $(\overline{VW_{ci+1j,i+1,j}})$ is calculated from feedback value of all $W(<C_{i+1,j}>, VW_{Ci+1j,i+1,j})$ as formula (2).

$$(\overline{VW_{ci+1j,i+1,j}}) \models \gamma(\overline{VW_{ci+1j,i+1,j}})_{t-1} + r_t \tag{2}$$

where t is time for that $<C_{i+1,j}>$ is generated by $W(<C_{ij}>, VW_{Cij,i,j})$.

When every weight function of input arc of the transition has gotten the value, each transition has a value of its action. The policy of the action selection needs to be considered. The simplest action selection rule is to select the service with the highest estimated state-action value, i.e. the transition corresponding to the maximum $VW_{Cij,i,j}$. This action is called a greedy action. If a greedy action is selected, the learner (agent) exploits the current knowledge. If selecting one of the non-greedy actions instead, agent intends to explore to improve its policy. Exploitation is to do the right thing to maximize the expected reward on the one play; meanwhile exploration may produce the greater total reward in the long run. Here, a method using near-greedy selection rule called ε-greedy method is used in action selection; i.e., the action is randomly selected at a small probability ε and selected the action which has the biggest $VW_{cij,i,j}$ at probability $1-\varepsilon$. Now, we show the algorithm of LPN which is listed in Table 1.

Algorithm 1. Weight function learning algorithm

Step 1. Initialization: Set all VW_{ij} and r of all input arc's weight function to zero.
Step 2. Initialize the learning Petri net. i.e. make the Petri net state as M_0.

Repeat i) and ii) until system becomes end state.

i. When a place gets a colored Token C_{ij}, there is a choice that which arc weight function is obeyed if the functions include this Token. This choice is according to selection policy which is ε greedy (ε is set according to execution environment by user, usually $0<\varepsilon<<1$).
A: Select the function which has the biggest $VW_{cij,i,j}$ at probability $1-\varepsilon$;
B: Select the function randomly at probability ε.

ii. The transition which the function correlates fires and reward is observed. Adjust the weight function value using $VW_{Cij,i,j} = VW_{Cij,i,jj} + \alpha[r + \gamma(\overline{VW_{ci+1j,i+1,j}}) - VW_{Cij,i,j}]$. At the same time, $\alpha[r + \gamma(\overline{VW_{ci+1j,i+1,j}}) - VW_{Cij,i,j}]$ is fed back to the weight function with generated C_{ij} as its reward for next time.

Table 1. Weight function learning algorithm in LPN

2.3.2. Continuous parameter learning

The delay time of transition is a continuous variable. So, the delay time learning is a problem of RL in continuous action spaces. Now, there are several methods of RL in continuous spaces: discretization method, function approximation method, and so on [4]. Here, discretization method and function approximation method are used in the delay time learning in LPN.

Discretization method

As shown in Figure 2 (i), the transition tr_1 has a delay time t_1. When p_1 has a token <$token_n$>, the system is at a state that p_1 has a Token. This time transition tr_1 is enabled. Because tr_1 has a delay time t_1, tr_1 doesn't fire immediately. After passing time t_1 and tr_1 fires, the token in p_1 is taken out and this state is terminated. Then, during the delay time of tr_1, the state that p_1 has a token continues.

Because the delay time is a continuous variable, the different delay time is discretized for using RL to optimize the delay time. For example, tr_1 in Figure 2 (i) has an undefined delay time t_1. Tr_1 is discretized into several different transitions which have different delay times (shown in Figure 2 (ii)) and every delay time has a value item Q. After Tr_1 fired at delay time t_{1i}, it gets a reward r immediately or after its subsequence gets rewards. The value of Q is updated by formula (3).

$$Q(P, Tr) \leftarrow Q(P, Tr) + \alpha[r + \gamma Q(P', Tr') - Q(P, Tr)] \tag{3}$$

where, $Q(P, Tr)$ is value of transition Tr at Petri net state P. $Q(P', Tr')$ is value of transition T' at next state P' of P. α is a step-size, γ is a discount rate.

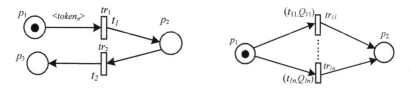

(i) The high-level time Petri net model   (ii) The discretization learning model for the delay time

Figure 2. Transformation form from high-level Petri net to the learning model

After renewing of Q, the optimal delay time will be selected. In Figure 2 (ii), when $tr_{11}, \ldots, tr_{1n}$ get value $Q_{11}, \ldots, Q_{1n}$, respectively, the transition is selected by the soft-max method according to a probability of Gibbs distribution.

$$\Pr\{t_i = t \mid p_i = p\} = \frac{e^{\beta Q(p, t)}}{\sum_{b \in A} e^{\beta Q(p, b)}} \tag{4}$$

where, $\Pr\{t_i = t \mid p_i = p\}$ is a probability selecting of transition t at state p, $\hat{a}$ is a positive inverse temperature constant and A is a set of available transitions.

Now, we found the learning algorithm of delay time of LPN using the discretization method. And it is listed in Table 2.

Transition's delay time learning algorithm 1 (Discretization method):
Step 1. Initialization: discretize the delay time and set $Q(p,t)$ of every transition's delay time to zero.
Step 2. Initialize Petri net, i.e. make the Petri net state as P_1.
Repeat (i) and (ii) until system becomes end state.
i. Select a transition using formula (4).
ii. After transition fired and reward is observed, value of $Q(p,t)$ is adjusted using formula (3).
Step 3. Step 3. Repeat Step2 until t is optimal as required.

Table 2. Delay time learning algorithm using the discretization method

Function approximation method

First, the transition delay time is selected randomly and executed. The value of the delay time is obtained using formula (3). When the system is executed m times, the data $(t_i, Q_i(p,t_i))$ $(i = 1, 2, ..., m)$ is yielded. The relation of value of delay time Q and delay time t is supposed as $Q = F(t)$. Using the least squares method, $F(t)$ will be obtained as follows. It is supposed that F is a function class which is constituted by a polynomial. And it is supposed that formula (5) hold.

$$f(t) = \sum_{k=0}^{n} a_k t^k \in F \tag{5}$$

The data $(t_i, Q_i(p,t_i))$ are substituted in formula (5). Then:

$$f(t_i) = \sum_{k=0}^{n} a_k t_i^k \ (i = 1, 2, ..., m ; m \geq n) \tag{6}$$

Here, the degree m of data $(t_i, Q_i(p,t_i))$ is not less than data number n of formula (5). According to the least squares method, we have (2.7).

$$||\delta||^2 = \sum_{i=1}^{m} \delta_i^2 = \sum_{i=1}^{m}[\sum_{k=0}^{n} a_k t_i^k - Q_i]^2 \Rightarrow \min \tag{7}$$

In fact, (7) is a problem which evaluates the minimum solution of function (8).

$$||\delta||^2 = \sum_{i=1}^{m}[\sum_{k=0}^{n} a_k t_i^k - Q_i]^2 \tag{8}$$

So, function (9), (10) are gotten from (8).

$$\frac{\partial ||\delta||^2}{\partial a_j} = 2\sum_{i=1}^{m}\sum_{k=0}^{n}(a_k t_i^k - Q_i)t_i^j = 0 \ \ (j = 0, 1, ..., n) \tag{9}$$

$$\sum_{i=1}^{m} \left(\sum_{k=0}^{n} t_i^{j+k} \right) a_k = \sum_{i=1}^{m} t_i^j Q_i \quad (j = 0, 1, \ldots, n). \tag{10}$$

Solution of Equation (10) a_0, a_1, ..., a_n can be deduced and $Q = f(t)$ is attained. The solution t^*_{opt} of $Q = f(t)$ which makes maximum Q is the expected optimal delay time.

$$\frac{\partial f(t)}{\partial t} = 0 \tag{11}$$

The multi-solution of (11) $t = t_{opt}$ ($opt = 1, 2, \ldots, n-1$) is checked by function (5) and a $t^*_{opt} \in t_{opt}$ which makes $f(t^*_{opt}) = \max f(t_{opt})$ ($opt = 1, 2, \ldots, n-1$) is the expected optimal delay time. t^*_{opt} is used as delay time and the system is executed and new $Q(p, t^*_{opt})$ is gotten. This (t^*_{opt}, $Q(p, t^*_{opt})$) is used as the new and the least squares method can be used again to acquire more precise delay time.

After the values of actions are gotten, the soft-max method is selected as the actions selection policy. And then, we found the learning algorithm of delay time of Learning Petri net using the function approximation method. And it is listed in Table 3.

Transition's delay time learning algorithm 2 (Function approximation method):
Step 1.   Step 1. Initialization: Set $Q(p, t)$ of every transition's delay time to zero.
Step 2.   Step 2. Initialize Petri net, i.e. make the Petri net state as P_1.
Repeat (i) and (ii) until system becomes end state.
i.   Randomly select the transition delay time t.
ii.   After transition fires and reward is observed, the value of $Q(p, t)$ is adjusted using formula (3).
Step 3.   Step 3. Repeat Step 2 until adequacy data are gotten. Then, evaluate the optimal t using the function approximation method.

Table 3. Delay time learning algorithm using the function approximation method

3. Applying LPN to robotic system control

3.1. Application for discrete event dynamic robotic system control

A discrete event dynamic system is a discrete-state, event-driven system in which the state evolution depends entirely on the occurrence of asynchronous discrete events over time [2]. Petri nets have been used to model various kinds of dynamic event-driven systems like computers networks, communication systems, and so on. In this Section, it is used to model Sony AIBO learning control system for the purpose of certification of the effectiveness of the proposed LPN.

AIBO voice command recognition system

AIBO (Artificial Intelligence roBOt) is a type of robotic pets designed and manufactured by Sony Co., Inc. AIBO is able to execute different actions, such as go ahead, move back, sit down, stand up and cry, and so on. And it can "listens" voice via microphone. A command

and control system will be constructed for making AIBO understand several human voice commands by Japanese and English and take corresponding action. The simulation system is developed on Sony AIBO's OPEN-R (Open Architecture for Entertainment Robot) [19]. The architecture of the simulation system is showed in Figure 3. Because there are English and Japanese voice commands for same AIBO action, the partnerships of voice and action are established in part (4). The lasted time of an AIBO action is learning in part (5). After an AIBO action finished, the rewards for correctness of action and action lasted time are given by the touch of different AIBO's sensors.

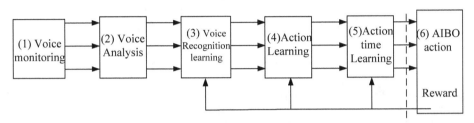

Figure 3. System architecture of voice command recognition

LPN model for AIBO voice command recognition system

In the LPN model for AIBO voice command recognition system, AIBO action change, action time are modeled as transition, transition delay, respectively. The human voice command is modeled by the different color Token. The LPN model is showed in Figure 4. The meaning of every transition is listed below: Tr_{input} changes voice signal as colored Token which describe the voice characteristic. Tr_{11}, Tr_{12} and Tr_{13} can analyze the voice signal. Tr_1 generates 35 different Token $VL_1....VL_{35}$ according to the voice length. Tr_2 generates 8 different Token $E2_1...E2_8$ according to the front twenty voice sample energy characteristic. Tr_3 generates 8 different Token $E4_1...E4_8$ according to the front forty voice sample energy characteristic [8]. These three types of the token are compounded into a compound Token $<VL_i> + <VE2_m> + <VE4_n>$ in p_2 [12].

Tr_{2j} generates the different voice Token. The input arc's weight function is $((<VL_i>+<VE2_m>+ <VE4_n>), VW_{Vlmn,2j})$ and the output arc's weight function is different voice Token. And voice Token will generate different action Token through Tr_{3j}. When $Pr_4 - Pr_8$ has Token, AIBO's action will last. Tr_{4j} takes Token out from $p_4 - p_8$, and makes corresponding AIBO action terminates. Tr_{4j} has a delay time DT_{4i}, and every DT_{4i} has a value VT_{4i}. Transition adopts which delay time DT_{4i} according to VT_{4i}.

Results of simulation

When the system begins running, it can't recognize the voice commands. A voice command comes and it is changed into a compound Token in p_2. This compound Token will randomly generate a voice Token and puts into p_3. This voice Token randomly arouses an action Token. A reward for action correctness is gotten, then, VW and VT are updated. For example, a compound colored Token $(<VL_i>+ <VE2_m> + <VE4_n>)$ fired Tr_{21} and colored Token

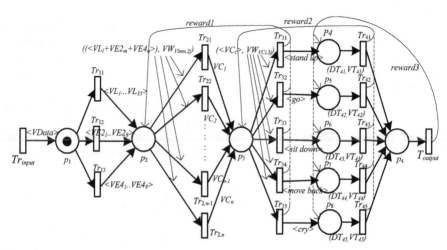

Figure 4. LPN model of voice command recognition

VC_1 is put into p_3. VC_1 fires T_{32} and AIBO acts "go". A reward is gotten according to correctness of action. $VW_{VC1,32}$ is updated by this reward and $VW_{VC1,32}$ updated value is fed back to p_2 as next time reward value of $(<VL_i>+ <VE_{2m}> + <VE_{4n}>)$ fired Tr_{21}. After an action finished, a reward for correctness of action time is gotten and VT is updated.

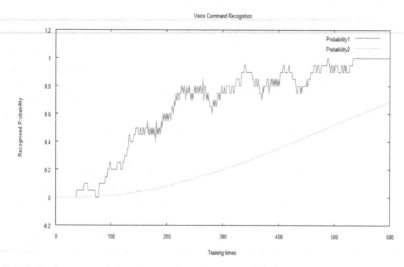

Figure 5. Relation between training times and recognition probability

Figure 5 shows the relation between training times and voice command recognition probability. Probability 1 shows the successful probability of recently 20 times training. Probability 2 shows the successful probability of total training times. From the result of simulation, we confirmed that LPN is correct and effective using the AIBO voice command control system.

3.2. Application for continuous parameter optimization

The proposed system is applied to guide dog robot system which uses RFID (Radio-frequency identification) to construct experiment environment. The RFID is used as navigation equipment for robot motion. The performance of the proposed system is evaluated through computer simulation and real robot experiment.

RFID environment construction

RFID tags are used to construct a blind road which showed in Figure 6. There are forthright roads, corners and traffic light signal areas. The forthright roads have two group tags which have two lines RFID tags. Every tag is stored with the information about the road. The guide dog robot moves, turns or stops on the road according to the information of tags. For example, if the guide dog robot reads corner RFID tag, then it will turn on the corner. If the guide dog robot reads either outer or inner side RFID tags, it implies that the robot will deviate from the path and robot motion direction needs adjusting. If the guide dog robot reads traffic control RFID tags, then it will stop or run unceasingly according to the traffic light signal which is dynamically written to RFID.

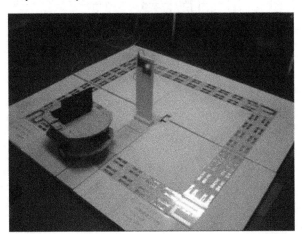

Figure 6. The real experimental environment

LPN model for the guide dog

The extended LPN control model for guide dog robot system is presented in Figure 7. The meaning of place and transition in Figure 7 is listed below:

P1 System starting state	P2 Getting RFID information
P3 Turning corner state	P4 Left adjusting state
P5 Right adjusting state	Tr1 Reading of the RFID environment
Tr2 Stop of the guide dog	Tr3 Guide dog runs
Tr4 Start of the turning corner state	Tr5 Start of left adjusting state
Tr6 Start of the right adjusting state	Tr7 Stop of the turning corner state
Tr8 Stop of the left adjusting state	Tr9 Stop of the right adjusting state

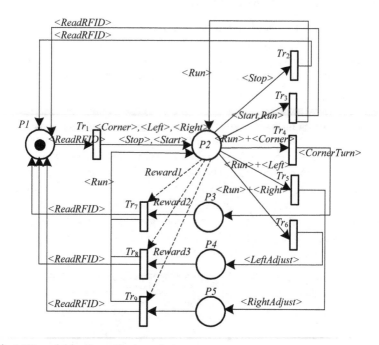

Figure 7. The LPN model for the guide dog robot

When the system begins running, it firstly reads RFID environment and gets the information, Token puts into P_2. These Tokens fire one of transition from Tr_2 to Tr_6 according to weight function on P_2 to Tr_2, ..., Tr_6. Then, the guide dog enters stop, running, turning corner, left adjusting or right adjusting states. Here, at P_3, P_4, P_5 states, the guide dog turns at a specific speed. The delay time of Tr_7-Tr_9 decide the correction of guide dog adjusting its motion direction.

Reward getting from environment

When Tr_7, Tr_8 or Tr_9 fires, it will get reward r as formula (12-b) when the guide dog doesn't get Token <Left> and <Right> until getting Token <corner> i.e. the robot runs according correct direction until arriving corner. It will get reward r as formula (12-a), where t is time from transition fire to get Token <Left> and <Right>. On the contrary, it will get punishment -1 as (12-c) if robot runs out the road.

$$r = \begin{cases} 1/e^t & \text{(a)} \\ 1 & \text{(b)} \\ -1 & \text{(c)} \end{cases} \qquad (12)$$

Computer simulation and real robot experiment

When robot reads the <Left>, <Right> and <corner> information, it must adjust the direction of the motion. The amount of adjusting is decided by the continuing time of the robot at the state of P_3, P_4 and P_5. So, the delay time of Tr_7, Tr_8 and Tr_9 need to learn.

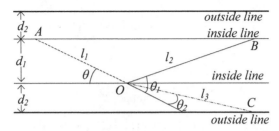

(i) Direction adjustment of the robot motion on the forthright road

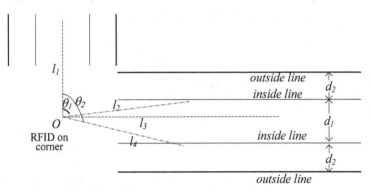

(ii) Direction adjustment of the robot motion at the corner

Figure 8. Direction adjustment of the guide dog robot motion

Before the simulation, some robot motion parameter symbols are given as:

v velocity of the robot
ω angular velocity of the robot
t_{pre} continuous time of the former state
    t adjusting time
    t_{post} last time of the state after adjusting

v, ω, t_{pre}, t_{post} can be measured by system when the robot is running. The delay time of Tr_7, Tr_8 and Tr_9, i.e. the robot motion adjusting time, is simulated in two cases.

1.   As shown in Figure 8 (i), when the robot is running on the forthright road and meets inside RFID line, its deviation angle θ is:

$$\theta = \arcsin(d_1/l_1) = \arcsin(d_1/(t_{pre} \bullet v)). \tag{13}$$

where d_1 and l_1 are width of area between two inside lines and moving distance between two times reading of the RFID, respectively (See Figure 8).

Robot's adjusting time (transition delay time) is t.

If $\omega t - \theta \geq 0$, then

$$t_{post} = \frac{d_1}{v\sin(\omega t - \theta)}, \tag{14}$$

else

$$t_{post} = \frac{d_2}{v\sin(\omega t - \theta)}. \tag{15}$$

Here, t_{post} is used to calculate reward r using formula (12). In the same way, the reward r can be calculated when the robot meets outside RFID line.

When the robot is running on the forthright road and meets the outside RFID line, the deviation angle θ is

$$\theta = \arcsin(d_2/(v \bullet t_{pre})), \tag{16}$$

Robot's adjusting time (transition delay time) is t.

If $\omega t - \theta \geq 0$, then

$$t_{post} = \frac{d_2}{v\sin(\omega t - \theta)}, \tag{17}$$

else the robot will runs out the road. And the reward r is calculated using formula (12).

2. As shown in Figure 8 (ii), when the robot is running at the corner, it must adjust $\theta = 90°$. If $\theta \neq 90°$, the robot will read <Left>, <Right> after it turns corner. Now, the case which the robot will read inner line <Left>, <Right> will be considered. If robot's adjusting time is t. If $\omega t - \theta \geq 0$, then

$$t_{post} = \frac{d_1}{2v\sin(\omega t - \theta)}, \tag{18}$$

else

$$t_{post} = \frac{d_2}{2v\sin(\omega t - \theta)} \tag{19}$$

Same to case (1), t_{post} is used to calculate reward r using formula (12). In the same way, the reward r can calculate when the robot meets outside RFID line. The calculation of reward, which is calculated from t, for other cases of direction adjustment of the robot is considered as the above two cases.

In this simulation, the value of the delay time has only a maximum at optimal delay time point. The graph of relation for the delay time and its value is parabola. So, when transition's delay time learning by function approximation method which states in section 2.2.3, the relation of the delay time and its value is assumed as:

$$Q = a_2 t^2 + a_1 t + a_0 . \tag{20}$$

Computer simulations of Transition's delay time learning algorithms were executed in the all cases of the robot direction adjusting. In the simulation of algorithm of discretization, the positive inverse temperature constant β is set as 10.0. After the delay time of different cases was learnt, it is recorded in a delay time table. Then, the real robot experiment was carried out using the delay time table which was obtained by simulation process.

Result of simulation and experiment

The simulation result of transition's delay time learning algorithm in two cases is shown in Figure 9.

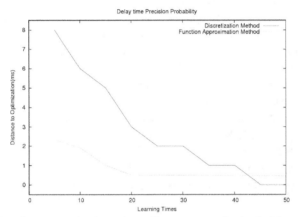

(i) Simulation result of moving adjustment on the forthright road

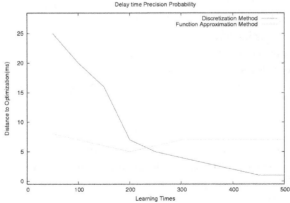

(ii) Simulation result of moving adjustment at the corner

Figure 9. Result of simulation for the guide dog robot

The simulation result of $\theta=5°$ for the robot moving adjustment on forthright road is shown in Figure 9 (i). The simulation result of robot moving adjustment at the corner is shown in Figure 9 (ii). From the result, it is found that the function approximation method can quickly approach optimal delay time than the discretization method, but the discretization method can approach more near optimal delay time through long time learning.

4. Construction of the learning fuzzy Petri net model

Petri net (PN) has ability to represent and analyze concurrency and synchronization phenomena in an easy way. PN approach can also be easily combined with other techniques and theories such as object-oriented programming, fuzzy theory, neural networks, etc. These modified PNs are widely used in the fields of manufacturing, robotics, knowledge based systems, process control, as well as other kinds of engineering applications [15]. Fuzzy Petri net (FPN), which combines PN and fuzzy theory, has been used for knowledge representation and reasoning in the presence of inexact data and knowledge based systems. But traditional FPN lacks of learning mechanism, it is the main weakness while modeling uncertain knowledge systems [25]. In this section, we propose a new learning model tool — learning fuzzy Petri net (LFPN) [7]. Contrasting with the existing FPN, there are three extensions in the new model: 1) the place can possess different tokens which represent different propositions; 2) these propositions have different degrees of truth toward different transitions; 3) the truth degree of proposition can be learned through the arc's weight function adjusting. The LFPN model obtains the capability of fuzzy production rules learning through truth degree updating. The artificial neural network is gotten learning ability through weight adjusting. The LFPN learning algorithm which introduces network learning method into Petri net update is proposed and the convergence of algorithm is analyzed.

4.1. The learning fuzzy Petri net model

Petri net is a directed, weighted, bipartite graph consisting of two kinds of nodes, called places and transitions, where arcs are either from a place to a transition or from a transition to a place. Tokens exist at different places. The use of the standard Petri net is inappropriate in situations where systems are difficult to be described precisely. Consequently, fuzzy Petri net is designed to deal with these situations where transitions, places, tokens or arcs are fuzzified.

The definition of fuzzy Petri net

A fuzzy place associates with a predicate or property. A token in the fuzzy place is characterized by a predicate or property belongs to the place, and this predicate or property has a level of belonging to the place. In this way, we may get a fuzzy proposition or conclusion, for example, *speed is low*. A fuzzy transition may correspond to an *if-then* fuzzy production rule for instance and is realized by truth values such as fuzzy inference algorithms [11, 20, 26].

Definition1 *FPN* is a 8-tuple, given by *FPN=<P, Tr, F, D, I, O, α, β* >

where:

$P = \{p_1, p_2, \ldots, p_n\}$ is a finite set of places;
$Tr = \{tr_1, tr_2, \ldots, tr_m\}$ is a finite set of transitions;
$F \subseteq (P \times Tr) \cup (Tr \times P)$ is a finite set of directional arcs;
$D = \{d_1, d_2, \ldots, d_n\}$ is a finite set of propositions, where proposition d_i corresponds to place p_i;
$P \cap Tr \cap D = \emptyset$; cardinality of (P) = cardinality of (D);
$I: tr \rightarrow P^\infty$ is the input function, representing a mapping from transitions to bags of (their input) places, noting as $*tr$;
$O: tr \rightarrow P^\infty$ is the output function, representing a mapping from transitions to bags of (their output) places, noting as $tr*$;
$\alpha: P \rightarrow [0, 1]$ and $\beta: P \rightarrow D$. A token value in place $p_i \in P$ is denoted by $\alpha(p_i) \in [0, 1]$. If $\alpha(p_i)=y_i$, $y_i \in [0, 1]$ and $\beta(p_i)= d_i$,, then this states that the degree of truth of proposition d_i is y_i.

A transition tr_k is enabled if for all $p_i \in I(tr_k)$, $\alpha(p_i) \geq th$, where th is a threshold value in the unit interval. If this transition is fired, then tokens are moved from their input place and tokens are deposited to each of its output places. The truth values of the output tokens are $y_i \bullet u_k$, where u_k is the confidence level value of tr_k. FPN has capability of modeling fuzzy production rules. For example, the fuzzy production rule (21) can be modeled as shown in Figure 10.

$$\text{IF } d_i \text{ THEN } d_j \text{ (with Certainty Factor (CF) } u_k) \tag{21}$$

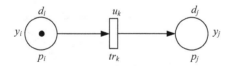

Figure 10. A fuzzy Petri net model (FPN)

The definition of LFPN

In a FPN, a token in a place represents a proposition and a proposition has a degree of truth. Now, three aspects of extension are done at the FPN and learning fuzzy Petri net (LFPN) is constructed. First, a place may have different tokens (Tokens are distinguished with numbers or colors) and the different tokens represent different propositions, i.e. a place has a set of propositions. Second, a place has a special token, i.e. there is a specified proposition. This proposition may have different degrees of truth toward different transitions tr which regard this place as input place $*tr$. Third, the weight of each arc is adjustable and used to record transition's input and output information.

Definition 3 *LFPN* is a 10-tuple, given by *LFPN= <P, Tr, F, D, I, O, Th, W, α, β>* (A LFPN model is shown in Figure 11).

where: *Tr, F, I, O* are same with definition of FPN.

$P=\{p_1, p_2,..., p_i,..., p_n,..., p'_1, p'_2,..., p'_i,..., p'_r\}$ is a finite set of places, where p_i is input place and p'_i is output places.

$D = \{d_{11}, ... , d_{1N}; d_{21}, ..., d_{2N}; ..., d_{ij}, ...; d_{n1}, ... , d_{nN}; d'_{11}, ... , d'_{1N}; d'_{21}, ..., d'_{2N}; ..., d'_{ij}, ...; d'_{n1}, ... , d'_{rN}\}$ is a finite set of propositions, where proposition d_{ij} is j-th proposition for input place p_i and proposition d'_{ij} is j-th proposition for output place p'_i.

$W =\{w_{11}, w_{12}, ..., w_{1k}, ..., w_{1m}; ...; w_{i1}, w_{i2}, ..., w_{ik}, ..., w_{im}; ... ; w_{n1}, w_{n2}, ..., w_{nm}; w'_{11}, w'_{12}, ..., w'_{1r}; ...; w'_{k1}, w'_{k2}, ..., w'_{kj} ’ ..., w'_{kr}; ... ; w'_{m1}, w'_{m2}, ..., w'_{mr}\}$ is the set of weights on the arcs, where w_{ik} is a weight from i-th input place to k-th transition and w'_{kj} is a weight from k-th transition to j-th output place.

$W =\{w_{11}, w_{12}, ..., w_{1k}, ..., w_{1m}; ...; w_{i1}, w_{i2}, ..., w_{ik}, ..., w_{im}; ... ; w_{n1}, w_{n2}, ..., w_{nm}; w'_{11}, w'_{12}, ..., w'_{1r}; ...; w'_{k1}, w'_{k2}, ..., w'_{kj} ’ ..., w'_{kr}; ... ; w'_{m1}, w'_{m2}, ..., w'_{mr}\}$ is the set of weights on the arcs, where w_{ik} is a weight from i-th input place to k-th transition and w'_{kj} is a weight from k-th transition to j-th output place.

$\alpha(d_{ij}, tr_k) \to [0, 1]$ and $\beta: P \to D$. When $p_i \in P$ has a special $token_{ij}$ and $\beta(token_{ij}, p_i) = d_{ij}$, the degree of truth of proposition d_{ij} in place p_i toward to transition tr_k is denoted by $\alpha(d_{ij}, tr_k) \in [0, 1]$. When tr_k fires, the probability of proposition d_{ij} in p_i is $\alpha(d_{ij}, tr_k)$.

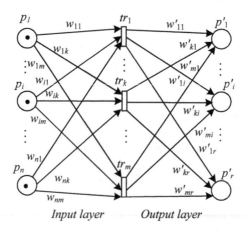

Input layer   **Output layer**

Figure 11. The model of learning fuzzy Petri net (LFPN)

$\alpha(d_{ij}, tr_k) \to [0, 1]$ and $\beta: P \to D$. When $p_i \in P$ has a special $token_{ij}$ and $\beta(token_{ij}, p_i) = d_{ij}$, the degree of truth of proposition d_{ij} in place p_i toward to transition tr_k is denoted by $\alpha(d_{ij}, tr_k) \in [0, 1]$. When tr_k fires, the probability of proposition d_{ij} in p_i is $\alpha(d_{ij}, tr_k)$.

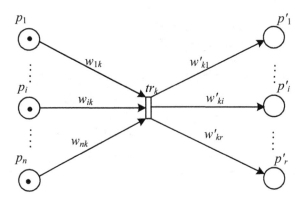

Figure 12. A LFPN model with one transition

$Th = \{th_1, th_2, ..., th_k, ..., th_m\}$ represents a set of threshold values in the interval $[0, 1]$ associated with transitions ($tr_1,\ tr_2, ...,\ tr_k, ...,\ tr_m$), respectively; If all $p_i \in I(tr_k)$ and $\alpha(d_{ij},\ tr_k) \geq th_k$, tr_k is enable.

As showed in Figure 12, when p_i has a $token_{ij}$, there is proposition d_{ij} in p_i. This proposition d_{ij} has different truth to $tr_1, tr_2, ..., tr_k, ..., tr_m$. When a transition tr_k fired, tokens are put into p'_1, ..., p'_r according to weight $w'_{k1}, ..., w'_{kr}$ and each of $p'_1, ..., p'_r$ gets a proposition.

Figure 11 shows a LFPN which has n-input places, m-transitions and r-output places. To explain the truth computing, transition fire rule, token transfer rule and fuzzy production rules expression more clearly, a transition and its relation arcs, places are drawn-out from Figure 11 and shown in Figure 12.

Truth computing As shown in Figure 12, w_{ik} is the perfect value for $token_{ij}$ when tr_k fires. When a set of $tokens= (token_{1j}, token_{2j}, ..., token_{ij}, ..., token_{nj})$ are input to all places of $*tr_k$, $\beta(token_{1j},\ p_1)= d_{1j}, ..., \beta(token_{nj},\ p_n)= d_{nj}$. $\alpha(d_{ij},\ tr_k)$ is computed using the degree of similarity between $token_{ij}$ and w_{ik} and calculation formula is shown in formula (22).

$$\alpha(d_{ij}, tr_k) = 1 - \frac{\left|w_{ik} - token_{ij}\right|}{\max(\left|w_{ik}\right|, \left|token_{ij}\right|)} \tag{22}$$

According to LFPN models for different systems, the token and weight value may have different data types. There are different methods for computing $\alpha(d_{ij},\ tr_k)$ according to data type. If value types of token and weight are real number, $\alpha(d_{ij},\ tr_k)$ is computed as formula (2). In Section 4, $\alpha(d_{ij},\ tr_k)$ will be discussed for a LFPN model which has the textual type token and weight.

Transition fire rule As shown in Figure 12, when a set of $tokens=(token_{1j}, token_{2j}, ..., token_{nj})$ are input to all places of $*tr_k$, and $\beta(token_{1j}, p_1)= d_{1j}, ..., \beta(token_{nj}, p_n)= d_{nj}$. If all $\alpha(d_{ij},\ tr_k)$ ($i=1$, 2, ..., n) $\geq th_k$ is held, tr_k is enabled. Maybe, several transitions are enabled at same time. If formula (23) is held, tr_k is fired.

$$\alpha(d_{1j},tr_k)\cdot\alpha(d_{2j},tr_k)\cdot...\cdot\alpha(d_{nj},tr_k)$$
$$=\max(\alpha(d_{1j},tr_h)\cdot\alpha(d_{2j},tr_h)\cdot...\cdot\alpha(d_{nj},tr_h)_{1\leq h\leq m}) \tag{23}$$

Token transfer rule As shown in Figure 12, after tr_k fired, token will be taken out from $p_1\sim p_n$. The token take rule is:

If $token_{ij} \leq w_{ik}$ is held, $token_{ij}$ in p_i will be taken out.
If $token_{ij} \geq w_{ik}$ is held, $token$ which equates $token_{ij}-w_{ik}$ will be left in p_i.

Thus, after a transition tr_k fired, maybe the enable transitions still exist in LFPN. An enable transition will be selected and fired according to formula (23) until there isn't any enable transition.

After tr_k fired, the token according w'_{ki} will be put into p'_i. For example, if the weight function of arc tr_k to p'_i is w'_{ki}, then $token$ which equates w'_{ki} will be put into p'_i.

Fuzzy production rules expression A LFPN is capable of modeling for fuzzy production rules just as a FPN. For example, as a case which states in **Transition fire rule** and **Token transfer rule**, when tr_k is fired, the below production rule is expressed:

IF d_{1j} AND d_{2j} AND ... AND d_{nj} THEN d'_{1k} AND d'_{2k} AND ... AND d'_{rk}

$$(CF=\alpha\ (d_{1i},\ tr_k\ )\bullet\alpha(d_{2i},\ tr_k\ )\bullet...\bullet\alpha(d_{ni},\ tr_k\ )) \tag{24}$$

The mathematical model of LFPN

In this section, the mathematical model of LFPN will be elaborated. Firstly, some conceptions are defined. When a $token_{ij}$ is input to a place p_i, it is defined event p_{ij} occurs, i.e. the proposition d_{ij} is generated and probability of event p_{ij} is $Pr(p_{ij})$. The fired tr_k is defined as event tr_k and probability of event tr_k occurrence is $Pr(tr_k)$. Secondly, we assume that each transition $tr_1, tr_2, ..., tr_k, ..., tr_m$ has the same fire probability in whole event space, then

$$Pr(tr_k) = \frac{1}{m} \tag{25}$$

And when event tr_k occurs, the conditional probability of p_{ij} occurrence is defined as $Pr(p_{ij} \mid tr_k)$, i.e. $á(d_{ij}, tr_k)$ which is the probability of proposition d_{ij} generation when tr_k fires.

When $p_1, p_2, ..., p_n$ have $token_{1j}, token_{2j}...token_{nj}$ and events $p_{1j}, p_{2j}, ..., p_{nj}$ occur. Then, $Pr(tr_k \mid p_{1j}, p_{2j}, ..., p_{nj})$ is:

$$Pr(tr_k \mid p_{1j},p_{2j},...,p_{nj}) = \frac{Pr(p_{1j},p_{2j},...,p_{nj} \mid tr_k)Pr(tr_k)}{\sum_{h=1}^{m} Pr(tr_h)Pr(p_{1j}p_{2j},...,p_{nj})} \tag{26}$$

When events $p_{1j}, p_{2j}, ..., p_{nj}$ occurred, there is one of transitions $tr_1, tr_2, ..., tr_k, ..., tr_m$ which will be fired, therefore

$$\sum_{h=1}^{m} Pr(tr_h)Pr(p_{1j},p_{2j},...,p_{nj}) = 1 \tag{27}$$

From (25), (26) and (27), (28') is gotten by the formula of full probability and Bayesian formula.

$$Pr(tr_k \mid p_{1j},p_{2j},...,p_{nj}) = \frac{1}{m}Pr(p_{1j},p_{2j},...,p_{nj} \mid tr_k)$$

$$= \frac{1}{m}Pr(p_{1j} \mid tr_k) \times Pr(p_{2j} \mid tr_k) \times ... \times Pr(p_{nj} \mid tr_k) \tag{28'}$$

$$= \frac{1}{m}\alpha(d_{1j},tr_k) \cdot \alpha(d_{2j},tr_k) \cdot ... \cdot \alpha(d_{nj},tr_k) \tag{28}$$

The transformation from (28') to (28) is according to definition of $\alpha(d_{ij}, tr_k)$. As shown in Figure 11, when p_1, p_2 , ..., p_n have $token_{1j}$, $token_{2j}$...$token_{nj}$, the occurring probability of transition tr_1, ..., tr_k, ..., tr_m are $\alpha(d_{1j}, tr_1)$ $\bullet \alpha(d_{2j}, tr_1)$ $\bullet...\bullet\alpha(d_{nj}, tr_1)/m$, ..., $\alpha(d_{1j}, tr_k)$ $\bullet\alpha(d_{2j}, tr_k)$ $\bullet...\bullet\alpha(d_{nj}, tr_k)/m$, ..., $\alpha(d_{1j}, tr_m)$ $\bullet\alpha(d_{2j}, tr_m)$ $\bullet...\bullet\alpha(d_{nj}, tr_m)/m$. Thus, the transition tr_k, which has maximum of $\alpha(d_{1j}, tr_k)$ $\bullet\alpha(d_{2j}, tr_k)$ $\bullet...\bullet\alpha(d_{nj}, tr_k)$, is selected and fired according to formula (23).

4.2. Learning algorithm for learning fuzzy Petri net

Learning algorithm

The learning fuzzy Petri net (LFPN) can be trained and made it learn fuzzy production rules. When a set of data input LFPN, a set of propositions are produced in each input place. For example, when token vectors ($token_{1j}$, $token_{2j}$, ..., $token_{nj}$) (j=1, 2, ..., N) input to $p_1 \sim p_n$, propositions d_{1j}, d_{2j}, ..., d_{nj} (j=1, 2, ..., N) are produced. To train a fuzzy production rule which is IF d_{1j} AND d_{2j} AND ... AND d_{nj} THEN d'_{1k} AND d'_{2k} AND ... AND d'_{nk}, there are two tasks:

1. $\alpha(d_{1j}, tr_k)\bullet\alpha(d_{2j}, tr_k)\bullet...\bullet\alpha(d_{nj}, tr_k)$ ($k\in\{1,2,...m\}$) need to be updated to hold formula (23);
2. 2) The output weight function of tr_k need to be updated for putting correct token to $p'_1 \sim p'_r$. Then, $\beta(p'_1) = d'_{1k}$, $\beta(p'_2) = d'_{2k}$, ..., $\beta(p'_r) = d'_{rk}$.

To accomplish these two tasks, the weights w_{1k}, w_{2k}, ..., w_{nk} and w'_{k1}, w'_{k2}, ..., w'_{kr} are modified by a learning algorithm of LFPN. Firstly, we define the training data set as $\{(X_1, Y_1), (X_2, Y_2), ..., (X_N, Y_N)\}$, where X is input token vector, Y is output token vector and X_j, Y_j is defined as $X_j=(x_{1j}, x_{2j}, ..., x_{nj})^T$, $Y_j=(y_{1j}, y_{2j}, ..., y_{rj})^T$, respectively. Thus,

$X=(X_1, X_2, ..., X_j, ..., X_N,)$, $Y=(Y_1, Y_2, ..., Y_j, ..., Y_N)$, i.e.

$$X=\begin{bmatrix} x_{11} & x_{12} & \cdots & x_{1j} & \cdots & x_{1N} \\ x_{21} & x_{22} & \cdots & x_{2j} & \cdots & x_{2N} \\ \vdots & \vdots & \vdots & \vdots & \vdots & \vdots \\ x_{n1} & x_{n2} & \cdots & x_{nj} & \cdots & x_{nN} \end{bmatrix} \quad Y=\begin{bmatrix} y_{11} & y_{12} & \cdots & y_{1j} & \cdots & y_{1N} \\ y_{21} & y_{22} & \cdots & y_{2j} & \cdots & y_{2N} \\ \vdots & \vdots & \vdots & \vdots & \vdots & \vdots \\ y_{r1} & y_{r2} & \cdots & y_{rj} & \cdots & y_{rN} \end{bmatrix}$$

Secondly, the weight $W_k=(w_{1k}, w_{2k}, \ldots, w_{nk})^T$ is the weight on arcs from $*tr_k$ to tr_k and $W'_k=(w'_{k1}, w'_{k2}, \ldots, w'_{kr})^T$ is the weight on arcs from tr_k to tr_k*. $W_1, \ldots, W_k, \ldots, W_m$ and $W'_1, \ldots, W'_k, \ldots, W'_m$ are the input and output arcs weight for $tr_1, \ldots, tr_k, \ldots, tr_m$. Thus,

$W=(W_1, W_2, \ldots, W_k, \ldots, W_m)$, $W'=(W'_1, W'_2, \ldots, W'_k, \ldots, W'_m)$, i.e.

$$W=\begin{bmatrix} w_{11} & w_{12} & \cdots & w_{1k} & \cdots & w_{1m} \\ w_{21} & w_{22} & \cdots & w_{2k} & \cdots & w_{2m} \\ \vdots & \vdots & \vdots & \vdots & \vdots & \vdots \\ w_{n1} & w_{n2} & \cdots & w_{nk} & \cdots & w_{nm} \end{bmatrix} \quad W'=\begin{bmatrix} w'_{11} & w'_{21} & \cdots & w'_{k1} & \cdots & w'_{m1} \\ w'_{12} & w'_{22} & \cdots & w'_{k2} & \cdots & w'_{m2} \\ \vdots & \vdots & \vdots & \vdots & \vdots & \vdots \\ w'_{1r} & w'_{2r} & \cdots & w'_{kr} & \cdots & w'_{mr} \end{bmatrix}$$

Lastly, in the learning algorithm, when tr_k is fired, the truth of $d'_{1j}, d'_{2j}, \ldots, d'_{rj}$ to tr_k are defined as $\alpha(d'_{1j}, tr_k)=1-|y_{1j}-w'_{k1}|/\max(|w'_{k1}|, |y_{1j}|)$, $\alpha(d'_{2j}, tr_k)=1-|y_{2j}-w'_{k2}|/\max(|w'_{k2}|, |y_{2j}|)$, $\ldots$, $\alpha(d'_{rj}, tr_k)=1-|y_{rj}-w'_{kr}|/\max(|w'_{kr}|, |y_{rj}|)$ according to definition 3. The learning algorithm of learning fuzzy Petri net is shown in Table 4.

Learning Algorithm of LFPN:
Step 1. W and W' are selected randomly.
Step 2. For every training data set $(X_j, Y_j)(j=1, 2, \ldots, N)$, subject propositions $d_{1j}, d_{2j}, \ldots, d_{nj}$ in $p_1\sim p_n$ and propositions $d'_{1j}, d'_{2j}, \ldots, d'_{rj}$ in $p'_1\sim p'_r$ are produced. Then do step 3 to step 7;
Step 3. For $i=1$ to n For $h=1$ to m do Compute $\alpha(d_{ij}, tr_h)$ according to formula (2);
Step 4. Compute maximum truth of transition 4.1 $Max=\alpha(d_{1j}, tr_1) \bullet \alpha(d_{2j}, tr_1) \bullet \ldots \bullet \alpha(d_{nj}, tr_1)$; $k=1$; 4.2 For $h=1$ to m do If $\alpha(d_{1j}, tr_h) \bullet \alpha(d_{2j}, tr_h) \bullet \ldots \bullet \alpha(d_{nj}, tr_h)>Max$ Then { $Max=\alpha(d_{1j}, tr_h) \bullet \alpha(d_{2j}, tr_h) \bullet \ldots \bullet \alpha(d_{nj}, tr_h)$; $k=h$; }
Step 5. Fire tr_k;
Step 6. Make $d_{1j}, d_{2j}, \ldots, d_{nj}$ have bigger truth to tr_k, $$W_k^{(new)} = W_k^{(old)} + \gamma(X_j-W_k^{(old)}) \qquad (29)$$ ($W_k^{(new)}$ is the vector W_k after update and $W_k^{(old)}$ is the vector W_k before updated. $\gamma\in(0,1)$ is learning rate.)
Step 7. Make $d'_{1j}, d'_{2j}, \ldots, d'_{rj}$ have bigger truth to tr_k, $$W'_k^{(new)} = W'_k^{(old)} +\gamma(Y_j-W'_k^{(old)}) \qquad (30)$$ ($W'_k^{(new)}$ is the vector W'_k after update and $W'_k^{(old)}$ is the vector W'_k before updated. $\gamma\in(0,1)$ is learning rate.)
Step 8. Repeat step 2-7, until the truth of $\alpha(d_{1j}, tr_k)$, $\alpha(d_{2j}, tr_k)$, $\ldots$, $\alpha(d_{nj}, tr_k)$ meet the requirement.

Table 4. Learning algorithm of learning fuzzy Petri net

Some details in the algorithm need to be elaborated further.

1. About the net construction: The number of input and output places can be easily set according to a real problem. It is difficult to decide a number of transitions when the net is initialized. When LFPN is used to solve a special issue, the number of transitions is initially set according to practical situation experientially. Then, transitions can be dynamically appended and deleted during the training. If an input data X_j has a maximal truth to tr_k but one or several $\alpha(d_{ij}, tr_k)(1{\leq}i{\leq}n)$ are less than th_k (threshold of tr_k), transition tr_k cannot fire according to definition 3. Thus, data X_j cannot fire any existed transition. This case means that W_1, W_2, ..., W_k, ..., W_m cannot describe the vector characteristic of X_j. Then, a new transition tr_{m+1} and the arcs which connect tr_{m+1} with input and output place are constructed. X_j can be set as weight W_{m+1} directly. Second, during a training episode, if there is no data in X_1, X_2, ..., X_N that can fire transition tr_d, it means that W_d cannot describe the vector characteristic of any data X_1, X_2, ..., X_N. Then, the transition tr_d and the arcs which connect tr_d with input and output place will be deleted.

2. About W and W' initialization: for promoting training efficiency at the first stage of training, W and W' are set randomly in $[X_{min}, X_{max}]$, $[Y_{min}, Y_{max}]$ (X_{min} is a vector which every components is minimal component of vector set X_1, X_2, ..., X_N; X_{max} is a vector which every components is maximal component of vector set X_1, X_2, ..., X_N; Y_{min}, Y_{max} are same meaning with X_{min}, X_{max}).

3. Training stop condition of the learning algorithm: According to application case, th_1, th_2, ..., th_k, ... th_m are generally set a same value th. When training begins, the threshold th is set low (for example 0.2), th increases as training time increasing. A threshold value th_{last} (for example 0.9) is set as training stop condition and algorithm is run until $\alpha(d_{1j}, tr_k) > th_{last}$, $\alpha(d_{2j}, tr_k) > th_{last}$ ...$\alpha(d_{nj}, tr_k) > th_{last}$. From transition appending analysis, we understand that number of transitions will near to the number of training data if the threshold of transition sets near to 1. In this case, results will be obtained more correctly but the training time and LFPN running time will increase.

Analysis for convergence of LFPN learning algorithm

In this section, the convergence of the proposed algorithm will be analyzed. In step 6 of the LFPN learning algorithm, the formula (29) is used for making Wk (new) approach Xj than Wk (old) when Xj fired a transition trk. It is proved as follows.

$$
\begin{aligned}
W_k^{(new)} &= W_k^{(old)} + \gamma(X_j - W_k^{(old)}) = W_k^{(old)} + \gamma X_j - \gamma W_k^{(old)} \\
X_j - W_k^{(new)} &= X_j - [W_k^{(old)} + \gamma(X_j - W_k^{(old)})] \\
&= X_j - W_k^{(old)} - \gamma X_j + \gamma W_k^{(old)} \\
&= (1 - \gamma)(X_j - W_k^{(old)})
\end{aligned} \tag{31'}
$$

Formula (11') is rewritten as a scalar type and the scalar type of $(X_j{-}W_k^{(old)})$ is used to divide both sides of formula (11'). We get formula (11).

$$\left(\frac{x_{ij} - w_{kj}^{(new)}}{x_{ij} - w_{kj}^{(old)}}\right)_{0 \le i \le n} = \left(\frac{(1-\gamma) \cdot \left(x_{ij} - w_{kj}^{(old)}\right)}{x_{ij} - w_{kj}^{(old)}}\right)_{0 \le i \le n} = 1 - \gamma \qquad (31)$$

Hence, W_k will converge to X_j after enough training times.

In LFPN learning algorithm, there may be a class of training data X_j which are able to fire same transition tr_k. In this case, W_k approaches to a class of data X_j and converges to a point in the class of data X_j according to formula (31).

Now, we will discuss the point in the class of data X_j where W_k converges to. Supposing, there are b_1 data which are in X_1, X_2, ..., X_j, ..., X_N and fire a certain transition tr_k at the first training episode. At the second training episode, there are b_2 data which fire tr_k, and so on. If the total training times is ep and the total number of data which fire tr_k is t, $t = \sum_{i=1}^{ep} b_i$. According to the order of the data fired tr_k, these t data are rewritten as X_{k1}, X_{k2}, ..., X_{kt}. The average of training data X_{k1}, X_{k2}, ..., X_{kt} is noted as $\overline{X}_k$. To record the updated process of W_k simply, the updated order of W_k is recorded as $W_{k1}, W_{k2}.... W_{kt}$.

The learning rate γ ($0 < \gamma < 1$) will decrease according to training time increasing, and it approaches to 0 at last because every training data cannot effect W_k too much in the last stage of training, else W_k will shake at the last stage of training. If learning rate γ is set as $1/(q+1)$ ($q>0$) when training begin, $1/(q+2)$, $1/(q+3)$, ..., $1/(q+t)$ are set as learning rate γ when tr_k is fired at 2, 3, ..., t time. Here, the initial values of W_k is set as $W_{k0}=W^{(0)} \times 1/q$, every component of $W^{(0)} \times 1/q$ is a random value in $[X_{min}, X_{max}]$. According to formula (29), we get

$$W_{k0} = \frac{1}{q} W^{(0)}$$

$$W_{k1} = W_{k0} + \frac{1}{q+1}(X_{k1} - W_{k0}) = \frac{1}{q} W^{(0)} - \frac{1}{q+1} \times \frac{1}{q} W^{(0)} + \frac{1}{q+1} X_{k1} = \frac{1}{q+1}(W^{(0)} + X_{k1})$$

$$W_{k2} = W_{k1} + \frac{1}{q+2}(X_{k2} - W_{k1}) = \frac{1}{q+1} W^{(0)} + \frac{1}{q+1} X_{k1}$$

$$-\frac{1}{q+1} \times \frac{1}{q+2} W^{(0)} - \frac{1}{q+1} \times \frac{1}{q+2} X_{k1} + \frac{1}{q+2} X_{k2}$$

$$= \frac{1}{q+2}(W^{(0)} + X_{k1} + X_{k2})$$

$$W_{kt} = W_{k,t-1} + \frac{1}{q+t}(X_{kt} - W_{k,t-1}) = \frac{1}{q+t-1} W^{(0)} - \frac{1}{q+t} \times \frac{1}{q+t-1} W^{(0)} +$$

$$\frac{1}{q+t-1} X_{k1} - \frac{1}{q+t} \times \frac{1}{q+t-1} X_{k1} + ... + \frac{1}{q+t-1} X_{k,t-1} - \frac{1}{q+t} \times \frac{1}{q+t-1} X_{k,t-1} + \frac{1}{q+t} X_{kt}$$

$$= \frac{1}{q+t}(W^{(0)} + X_{k1} + \ldots + X_{k,t-1} + X_{kt}) \tag{32}$$

When the training time increases, the training data set X_{k1}, X_{k2}, ..., X_{kt} can be looked as very large, i.e. t is large.

$$\lim_{t \to \infty} W_{kt} = \lim_{t \to \infty} \frac{1}{q+t}(W^{(0)} + X_{k1} + \ldots + X_{k,t-1} + X_{kt}) \tag{33}$$

Generally, q is a small positive constant and t is large. Then,

$$\lim_{t \to \infty} W_{kt} \approx \lim_{t \to \infty} \frac{1}{t}(W^{(0)} + X_{k1} + \ldots + X_{k,t-1} + X_{kt})$$

$$= \lim_{t \to \infty} \frac{1}{t} W^{(0)} + \lim_{t \to \infty} \frac{1}{t}(X_{k1} + \ldots + X_{k,t-1} + X_{kt})$$

$$\approx \lim_{t \to \infty} \frac{1}{t}(X_{k1} + \ldots + X_{k,t-1} + X_{kt}) = \overline{X}_k \tag{34}$$

From formula (14) will be gotten:

$$W_k \to \overline{X}_k \tag{35}$$

In the same way, $W_k \to \overline{X}_k$ ($k=1$, 2, ..., m) and $W'_k \to \overline{Y}_k$ ($k=1$, 2, ..., m) can be proved. Consequently, the learning algorithm of LFPN converges.

Now, we will analyze the convergence process and signification of convergence.

1. X_{k1}, X_{k2}, ..., X_{kt} fire a certain transition tr_k at training time. As the training time increase, there are almost same data which fire the transition tr_k in every training time. These data belong to a class k. We suppose that these data are X_{k1}, X_{k2}, ..., X_{ks}. When training begins, supposing, there is data X_u which does not belong to X_{k1}, X_{k2}, ..., X_{ks} but fires tr_k. But, when training times increase, W_k will approach to X_{k1}, X_{k2}, ..., X_{ks} and the probability which X_u fires tr_k will decrease. Hence, this type data X_u is very small part of X_{k1}, X_{k2}, ..., X_{kt}. X_u little affects to W_k. On the other hand, when training begins, there is X_{ke} which belongs to X_{k1}, X_{k2}, ..., X_{ks} but doesn't fire transition tr_k. But, when training times increase, the probability which X_{ke} fires tr_k increases, then, X_{k1}, X_{k2}, ..., X_{ks} can be approximately looked firing tr_k according to the training. $\overline{X}_k$ is denoted as the average of training data X_{k1}, X_{k2}, ..., X_{ks}.

2. In the convergence demonstration, we use a special series of learning rate γ. Form the analysis in 1), X_{k1}, X_{k2}, ..., X_{ks} can be looked as a class data which fires one transition tr_k. The data series X_{k1}, X_{k2}, ..., X_{kt} can be looked as iterations of X_{k1}, X_{k2}, ..., X_{ks}. W_k can converge to a point near $\overline{X}_k$ with any damping learning rate series γ.

3. After training, $W_k=(w_{1k}, w_{2k}, \ldots, w_{nk})$ comes near to the average of data which belong to class k, i.e., $W_k \approx \overline{X}_k = (\overline{x}_{1k}, \overline{x}_{2k}, \ldots, \overline{x}_{nk})$. When a data X_{kj} belong to class k comes, X_{kj} will

have same vector characteristic with X_{k1}, X_{k2}, ..., X_{ks}, i.e. $x_{1,kj}$, $x_{2,kj}$, ..., $x_{n,kj}$ are near to w_{1k}, w_{2k}, ..., w_{nk}. Then, each component $x_{i,kj}$ ($1 \leq i \leq n$) of this data X_{kj} will have bigger similarity to w_{ik} ($1 \leq i \leq n$) than i-th components of other weight W according to formula (2). X_{kj} will have biggest truth to tr_k according to formula (2). Thus, when data X_{kj} which belongs to class of X_{k1}, X_{k2}, ..., X_{ks} inputs to LFPN, it will fire tr_k correctly and product correct output.

5. Web service discovery based on learning fuzzy Petri net model

Web services are used for developing and integrating highly distributed and heterogeneous systems in various domains. They are described by Web Services Description Language (WSDL). Web services discovery is a key to dynamically locating desired Web services across the Internet [16]. It immediately raises an issue, i.e. to evaluate the accuracy of the mapping in a heterogeneous environment when user wants to invoke a service. There are two aspects which need to evaluate. One is functional evaluation. The service providing function should be completely matched with user's request; another aspect is non-functional evaluation, i.e. Quality of Service (QoS) meets user's requirement. UDDI (Universal Description, Discovery and Integration) is widely used as a kind of discovery approach for functional evaluation. But, as the number of published Web services increases, discovering proper services using the limited description provided by the UDDI standard becomes difficult [17]. And UDDI cannot provide the QoS information of service. To discover the most appropriate service, there are necessary to focus on developing feasible discovery mechanisms from different service description methods and service execution context. Segev proposed a service function selection method [21]. A two-step, context based semantic approach to the problem of matching and ranking Web services for possible service composition is elaborated. The two steps for service function selection are Context extraction and Evaluation for Proximity degree of Service. Cai proposed service performance selection method [3]. The authors used a novel Artificial Neural Network-based service selection algorithm according to the information of the cooperation between the devices and the context information. In this paper, we aim at analyzing different context of services and constructing a services discovery model based on the LFPN. Firstly, different service functional descriptions are used to evaluate service function and an appropriate service is selected. Secondly, context of QoS is used to predict QoS and a more efficient service is selected. Data of QoS is real number and LFPN learning algorithm is directly used. But service function description is literal. Therefore, a Learning Fuzzy Petri Net for service discovery model is proposed for keyword learning based on LFPN.

5.1. Web services discovery model based on LFPN

To map a service's function accurately, free textual service description, WSDL description, Web service's operation and port parameters which are drawn from WSDL are used as input data here. Because the input data type is keyword, the proposed LFPN cannot deal with this type of data. Consequently, a Learning Fuzzy Petri Net for Web Services Discovery model (LFPNSD) is proposed. LFPNSD is a 10-tuple, given by LFPNSD = <P, Tr, F, W, D, I, O, Th, α, β > (as shown in Figure 13.)

where: Tr, I, O, Th, β are same with definition of LFPN.
P= {P_{input}}∪{P_{output}}={P_{11}, P_{12}, P_{13}}∪{P_{21}, P_{22}, P_{23}, P_{24}}
F ⊆ (P_{input}×Tr)∪(Tr×P_{output})
W=F→ $Keywords^+$, where weight function on P_{input}×Tr are different keywords of service description and weight function on Tr×P_{output} are different service invoking information.
D = {$d_{11,a}$, $d_{12,b}$, $d_{13,c}$}∪{$d_{21,e}$, $d_{22,f}$, $d_{23,g}$, $d_{24,h}$ } is a finite set of propositions, where proposition $d_{11,a}$ is that P_{11} has a service description tokens; proposition $d_{12,b}$ is that P_{12} has a free textual description tokens; proposition $d_{13,c}$ is that P_{13} has a service operation and port parameters tokens. And the propositions $d_{21,e}$, $d_{22,f}$, $d_{23,g}$, $d_{24,h}$ are that P_{21}, P_{22}, P_{23}, P_{24} have different invoking information tokens of services.

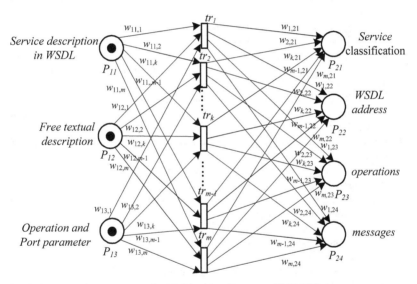

Figure 13. The learning fuzzy Petri net for Web service discovery (LFPNSD)

$\alpha(d_{ij}, tr_k)$→ [0, 1]. $\alpha(d_{ij}, tr_k)=y_i$∈ [0, 1] is the degree of truth of proposition d_{ij} to tr_k. $\alpha(d_{ij}, tr_k)$ is computed by bellow rules: if input description has n keywords and the w_{ik} on arc P_i to tr_k has s same keywords, the degree of similarity between weight keywords and input description keywords is expressed as:

$$\alpha\left(d_{ij}, tr_k\right) = 1 - \frac{|n-s|}{\max(n,s)} \tag{36}$$

The fire rule of transition: if $\alpha(d_{11,a}, tr_k)$ •$\alpha(d_{12,b}, tr_k)$ •$\alpha(d_{13,c}, tr_k)$ =max(($\alpha(d_{11,a}, tr_i)$ •$\alpha(d_{12,b}, tr_i)$ •$\alpha(d_{13,c}, tr_i))_{1≤i≤m}$) and all of $\alpha(d_{11,a}, tr_k)$, $\alpha(d_{12,b}, tr_k)$, $\alpha(d_{13,c}, tr_k)$ are bigger than a threshold value th, then tr_k fires, the tokens in P_{11}~P_{13} are taken out and tokens which according to $w_{k,21}$, $w_{k,22}$, $w_{k,23}$, $w_{k,24}$ are put into P_{21}~P_{24}.

As shown in Figure 13, service free textual description, WSDL description and operation and port information are used as input vector in the learning algorithm. And, service classification, WSDL address, all of service operation names and service SOAP messages are used as output vector. Because the training data type is the keyword, the learning algorithm of LFPN is developed into a learning algorithm of LFPNSD. The learning algorithm of learning fuzzy Petri net for Web service discovery is shown in the table 5.

Learning Algorithm of LFPNSD:
Step 1. Make all weights on arcs be ⊛;
Step 2. For every service in training data set,
Repeat:
2.1 Get free textual description; Draw out WSDL description and operation and port name from WSDL;
2.2 Set service textual description, WSDL description, operation and port information as input vector;
2.3 Compare the input with the keywords on the weight of input arc:
If every keyword in weight is in the input data, then compute $\alpha(d_{ij}, tr_k)$ according to formula (16), else set $\alpha(d_{ij}, tr_k) = 0$.
If each of $\alpha(d_{ij}, tr_1)$, $\alpha(d_{ij}, tr_2)$, ..., $\alpha(d_{ij}, tr_{m-1})$ equates 0 and the weight of tr_m is ⊛, then set $\alpha(d_{ij}, tr_m) = 1$.
If each of $\alpha(d_{ij}, tr_1)$, $\alpha(d_{ij}, tr_2)$, ..., $\alpha(d_{ij}, tr_{m-1})$ equates 0⊛and tr_m doesn't exist, a new transition tr_m and the arcs which connect tr_m with input and output place are constituted, set weight of arcs to be ⊛⊛and $\alpha(d_{ij}, tr_m) = 1$.
2.4 If $\alpha(d_{11,a}, tr_k) \bullet \alpha(d_{12,b}, tr_k) \bullet \alpha(d_{13,c}, tr_k) = \max((\alpha(d_{11,a}, tr_i) \bullet \alpha(d_{12,b}, tr_i) \bullet \alpha(d_{13,c}, tr_i))\ 1 \leq i \leq m)$, then tr_k fires.
2.5 If the tr_k fired, get a keyword in service description but not in the weight, and add it into the weight.
If training time is t and the weight is ⊛, t keywords in service description are gotten and they are added into the weight.
2.6 If the tr_k fired, compare out training data (service classification, WSDL address, service operation and message) with the weight of $w_{k,21}$, $w_{k,22}$, $w_{k,23}$, $w_{k,24}$, and calculate and record the correct rate of output.
2.7 Update $w_{k,21}$, $w_{k,22}$, $w_{k,23}$, $w_{k,24}$ according to output of training data.
Step 3. Repeat step 2, until each $\alpha(d_{11,a}, tr_k)$, $\alpha(d_{12,b}, tr_k)$, $\alpha(d_{13,c}, tr_k)$ meets the requirement value th_k.

Table 5. Learning algorithm of learning fuzzy Petri net for Web service discovery

Discussion:

1. We discuss about the learning rate γ in the learning algorithm of LFPNSD. In the algorithm, the keyword is learned and added into weights one by one. Hereby, $X_j - W_k$ (new) $= 1$ and $X_j - W^{(old)}$ equates the difference between the number of input data keywords and the number of keywords on arc weight. Because $X_j - W^{(old)}$ is not constant, the learning rate γ is different at each learning episode. For example, when input data has 10 keywords and arc weight has 6 keywords firstly, one keyword is learnt from input data and added into weight. In this case, the learning rate is $1/(10-6)=0.25$.

2. If keyword isn't learning one by one, the keywords on W_1, W_2, ..., W_k, ..., W_m will do not balance at beginning stage of training. Then, the similar but different description

services have unbalance probability to fire transition at beginning stage of training. This makes the similar but different description services improperly fire a transition which has more keywords on its weight. It makes training efficiency lower.

3. In step 2.3 of algorithm, when each of $\alpha(d_{ij}, tr_1)$, $\alpha(d_{ij}, tr_2)$, ..., $\alpha(d_{ij}, tr_{m-1})$ equates 0, it means all weights on transition $tr_1 \sim tr_{m-1}$ cannot describe this service. Therefore, it is a new type service. If there is a transition which has weight arc, it is used to record the new type service; else a new transition needs to be constructed.

5.2. The result of simulation

The two simulations are carried out. One is a more efficient service selection through QoS prediction using LFPN. The other is a service selection for appropriate function using LFPNSD.

Simulation for more efficient Web service selection

During the process of Web services discovery, there are maybe several services which have same function. One service which has the best QoS needs to be select. Hereby, the service performance context is used to predict the QoS value for next execution of service. If the prediction is precise enough, an appropriate service maybe selected.

In this simulation, LFPN is used as learning model for predicting service execution time which is main part of QoS. There are 11 inputs and 1 output in this model. 11 inputs include 10 data which are last 10 times execution time of a service and one data which is reliability of the service. The output is a prediction for execution time of service's next execution. 10 transitions of LFPN is set when initialization.

A Web service performance dataset is employed for simulation. This dataset includes 100 publicly available Web services located in more than 20 countries. 150 service users executed about 100 invocations on each Web service. Each service user recorded execution time and invocation failures in dataset [27]. We selected one use's invocation data as training data. Last 10 times execution time and reliability of each service was set as input and next time execution time was set as output. 20 sets of training data were selected for each of 100 services.

The initial threshold is selected as 0.2 and the threshold is increased 0.001 at every training episode. The initial learning rate is set as 1/1.1 for every transition. The learning rate is $1/(0.1+t)$ when a transition fired t times. Prediction result and training output data are noted as $Output_{predict}$ and $Output_{training}$. Prediction precision probability Pre_{pro} is used to evaluate the precision result. And the precision probability is computed using:

$$Pre_{pro} = 1 - (\,|\,Output_{predict} - Output_{training}\,|\,/\,Output_{training}).$$

Three different training stop conditions are set as that three threshold values equal to 0.7, 0.8, and 0.9. The simulation result is listed in Table 6. Here, the number of service, which their execution time is precisely predicted, increased with the training threshold value increasing.

In the paper [3], the authors improved the traditional BP algorithm based on three-term method consisting of a learning rate, a momentum factor and a proportional factor for predicting service performance according to service context information. In this paper, this model is used to predict service execution time. The training data is same to LFPN's. And the learning rate is 0.6, momentum factor 0.9, proportional factor 1 and training times is 10,000. We compared the simulation result of the method of [3], i.e. the conventional method, with that of LFPN in Table 7. From Table 7, it is shown that Web service number of high precision in LFPN's prediction is bigger than the number of BP algorithm's prediction and Web service number of low precision in LFPN's prediction is smaller that BP algorithm's prediction. Hereby, the result of LFPN is better than result of three term's BP algorithm.

Precision	0.99~1	0.98~0.99	0.95~ 0.98	0.9~0.95	0.8~0.9	0.7~0.8	0.6~0.7	0~0.6
Number of Web services (th= 0.9)	21	14	17	15	10	8	9	6
Number of Web services (th= 0.8)	17	12	14	11	10	12	10	14
Number of Web services (th= 0.7)	10	10	16	8	8	11	19	18

Table 6. Prediction ability of LFPN

Precision	0.99~1	0.98~0.99	0.95~0.98	0.9~0.95	0.8~0.9	0.7~0.8	0.6~0.7	0~0.6
Number of Web services using the LFPN(th=0.9)	21	14	17	15	10	8	9	6
Number of Web services using the conventional method	6	7	15	18	20	12	10	12

Table 7. Prediction ability compares for two methods

Simulation for selection of Web service's function

In this simulation, LFPNSD is used as leaning model. The benchmark Web services which listed at www.xmethods.net are used as training data. Each service of these 260 services has a textual description and its WSDL address. And, we can get WSDL description, operation and port parameters from the WSDL. We want to classify the Web service into four classes: 1) business, 2) finance, 3) nets and 4) life services. After training, Web services are invoked by natural language request [14]. The natural language is decompounded into three inputs of this model. For example, we want to get a short message service (SMS) for sending a message to a mobile phone. The nature language of this discovery is input and decomposed into three parts: 1) WSDL description: send a message to a mobile phone; 2) free textual service description: sending a message to a mobile phone through the Internet; 3) operation and port parameters maybe have operation names: send messages, send message multiple recipients, and so on; port names send service SOAP, and so on.

In this simulation, we firstly set 100 transitions for LFPNSD model. The training stop condition is th_k $(1 \leq k \leq m) \geq 0.6$. The service selection precision is recorded after every time of training. As shown in Figure 14 and 15, using LFPNSD model and its learning algorithm described in Section 5.1, every service class precision probability raised to more than 0.9 when the training time reaches to 10.

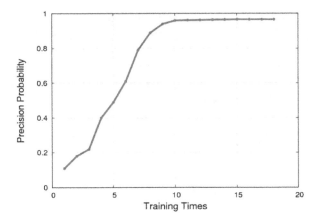

Figure 14. The results of simulation using LFPNSD and its learning algorithm– Discovery Precision Probability for total services

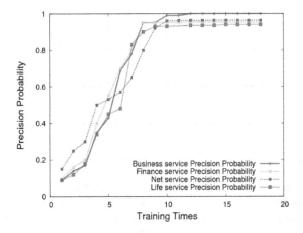

Figure 15. The results of simulation using LFPNSD and its learning algorithm – Discovery Precision Probability for classification services

A method for evaluating the proximity of services is proposed [21]. In the method, WSDL document is represented as $D^{wsdl}=\{t_1, t_2, ..., t_{wsdl}\}$ and $D^{desc}=\{t_1, t_2, ..., t_{desc}\}$ represents the textual description of the service. Because there is another descriptor of operation and port parameters in LFPNSD model, we add this descriptor as $D^{op\&port}=\{t_1, t_2, ..., t_{op\&port}\}$ in order to compare two methods. Here, t_{wsdl}, t_{desc} and $t_{op\&port}$ are last keyword of WSDL, textural description and operation and port parameters. In the proximity of services method, the descriptor of natural language request which is provided by a user is D_{user} and descriptor of invoked service is D_{inv}. The three Context Overlaps (CO) are defined as same keywords between D^{wsdl}_{user}, D^{desc}_{user}, $D^{op\&port}_{user}$ and D^{wadl}_{inv}, D^{desc}_{inv}, $D^{op\&port}_{inv}$. The proximity of user requested service and invoked service is defined as a root of sum of three CO's squares. When a user invoking comes, it is compared with all services in services repository. Then, one service in D_{inv}, which has the biggest proximity value with D_{user}, was selected. We compared the discovery precision probability of this method (conventional method) with the proposed LFPNSD. The simulation results are shown in Figure 16. The LFPNSD method yielded higher precision probabilities than the conventional method proposed in [21]. Especially when the service number of Web services' repository becomes more than 88, the difference is much more significant. Here, a correct service is selected in 14 services, 24 services, 37 services, 54 services, 88 services, 151 services just as they were used in [21].

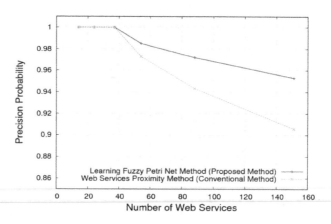

Figure 16. Comparison of two discovery methods

6. Conclusion

In this chapter, Learning Petri net (LPN) was constructed based on High-level Time Petri net and reinforcement learning (RL). The RL was used for adjusting the parameter of Petri net. Two kinds of learning algorithm were proposed for Petri net's discrete and continuous parameter learning. And verification for LPN was shown. LPN model was applied to dynamical system control. We had used the LPN in three robot systems control - the AIBO, Guide Dog. The LPN models were found and controlled for these robot systems. These robot systems could adjust their parameters while system was running. And the correctness and effectiveness of our proposed model were confirmed in these experiments. LPN model was improved to the hierarchical LPN model and this improved hierarchical LPN model was applied to QoS optimization of Web service composition. The hierarchical LPN model was constructed based on stochastic Petri net and RL. When the model was used, the Web service composition was modeled with stochastic Petri net. A Web service dynamical composing framework is proposed for optimizing QoS of web service composition. The neural network learning method was used to Fuzzy Petri net. Learning fuzzy Petri net (LFPN) was proposed. Contrasting with the existing FPN, there are three extensions in the new model: the place can possess different tokens which represent different propositions;

these propositions have different degrees of truth toward different transitions; the truth degree of proposition can be learnt through adjusting of the arc's weight function. The LFPN model obtains the capability of fuzzy production rules learning through truth degree updating. The LFPN learning algorithm which introduced network learning method into Petri net update was proposed and the convergence of the algorithm was analyzed. The LFPN model was used into discovery of Web service. Using the LFPN model, different service functional descriptions are used to evaluate service function and an appropriate service is selected firstly, Secondly, context of QoS is used to predict QoS and a more efficient service is selected.

In the future, the different intelligent computing methods will be used into Petri net for constructing different type of LPN. The efficient different types of LPN used in different special area will be compared and an efficient LPN model for solving various problems will be founded.

Author details

Liangbing Feng, Masanao Obayashi, Takashi Kuremoto and Kunikazu Kobayashi
Division of Computer Science & Design Engineering, Yamaguchi University, Ube, Japan

Liangbing Feng
Shenzhen Institutes of Advanced Technology, Shenzhen, China

7. References

[1] Konar A., Chakraborty U. K. and Wang P. P. Supervised Learning on a Fuzzy Petri Net. Information Sciences 2005; Vol.172, No.3-4, 397-416.

[2] Hrúz B., Zhou M.C. Modeling and Control of Discrete-event Dynamic Systems: with Petri Nets and Other Tools. Springer Press. London, UK, 2007.

[3] Cai H., Hu X., Lu Q. and Cao Q. A Novel Intelligent Service Selection Algorithm and Application for Ubiquitous Web Services Environment. Expert Systems with Applications 2009; Vol. 36, No. 2, 2200-2212.

[4] Doya, K. Reinforcement Learning in Continuous Time and Apace, Neural Computation, 2000; Vol.12, No.1, 219–245.

[5] Feng L. B, Obayashi M., Kuremoto T. and Kobayashi K. A Learning Petri Net Model Based on Reinforcement Learning. Proceedings of the 15th International Symposium on Artificial Life and Robotics (AROB2010); 290-293.

[6] Feng L. B., Obayashi M., Kuremoto T. and Kobayashi K. An Intelligent Control System Construction Using High-Level Time Petri Net and Reinforcement Learning. Proceedings of International Conference on Control, Automation, and Systems (ICCAS 2010); 535 – 539.

[7] Feng L. B., Obayashi M., Kuremoto T. and Kobayashi K. A learning Petri net Model. IEEJ Transactions on Electrical and Electronic Engineering 2012; Volume 7, Issue 3, pages 274–282.

[8] Frederick J. R. Statistical Methods for Speech. The MIT Press. Cambridge, Massachusetts, USA, 1999.

[9] Guangming C., Minghong L., Xianghu W. The Definition of Extended High-level Time Petri Nets. Journal of Computer Science 2006; 2(2):127-143.

[10] Hirasawa K., Ohbayashi M., Sakai S., Hu J. Learning Petri Network and Its Application to Nonlinear System Control. IEEE Transactions on Systems, Man and Cybernetic, Part B: Cybernetics, 1998; 28(6), 781-789.

[11] VIRTANEN H. E. A Study in Fuzzy Petri Nets and the Relationship to Fuzzy Logic Programming, Reports on Computer Science and Mathematics, No. 162, 1995.

[12] Yan H. S., Jian J. Agile concurrent engineering. Integrated Manufacturing Systems 1999; 10(2): 103-113.

[13] Wang J. Petri nets for dynamic event-driven system modeling. Handbook of Dynamic System Modeling 2007; Ed: Paul Fishwick, CRC Press, 1-17.

[14] Lim J. H., Lee. K. H. Constructing Composite Web Services from Natural Language Requests, Web Semantics: Science, Services and Agents on the World Wide Web 2010; Vol. 8, No.1, 1-13.

[15] Li X., Yu W., and Rsano F. L. Dynamic Knowledge Inference and Learning under Adaptive Fuzzy Petri Net Framework, IEEE Transactions on System, Man, and Cybernetics-Part C 2000; Vol. 30, No.4, 442-450.

[16] Papazoglou M.P., Georgakopoulos D. Service-Oriented Computing, Communications of the ACM, 2003; 46(10), 25-65.

[17] Platzer C. and S. Dustdar. A Vector Space Search Engine for Web Services, Proc. Third European Conf. Web Services (ECOWS'05) 2005, 62-71.

[18] Sutton R. S., Batto A. G. Reinforcement learning: An Introduction. The MIT Press, Cambridge, Massachusetts, USA, 1998.

[19] Sony OPEN-R programming group, OPEN-R programming introduction. Sony Corporation, Japan, (2004).

[20] Tzafesta S.G., Rigatos G.G. Stability analysis of an adaptive fuzzy control system using Petri nets and learning automata. Mathematics and computers in Simulation 2000; Vol. 51. No. 3. 315-339.

[21] Segev A. and E. Toch. Context-Based Matching and Ranking of Web Services for Composition, IEEE Transaction on Services computing 2009;, Vol.2, No.3, 210-222.

[22] Baranaushas V., Sarkauskas K. Colored Petri Nets-Tool for control system Learning. Electronics and Electrical Engineering 2006; 4(68):41-46.

[23] Victor R. L. Shen. Reinforcement Learning for High-level Fuzzy Petri Nets, IEEE Transactions on System, Man, and Cybernetics-Part B 2003; Vol.33, No.2, 351-361.

[24] Pedrycz W. and Gomide F. A Generalized Fuzzy Petri Net Model, IEEE Transaction on Fuzzy System 1994; Vol.2, No.4, 295-301.

[25] Xu H., Wang Y., and Jia P. Fuzzy Neural Petri Nets, Proceedings of the 4th International Symposium on Neural Networks: Part II--Advances in Neural Networks, 2007; 328 – 335.

[26] Ding Z. H., Bunke H., Schneider M. and A. Kandel. Fuzzy Time Petri net Definitions, Properties, and Applications, Mathematical and Computer Modeling, 2005, Vol. 41, No. 2-3, 345-360.

[27] Zheng Z. B., Lyu M. R. Collaborative Reliability Prediction for Service -Oriented Systems, Proceedings of the ACM/IEEE 32nd International Conference on Software Engineering (ICSE2010), 35 – 44.

Permissions

The contributors of this book come from diverse backgrounds, making this book a truly international effort. This book will bring forth new frontiers with its revolutionizing research information and detailed analysis of the nascent developments around the world.

We would like to thank Pawel Pawlewski, for lending his expertise to make the book truly unique. He has played a crucial role in the development of this book. Without his invaluable contribution this book wouldn't have been possible. He has made vital efforts to compile up to date information on the varied aspects of this subject to make this book a valuable addition to the collection of many professionals and students.

This book was conceptualized with the vision of imparting up-to-date information and advanced data in this field. To ensure the same, a matchless editorial board was set up. Every individual on the board went through rigorous rounds of assessment to prove their worth. After which they invested a large part of their time researching and compiling the most relevant data for our readers. Conferences and sessions were held from time to time between the editorial board and the contributing authors to present the data in the most comprehensible form. The editorial team has worked tirelessly to provide valuable and valid information to help people across the globe.

Every chapter published in this book has been scrutinized by our experts. Their significance has been extensively debated. The topics covered herein carry significant findings which will fuel the growth of the discipline. They may even be implemented as practical applications or may be referred to as a beginning point for another development. Chapters in this book were first published by InTech; hereby published with permission under the Creative Commons Attribution License or equivalent.

The editorial board has been involved in producing this book since its inception. They have spent rigorous hours researching and exploring the diverse topics which have resulted in the successful publishing of this book. They have passed on their knowledge of decades through this book. To expedite this challenging task, the publisher supported the team at every step. A small team of assistant editors was also appointed to further simplify the editing procedure and attain best results for the readers.

Our editorial team has been hand-picked from every corner of the world. Their multi-ethnicity adds dynamic inputs to the discussions which result in innovative outcomes. These outcomes are then further discussed with the researchers and contributors who give their valuable feedback and opinion regarding the same. The feedback is then collaborated with the researches and they are edited in a comprehensive manner to aid the understanding of the subject.

Apart from the editorial board, the designing team has also invested a significant amount of their time in understanding the subject and creating the most relevant covers. They scrutinized every image to scout for the most suitable representation of the subject and create an appropriate cover for the book.

The publishing team has been involved in this book since its early stages. They were actively engaged in every process, be it collecting the data, connecting with the contributors or procuring relevant information. The team has been an ardent support to the editorial, designing and production team. Their endless efforts to recruit the best for this project, has resulted in the accomplishment of this book. They are a veteran in the field of academics and their pool of knowledge is as vast as their experience in printing. Their expertise and guidance has proved useful at every step. Their uncompromising quality standards have made this book an exceptional effort. Their encouragement from time to time has been an inspiration for everyone.

The publisher and the editorial board hope that this book will prove to be a valuable piece of knowledge for researchers, students, practitioners and scholars across the globe.

List of Contributors

Dejan Gradišar
Jožef Stefan Institute, Slovenia

Gašper Mušič
Faculty of Electrical Engineering, University of Ljubljana, Slovenia

Yen-Liang Pan
Department of Avionic Engineering, R.O.C. Air Force Academy, Taiwan, R.O.C.

Belhassen Mazigh
Faculty of sciences, Department of Computer Sciences, 5000, Monastir, Tunisia

Abdeljalil Abbas-Turki
Laboratoire SET, Université de Technologie de Belfort Montbéliard, Belfort, France

Tiago Facchin and Miguel Afonso Sellitto
Universidade do Vale do Rio do Sinos - UNISINOS, Brazil

Geńichi Yasuda
Nagasaki Institute of Applied Science, Japan

Chongyi Yuan
School of Electronics Engineering and Computer Science, Peking University, Beijing, China

Iwona Grobelna
University of Zielona Góra, Poland

Liangbing Feng, Masanao Obayashi, Takashi Kuremoto and Kunikazu Kobayashi
Division of Computer Science & Design Engineering, Yamaguchi University, Ube, Japan

Liangbing Feng
Shenzhen Institutes of Advanced Technology, Shenzhen, China

Printed in the USA
CPSIA information can be obtained
at www.ICGtesting.com
JSHW011400221024
72173JS00003B/359